ESCALANTE'S DREAM

ALSO BY DAVID ROBERTS

Limits of the Known

Alone on the Wall
(with Alex Honnold)

The Lost World of the Old Ones:
Discoveries in the Ancient Southwest

Alone on the Ice:
The Greatest Survival Story in the History of Exploration

The Mountain:
My Time on Everest (with Ed Viesturs)

The Will to Climb:
Obsession and Commitment and the Quest to Climb Annapurna
(with Ed Viesturs)

Finding Everett Ruess:
The Life and Unsolved Disappearance of a
Legendary Wilderness Explorer

K2: Life and Death on the World's Most Dangerous Mountain
(with Ed Viesturs)

The Last of His Kind: The Life and Adventures of Bradford Washburn,
America's Boldest Mountaineer

Devil's Gate:
Brigham Young and the Great Mormon Handcart Tragedy

No Shortcuts to the Top:
Climbing the World's 14 Highest Peaks
(with Ed Viesturs)

Sandstone Spine:
Seeking the Anasazi on the First Traverse of the Comb Ridge

On the Ridge Between Life and Death:
A Climbing Life Reexamined

ESCALANTE'S DREAM

On the Trail of the Spanish Discovery of the Southwest

David Roberts

W. W. NORTON & COMPANY

Independent Publishers Since 1923

NEW YORK ★ LONDON

For information about permission to reproduce selections from this book, write to
Permissions, W. W. Norton & Company, Inc., 500 Fifth Avenue, New York, NY 10110

For information about special discounts for bulk purchases, please contact
W. W. Norton Special Sales at specialsales@wwnorton.com or 800-233-4830

Manufacturing by Lake Book
Book design by Lovedog Studio
Production manager: Anna Oler

Library of Congress Cataloging-in-Publication Data

Names: Roberts, David, 1943–
Title: Escalante's dream : on the trail of the Spanish discovery of the Southwest /
David Roberts.
Description: First edition. | New York : W. W. Norton & Company, 2019. |
Includes bibliographical references and index.
Identifiers: LCCN 2019006079 | ISBN 9780393652062 (hardcover)
Subjects: LCSH: Domínguez-Escalante Expedition (1776) | Roberts, David, 1943–
—Travel—Southwest, New. | Southwest, New—Description and travel. | Four
Corners Region—Description and travel. | Southwest, New—Discovery and explo-
ration—Spanish. | Domínguez, Francisco Atanasio, active 1776. | Vélez de Escalante,
Silvestre, –1792. | Explorers—Southwest, New—Biography. | Explorers—Spain—
Biography. | Franciscans—Southwest, New—Biography.
Classification: LCC F799 . R63 2019 | DDC 979/.01—dc23
LC record available at https://lccn.loc.gov/2019006079

W. W. Norton & Company, Inc., 500 Fifth Avenue, New York, N.Y. 10110
www.wwnorton.com

W. W. Norton & Company Ltd., 15 Carlisle Street, London W1D 3BS

1 2 3 4 5 6 7 8 9 0

Contents

For Sharon—

Because you are there

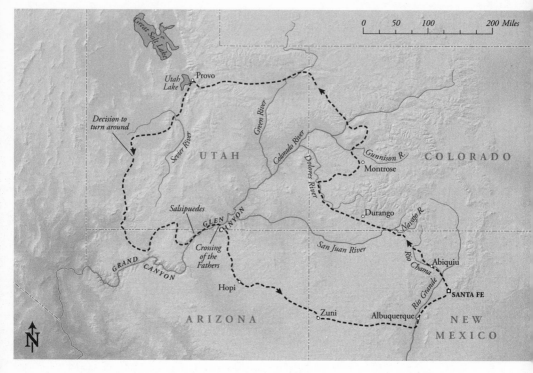

Route followed by the Domínguez–Escalante expedition, July 29, 1776, to January 2, 1777.
Courtesy of Adam Stack.

Author's Note

THE RIO GRANDE VALLEY ALL THE WAY UP TO WHAT IS
today north-central New Mexico was a Spanish colony from 1598, as
was much of southern Arizona up to the mission at San Xavier del
Bac, from 1692. Both regions, of course, are today parts of the American Southwest. In crediting the Domínguez–Escalante expedition
with "the Spanish discovery of the Southwest," as I do in the subtitle
to this book and several times in the text, I mean to evoke the greater
Southwest—the convoluted and magnificent landscape of deep canyons and towering buttes and alpine mountains ranging from the San
Juans to the Wasatch, from Canyonlands to the Grand Canyon, from
the lakes of northern Utah to the plains of northern Arizona. It was
the Spanish discovery of this vast country, known before 1776 only
to the indigenous Native Americans, that the Franciscan padres and
their ten companions accomplished.

ESCALANTE'S DREAM

Chapter One

ABIQUIU AND BEYOND

THE THREE-QUARTER MOON HAD CREPT INTO THE WEST when my nightmare arrived.

It was September 2, 2017. That morning my wife, Sharon, and I had left Santa Fe on what promised to be a six-week journey, following the fugitive trail of the twelve-man expedition that had passed this way 241 years before. Our voyage was one that would have seemed almost tame to me throughout my adult life—until two years earlier, when cancer had abruptly redefined all my notions of the possible. Now I knew that our forty days in pursuit of Domínguez and Escalante posed as stern a challenge as I dared to engage.

We had driven north on Highway 84, through the crossroads town of Española, along the Chama River, arriving after some 45 miles at the sleepy village of Abiquiu, famed for Georgia O'Keeffe's obsession with cow skulls, local flowers, and the old mission church. From there we had headed south on a dirt road that climbed out of a tight canyon to emerge on a glorious grassy plateau—land still held by the descendants of the benefactors of an old Spanish land grant. After some 10 miles we had crossed into the Santa Fe National Forest. Around 5 PM we found the perfect roadside campsite, at 8,000 feet under the soaring ponderosas, with open views east to a far rim of the forest and west to Cerro Pedernal, the volcanic mountain from which the ancients had extracted chert and obsidian to craft their dart points and arrow-heads. We set up our tent, gathered sticks for a fire, and sat in our ten-dollar Walmart camp chairs sipping Pilsner Urquells as the sun slipped toward the horizon. I was as happy as I had been in months.

It was Saturday night. The previous evening, an old friend who lives in Santa Fe, on learning about our plans, had warned us that Española was the center of opioid and alcohol excess in northern New Mexico. As she wished us well, she parted with that timeless admo-nition, "Be careful."

I was inclined to dismiss our friend's malaise, recognizing in it, along with statistical accuracy, an ancient bias against Hispanic life-ways promulgated by the Anglos who ran New Mexico after 1848. But Sharon was troubled. Unable to sleep during our last night in Santa Fe, she got up and Googled "Española—opioids—crime" on her iPhone. I slept on oblivious. In the morning, she haltingly shared her worries. I pointed out that we would pass through Española in the afternoon and that wherever we car-camped, it would be well beyond the range of the region's most malevolent junkies.

Since we had set up camp, only a single vehicle had passed by on the dirt road, a pickup headed at dusk, I guessed, for home or some other civilized refuge. But paradoxically, when almost no cars pass your campsite, the advent of a single one, announced by distant engine noise, then by the beams of headlights bouncing among the trees, seems faintly ominous.

I had unconsciously absorbed Sharon's fears. In the night, a dream delivered a black SUV that stopped just yards away from our tent. Instead of hiding or fleeing, I got up to greet the strangers. Several bearded men wearing camo stepped out of the vehicle. They carried their guns nonchalantly in their hands or slung across their backs. One of them surveyed our campsite. "We just need something to eat," he said.

"But is it deer season?" I asked.

"No."

I fought down a thread of panic. "I've camped out," I said, "for sixty years now."

"Not much left then, is there?"

The sun rose at its appointed hour over the far rim in the east. Bundled against the cold, I put a pot of water on our two-burner stove to heat for coffee. Slowly the pallor of the nightmare dissolved. But I didn't tell Sharon about the visitation in the night until the next day.

*   *   *

To ECHO MACAULAY, every schoolboy knows about the journey across the continent launched by Lewis and Clark in 1804, as the Corps of Discovery fulfilled Thomas Jefferson's mandate to learn just what kind of territory the United States had bought from France the preceding year. Twenty-eight years before Lewis and Clark set out from St. Louis, a pair of Franciscan priests led a much smaller cadre of men on a monumental exploration through some of the most spectacular and difficult terrain in the future United States, in the process actually discovering more land unknown to non-natives than Lewis and Clark did. Yet not even Macaulay's brightest pupil today has more than the haziest grasp of the extraordinary journey led by Domínguez and Escalante in 1776. The journals kept by Lewis and Clark are disjointed, preoccupied with minutiae, and myopic about the shape of the great voyage, and Clark's command of spelling, grammar, and punctuation is so shaky that his passages often verge on the illiterate. America's most famous expedition of discovery is best absorbed today via such excellent second-hand narratives as Bernard DeVoto's *The Course of Empire* or Stephen Ambrose's *Undaunted Courage*. But Escalante's journal—coherent, succinct, yet full of curious asides and observations—is far more readable than any of the several commentaries about the Spaniards' journey written by latter-day historians. In the words of DeVoto, the journal is "a poem, dramatized against the backdrop of the rock deserts." The expedition itself, despite its harrowing tribulations and a life-or-death denouement, seemed to DeVoto a "sunnily stupendous journey." What's more, the team's cartographer, Bernardo Miera y Pacheco, drew an extraordinary map that is an artistic masterpiece in its own right. It remained the best chart of the greater Southwest until the middle of the nineteenth century.

In 1951, Herbert E. Bolton became the first historian to engage Domínguez and Escalante at book length. About the padres as explorers, he wrote, "For the opening of new vistas they belong with Coronado and the splendid wayfarers of Mexico and South America. For their relations with the strange peoples encountered they stand in a class almost by themselves."

No book yet written about the Domínguez–Escalante journey has gone beyond a paraphrase of the journal and a summary of the expedition's results. My intention in *Escalante's Dream* is to cross-examine the padre's account at every turn, to wonder what was going on whenever the explorers made a strange decision or engaged in a puzzling interaction with Native Americans met along the way, and to dig below the surface of the conflicts among and characters of the twelve men on the team. And as Sharon and I retrace the 1776 journey through forty days in the fall of 2017, I intend to treat our own adventure as a parallel expedition 241 years later—a road trip through a world Domínguez and Escalante could never have foreseen.

Silvestre Vélez de Escalante was born in 1749 in Cantabria, a green, hilly province in northern Spain. He was a *montañes*, a highlander, and had he stayed in his native land he might well have whiled away his years as a shepherd or a farmer. We know very little about the man's early life, but by the late 1760s he had arrived in Mexico City. There, at only eighteen, he became a friar in the order of Saint Francis of Assisi. From 1598 onward, it had been Franciscans who took charge of the religious life of New Spain's northernmost colony, and their highest duty and keenest passion had to do with bringing the salvation of the Redeemer into the hearts and souls of the "benighted" natives the Spaniards found when they arrived.

Escalante was second in command of the bold expedition on which

he embarked in July 1776—the same month that fifty-six ardent rebels convened in a hall in Philadelphia to sign a ringing declaration
of their freedom from the tyranny of King George III. We know as
little about the expedition's commander, another friar named Francisco Atanasio Domínguez, as we do about Escalante. But because it
was the latter man who wrote the official journal—virtually the sole
primary document from the adventure to come down to us—we have
something like a direct pipeline to the thoughts and feelings of the
exploit's junior leader.

As many commentators have pointed out, we should refer to
Domínguez's lieutenant not as "Escalante" but as "Vélez," since the
"de Escalante" of his name merely identified where he was from—as
in Shakespeare's John of Gaunt. Likewise, of course, with Francisco
Vázquez de Coronado. But calling the conquistador who led the first
great exploration of what would become the American Southwest
"Vázquez" would simply confuse the reader. The name Escalante,
like that of Coronado, has been attached to all kinds of places in the
Southwest, and to insist on "Vélez" here would be to err on the side
of pedantry.

As Sharon and I retraced the route of the long-ago journey, and
read and reread the entries that dealt with each stage of the voyage, I
often wondered what kind of role fear had played in the men's lives.
Because the expedition turned into a survival ordeal, reducing the
twelve men to the most desperate conditions, I knew that terror and
doom must have ridden beside them on their played-out horses. But
the diary is for the most part laconic about their hardships.

On our own journey, the risks were minimal. A bad dream about
creepy gunslingers arriving at our camp in the night bore only the
faintest subconscious echo of the real threats that had shadowed
travelers in the wilderness in previous centuries. Normally, Spanish
expeditions crossing the badlands of the American Southwest—most
notably the Jornada del Muerto between El Paso and Santa Fe, a
gauntlet that invited attack by Apaches and Comanches—traveled

heavily armed. Among the ten men who set off to the north from Santa Fe in 1776, there were no soldiers. And though Escalante never records what weapons the men carried, the few references to firearms surface only when the starving men used muskets to fell a bison here or celebrate a river crossing there.

The journal does not suppress the tribulations the men endured, especially during the second half of the journey. Terrible cold, even in September; grim trudges across prairies devoid of firewood or water; confusion in canyons and forests as the men suspect they're lost—these and other depredations come to vivid life in the pages of the journal. But against the threat of even more insidious dangers, Escalante wore a suit of invisible armor: his faith.

In 1775, the twenty-five-year-old priest was assigned to the pueblo of Zuni far to the southwest of Santa Fe—in historian John Kessell's pithy phrase, to Spanish minds "the Siberia of New Mexico." Yet he decided, in the hope of making conversions among an even more remote community of natives, to make a journey to Hopi, 130 miles farther west.

Escalante's mission was an utter failure. Not a single Indian was persuaded by his earnest sermons, translated by a local, to give up his allegiance to Maasaw and the kachinas and become a Christian. As he prepared to return to Zuni, a sympathetic Hopi told Escalante that he had overheard a group of Navajos plotting to lie in wait along the trail to ambush and massacre his small party.

Escalante was unfazed. "I replied that I was very grateful to him for the warning, [but that] . . . he was to tell them from me that even all of them were too few to carry out their intention; that if they liked, they might seek the aid of other tribes, but even if many went forth, they would have an exceedingly costly trial of their weakness and my safeguard." The informant, thinking that Escalante had misunderstood the Navajo threat or given no credence to his words, called upon other Hopi to witness his warning. The friar doubled down, saying that "though I believed him, I was not worried, nor should he be, because I trusted in God Who is infinitely more powerful than all the men there ever were, are, or will be."

* * *

SPAIN'S EXPLORATION OF what would become the western United States began with Coronado's *entrada*, from 1540 to 1542. It is a measure of just how ambitious the conquistadors were, how hungry for new land, that only nineteen years after Cortés had completed his astonishing conquest of the Aztec empire centered around Tenochtitlan (today's Mexico City), the Spaniards were pushing the borders of terra incognita more than a thousand miles to the northwest.

Coronado's adventure was launched in response to one of the strangest and most unlikely journeys ever accomplished by Europeans in the New World. One day in 1536, four Spaniards stumbled into the colonial outpost of Culiacán in today's Mexican state of Sinaloa. Alvar Nuñez Cabeza de Vaca and his three weary companions were the sole surviviors of an expedition of some 600 men that had come to grief along the west coast of Florida in 1528. For eight years, the four survivors had wandered among Indian tribes, sometimes as slaves, sometimes as shamans revered for their magical gifts, as they made their way across 2,500 miles of unmapped terrain from the Gulf Coast to the Pacific.

Although at first they were suspected of making up their outlandish tale, the four vagabonds brought electrifying news of unknown lands and tribes that whetted the Spanish imagination. Driven by an unquenchable thirst for gold and silver, but also by a zeal to convert pagans to the true faith, the governors of New Spain sent out a scouting mission in 1539. The party was led by a Franciscan, Fray Marcos de Niza (a missionary model for Domínguez and Escalante two and a half centuries later), and guided by Esteban, a Moor from North Africa, originally a Spanish slave, who had been one of Cabeza de Vaca's companions on that epic journey of survival.

All across the wilderness the four refugees traversed, Esteban spurred bewildered curiosity among the Indians. Who was he, this brown-skinned stranger traveling with his white-skinned comrades, speaking the same strange tongue as they did? The Moor had a remarkable gift for picking up native languages, so during their desperate journey it was he who best communicated with the Indians. By some he was treated as a servant to be starved and tormented, while to others he was a healer with occult and wondrous powers.

In 1539, his success among the "savages" must have gone to Esteban's head. Impetuously he rode several days ahead of the cautious priest and the main party, and while he announced the coming of white men who would "instruct [the natives] about things divine," he also demanded tribute in the form of turquoise and women. Somewhere in what is today the greater Southwest, Esteban rubbed his temporary hosts the wrong way. In the words of historian Andrés Reséndez, those Indians "deliberated for three days about what to do and finally chose to kill him." Despite this setback, Fray Marcos de Niza rode in sight of some large native settlement, where he later claimed to have seen from afar buildings made of gold, festooned with precious jewels.

This doubtful sighting reinforced the enduring legend of the Seven Cities of Cíbola, or the Seven Cities of Gold. A persistent oral tradition has it that Esteban's fatal encounter occurred at the New Mexico pueblo of Zuni, though some scholars doubt the connection.

On a warm September day in 2002, a Zuni woman named Lena Tsethlikai guided me to Hawikuh, the village in which, if the oral tradition has it right, Esteban met his doom. Though the site lies in ruins today, in the sixteenth century it was one of six villages that made up the prosperous pueblo of Zuni. No one knows how long those people have dwelled in their current location, but the fact that the Zuni language is an isolate—a tongue related to no other language anywhere in the world—suggests a geographic stability lasting 8,000 years or longer.

With Tsethlikai, I strolled across the furrows and swales of the ruin, which is normally off-limits to Anglos. The ground was covered with polychrome potsherds, and scores of crumbling walls, the purplish building stones scattered on either side, outlined the layout of the ancient town. The site lay open to the distant horizon on the southwest, the direction from which the Spaniards would have come.

I asked Tsethlikai what had happened here in 1539. As a young girl, she had been told the story by her father. "At first the Zuni thought he was a great man," she said. "They liked the parrot feather plumes that he had. They thought he must be an important man.

"But Esteban came to look around and see what was here. He started demanding food and shelter. Then he started wanting our women. That's why the Zunis got mad and killed him."

*   *   *

THE EXPEDITION LED by Coronado amounted to a virtual army, as 400 armed men, more than 1,300 Indian allies, and four Franciscan priests, driving hundreds of cattle, sheep, goats, and pigs, marched slowly north beyond Culiacán toward the rumored lands in the north. In July 1540 the forces reached Hawikuh. When the Zuni forbade entry into the pueblo, Coronado attacked, in only days completing what he grandiosely called "the Conquest of Cíbola." But the leader was disgusted to discover that Marcos de Niza's golden walls were made of mud and stones.

During the next two years, Coronado ranged all over what would become New Mexico, frustrated again and again in his search for gold and silver. When Puebloans offered him their most precious substance, turquoise, he redoubled his disgust. In 1541, an Indian whom the Spaniards called the Turk filled Coronado's ears with honeyed tales of a land called Quivira, far to the east, where the chief drank from golden cups hanging from trees. It is now clear that Puebloans invented Quivira in hopes of luring the despotic conquistador far away from their homeland. With the Turk as his guide, Coronado spent months marching across the Texas panhandle and western

Kansas, discovering instead of fabled Quivira only a succession of "wretched," nearly naked tribes. When at last he gave up the eastern quest, Coronado ordered the Turk strangled.

Among the expedition's dubious achievements was the European discovery of the Grand Canyon, when a lieutenant, García López de Cárdenas, guided by Hopi men, came to the South Rim as he sought a route westward to the Pacific. At first glance, Cárdenas completely misjudged the size of the colossal gorge. Guessing that the river threading the canyon bends below was only waist- or shoulder-deep, he sent several men out to scout, expecting their return in hours. When they regained the rim after three days, exhausted, their clothes torn to shreds, with the news that the great river was unfordable, an exasperated Cárdenas gave up his mission.

(A trenchant footnote to the Spanish discovery of the Grand Canyon: 317 years would elapse before the first Anglo-American reached the edge of the great abyss. In 1857, in the vicinity of today's Hualapai reservation, U.S. Army Lieutenant Joseph Ives gazed down at the river and the canyon below, before turning back in disgust as vehement as that of his Spanish predecessor. Wrote Ives in his government report, "Ours has been the first, and will doubtless be the last, party of whites to visit this profitless locality.")

Coronado's long foray through New Mexico decimated the native populations. In the Tiguex War, the Spaniards wiped out a whole complex of Pueblo villages, killing hundreds of inhabitants. Despite the conquistador's savagery, his expedition was a monumental campaign of exploration and discovery. Historians today devote whole conferences to figuring out just what Coronado did and where he went.

But on its return to Mexico City, the expedition was castigated as an expensive failure. For his pains, Coronado suffered bankruptcy and prosecution by the government for war crimes. Though he was acquitted, he never recovered from injuries suffered on the expedition, and died in infamy in 1554.

In the aftermath of Coronado, an ambivalence about New Mexico lingered for decades. Not until 1582 did an expedition set out with the aim of turning that northern hinterland into a colony. The first five such attempts came nowhere near success. The last and most feckless of them ended bathetically, out on the eastern plains, after one of its two leaders stabbed the other to death—prompting Indians to wipe out the whole party.

It was not until 1598, fifty-six years after Coronado limped back to Mexico City, that an army under Don Juan de Oñate rode up the Rio Grande and forced one pueblo after another to succumb to Spanish rule. Oñate was at least as merciless and violent a conquistador as Coronado. His advent is seared into the collective memory of Acoma pueblo. In December, the proud residents of its mesa-top redoubt resisted the attack of Oñate's lieutenant, killing him and ten of his soldiers in hand-to-hand combat. A month later, Oñate enacted his revenge. With a force of 70 armed and mounted men, he overcame the defenses of the pueblo fortress and set fire to the buildings. Between 600 and 800 Acomans—men, women, and children—died.

Even this rout was not punishment enough to tame Oñate's rage. After the battle, he decreed that every Acoma man over the age of twenty-five should have his right foot cut off, at the onset of a sentence of twenty years of slavery. Women older than twelve and all the younger men likewise were to serve for two decades as slaves. Only girls and boys younger than twelve were spared, assigned to become "servants" in Spanish households. At least sixty Acoma girls ended up as slaves in Mexico, torn for the rest of their lives from their families.

Oñate's conquest launched eight decades of colonial bondage for New Mexico's Puebloans. From Coronado onward, the Spanish distinguished between two distinct species of natives in this new land. The *indios de pueblos* claimed a higher rung on the ladder of presumed ascent toward civilization, for in building permanent settlements—"pueblos," or towns, of stone and mortar—they demonstrated a nascent aptitude for humanity. As such, they were viable candidates for conversion to the Catholic Church. Nomads such as Utes, Apaches,

Navajos, and Comanches, on the other hand, were *indios barbaros,* beyond hope of salvation (if indeed they even possessed souls), to be eliminated rather than brought into the Catholic fold.

Under Oñate's rule, New Mexico imposed a pair of legal obligations on the Puebloans that often reduced their existence to a fight for survival. *Encomienda* entitled each Spanish colonist to exact a tribute from a designated number of Indians in the form of goods—usually the staple crop of maize (corn) or the hides of animals. *Repartimiento* granted the colonists a similar tribute in the form of unpaid labor. These twin burdens were not the invention of Oñate; they sprang from a tradition dating back even before the discovery of the New World, to Hispanic dominion over the Moors. In exchange for these subjugations, the Spaniards promised the Puebloans protection against nomad raiders, but so small were the numbers of colonists in and around Santa Fe, so poorly armed and trained, that Comanche and Apache attacks still took their regular toll.

From the founding of the new colony through the first eighty years of the seventeenth century, it was Franciscan friars, rather than Jesuits or Dominicans, who fulfilled the divine mandate to bring the word of God into the hearts and minds of natives who for centuries had gathered in their kivas and plazas to worship "foolish idols" and practice their "hideous rites." From the start, the Puebloans were mystified and misled by the twin rule of church and state. For it was not at all clear whether the demands of the colony's governor and soldiers were to be obeyed, or the exhortations of the priests.

Despite the apparent smoothness of Oñate's conquest, New Mexico got off to a bad start. An air of demoralization quickly set in among the ranks of new settlers. Not only was there no gold or silver to be mined in the hills rising on either side of the Rio Grande, but crops and livestock suffered under the fickle climate of this arid land. Near starvation became the normal state of existence for the Indians and even for the poorer colonists, many of whom gave up and returned to the more fruitful colonies to the south. By 1608, the Spanish population of New Mexico had dwindled to about 200. In that year, one of the great historical ironies in the long pageant of European subjugation of the tribes of North America unfolded.

Chastened by the dismal reports of life in New Mexico that messengers carried south to the capital, in 1608 the viceroy in Mexico City sent a report to the Council of the Indies in Madrid summing up conditions in the new colony. On September 13, that body formally recommended the immediate and complete abandonment of Nuevo México.

How different the history of the American Southwest would have been had the Council's recommendation been carried out! Might the first invaders to disturb the balance of power and territory among the many tribes who roamed and settled the canyons, plains, and mountains between the Rio Grande and the Colorado River have been the lawless, mostly illiterate mountain men of the 1820s and '30s?

It was not to be. Alarmed by the Council's declaration, the Franciscan friars of New Mexico thwarted the abandonment. A single fact-finding priest, Fray Lázaro Ximénez, returned to Mexico City in December 1608 claiming that no fewer than 7,000 Indians had been converted and baptised in the short decade of Spanish rule. (That total is highly suspect, even if scores of Puebloans may have submitted to the strange rituals of the catechism and immersion in water that the blue-robed magicians dispensed, with little notion of what such acts signified.) To leave a converted Indian without spiritual guidance, allowing him to lapse back into the sorcery of the kachinas, would be to commit a misdeed far more grievous than simply to turn Spain's back on natives who had never emerged from their aboriginal ignorance.

So persuasive was this argument that the Council pondered a plan to transplant all 7,000 of the converted Puebloans to New Spain, where the Franciscans might continue to minister to their souls. Instead, the Crown declared the spiritual cost of giving up on the colony unbearable. No matter how marginal New Mexico remained, no matter the hardships the settlers must continue to undergo, the struggling colony must not be abandoned.

In theory, the governor of the colony, appointed by the viceroy of New Spain, was in charge. But the more ambitious Franciscan friars wielded powers that sometimes trumped those of their civilian rivals. The priests' ultimate weapon was to threaten to send reports of treason or corruption back to Mexico City. Several of those prelates were infected by a grandiosity that verged on madness, such as Fray Isidro Ordoñez, who proclaimed to a Santa Fe congregation in 1613, "Let no one persuade with vain words that I do not have the same power and authority that the Pope in Rome has, or that if his Holiness were [here] in New Mexico he could do more than I."

Throughout the first eighty years of the seventeenth century, power-hungry priests and governors attacked one another as they claimed supreme command of the unstable colony. The Puebloans who bore the brunt of this misrule observed it in stunned bewilderment. Although a few of the priests treated the Indians with kindess and curiosity, on the whole the Franciscans made demands on the natives that exceeded the most draconian requirements meted out by the governors. Centuries before even the first glimmerings of cultural relativism came into vogue, the men of God could muster only outrage as they beheld the workings of a religion based on a polytheistic cosmos whose supernatural emissaries—the kachinas—regulated human destiny. When impassioned arguments in the form of sermons proclaimed in the newly built churches failed to enlighten the Puebloans, all too often force became the last resort.

Perhaps the most notorious such treatment took place at Hopi in 1655. The resident padre, Salvador de Guerra, flew into a fury when he caught a man from the ancient village of Oraibi, whose Spanish name was Juan Cuna, performing "a sinful act of idolatry." According to three witnesses who later testified in Guerra's trial, the priest first gave Cuna "many kicks and punches, from which he was bathed in blood." Next the padre tied the Hopi to a stepladder and "whipped him with much severity and many times on the back, belly, and all the other parts of his body." As if this were not punishment enough, Guerra finally "scalded [Cuna] from head to foot with a large lump of turpentine, and burned him with it."

Having doled out his treatment, the padre ordered Cuna to walk under guard 25 miles from Oraibi to Awatovi, the outlying village where Hopi's *penitenciados*, or convicts, were sequestered. On the way, unable to take another step, "unconscious and speechless," the wretched native died of his wounds.

This was too much for the chief custodian of New Mexico's missions. Brought to trial, Guerra, who denied punishing Cuna more vigorously than by giving him a single slap on the face, was sentenced to deportation to Mexico City. Historians doubt whether that verdict was ever carried out. By 1659, Guerra was once more in the pulpit, first at Taos pueblo, then at Isleta, where he continued to wage his relentless battle against pagan idolatry.

Throughout the first eight decades of the seventeenth century, the Puebloans under the Spanish yoke, from Hopi to Taos, bore all manner of mistreatment and subjugation from both church and state. So silently did they guard their suffering that the authorities never suspected that anything was brewing. The twenty-sixth governor of New Mexico later swore, in utter consternation, that the colony of which he was in charge had been flourishing in a state of unbroken "peace and tranquility."

Everything changed on a single day.

* * *

IN THE COLONIAL history of the Americas, there is nothing quite like the Pueblo Revolt. In near-total secrecy, a visionary shaman named Popé, from San Juan pueblo north of Santa Fe, concocted a brilliant plot with village leaders all the way from Taos to Hopi, a distance of more than 350 miles. Runners carried knotted cords to each of the far-flung pueblos, telling the village headmen to untie one knot each

day until none were left. On that day, August 10, 1680, the grievances of eighty-two years of oppression burst into flame. Warriors
in the pueblos killed 380 settlers, including women and children,
meeting only token resistance. Of the 33 Franciscan friars stationed
across New Mexico, 21 were slain. The rebels reserved their cruelest
killings for the priests—as, for instance, at Jemez, where Fray Juan
de Jesús was stripped naked, tied to a pig's back, and paraded along
a gauntlet of kicks and blows before he was dispatched with a sword
through the heart.

The outrage that dictated such vengeance took shape in the destruction and defilement of the churches. In the wreckage at Sandia, for
example, stunned eyewitnesses reported finding a statue of Saint
Francis with his arms hacked off, as well as paintings of saints and
the holy communion table smeared with human excrement. Many of
the churches were burned to the ground.

Under the colony's witless governor, Antonio de Otermín, nearly
1,000 Spaniards who had survived the initial attack took refuge in a
stockade at the center of Santa Fe. After five days of siege by an army
of Puebloan warriors, those colonists were allowed to retreat down
the Rio Grande toward El Paso. Otermín bewailed his misfortune by
declaring the revolt a "lamentable tragedy, such as has never before
happened in the world."

In the rebellion triggered by Popé's apocalyptic vision, New
Mexico was purged of Spaniards to the last woman and child. Never
before had the famously autonomous pueblos collaborated in such a
joint campaign, nor would they ever do so again. For twelve years
the Pueblo world basked in a freedom it had not known since before
Coronado's massive invasion in 1540.

It is often said that history is written by the victors. But because
the only languages the Puebloans knew were oral ones, that formula
cannot be affixed to the events of 1680 to 1692.

In 2004, I published a book about the Pueblo Revolt, after more
than two years of research among archives and libraries and on the

ground in New Mexico and Arizona. By then, I knew how insular the twenty-one pueblos that survive today tend to be, how fiercely their people guard their sacred or secret lore. But somewhat naively, I assumed that the twelve-year span of freedom from Spanish rule ought to be the pueblos' proudest accomplishment, and that testimony about that glorious liberation might be forthcoming from the descendants of the men and women who had carried it out.

Instead, I ran head on into a wall of bureaucratic avoidance. At one pueblo after another, whatever person I approached in the tribal headquarters about how to proceed with my inquiry responded with some variant of "You'll have to bring that up with the tribal council." Or with the governor. But a meeting with those officials seemed impossible to arrange.

I decided to focus my effort on Jemez, which before 1680 had borne afflictions under Spanish tyranny at least as dire as those endured at any of the twenty other pueblos. It took me two months to set up a meeting with the Cultural Committee at Jemez. During two hours in the conference room of the governor's office, I was met with a reception that ran the gamut from stony silence to private exchanges in Towa (spoken only at Jemez) to overt hostility. Near the end of my trial by distrust, one member of the council leaned back in his chair, squinted at me, and demanded, "What's in it for Jemez?" Another man explained, "We just don't want to get screwed . . . again." The first fellow added, "The thing that really bothers me is that you keep talking about 'my book.' This is all about you."

Late that evening, I staggered out of the conference room with the injunction to put my request in writing in a letter to Jemez's lieutenant governor. I never bothered.

By the end of my research, the fruit of my attempts to talk to Puebloans about the revolt was limited to interviews with five men and women who had gone beyond their home education to pursue graduate degrees at Anglocentric universities. They were, in a sense, historians and artists with one foot in each of the two New Mexican worlds. That, along with a few published works by Puebloans that touched on the Revolt and the weirdly skewed Spanish records of Puebloans captured during campaigns to reconquer the colony, who were compelled (often by torture) to explain what had brought on the blitzkrieg of the Revolt and how life in the pueblos had been led during the next twelve years, comprised the sum of my understanding from primary sources about what several scholars have called "the greatest event in New Mexico's history."

Popé's vision had postulated that after the revolt, the people must forswear any taint of things introduced by the Spanish. But having grown accustomed to beef and pork and mutton, to cherries and peaches and chile peppers, to wool for weaving and horses to ride, Puebloans found it difficult to give up the Spanish lifeway altogether. Popé had gone so far as to decree that his people should wade naked into rivers and scrub their bodies with yucca root to undo the curse of baptism.

Rumors filtered down after 1692 that, rather than revert to Puebloan egalitarianism, the leaders of the Revolt had been corrupted by power and wealth, becoming, in the worst cases, "more Spanish than the Spanish." And the brief unification that Popé had wrought with the knotted cords collapsed, as pueblos began to war with one another. So hazy is the record of the twelve-year interregnum in New Mexico that some scholars have wondered whether Popé even existed, except as the composite legend of the most forceful of the shamans and warriors who engineered the great rebellion.

Most surprising to me were the hints I gathered from one pueblo after another that younger men and women today really knew very little about the Revolt. If as children or adolescents they had shown interest in that long-ago upheaval of the Puebloan world, their elders discouraged their curiosity. It had been a bad time; bad things had happened back then. This veil over the past sprang in part from a deep Puebloan belief that strife and killing are inherently evil, that the Revolt had disturbed the harmony of the cosmos. But it seemed to derive as well from inklings that freedom and power after 1680 had bred their own corruption, had turned allies against one another, had sown chaos instead of peace.

In any event, the reconquest of New Mexico came at the hands of a general named Diego José de Vargas. In 1692, he marched up the Rio Grande at the head of a sizable army, winning the submission of one pueblo after another, aided by the recruitment of Puebloan warriors who were happy to attack neighbors against whom they nursed grievances. On September 13, Vargas erected a cross in the Santa Fe plaza and proclaimed the retaking of New Mexico complete.

From the relative ease of Vargas's initial campaign has come down to us the myth of the Bloodless Reconquest. In reality, the pacification of the pueblos dragged on for four more years, during which Vargas attacked and later punished and executed the natives who dared to resist. All in all, his campaign was every bit as violent and cruel as Oñate's.

Yet a pageant launched in 1712 still unfolds each September in the twelve-day Fiesta of Santa Fe, during which the myth is reenacted, complete with the knighting and coronation of a Vargas impersonator and a procession that carries La Conquistadora, a wooden statue of the Virgin Mary, through the streets before reinstalling it in the basilica of the cathedral. Beloved by many Hispanic descendants of the conquerors, the Fiesta is resented and abhorred by most Puebloans.

Thus the brilliantly executed liberation of New Mexico from its Spanish rulers lasted only a little more than a decade. The reconquest was inevitable, of course, given Spanish superiority in arms and wealth to the material power of the native people. The Pueblo Revolt might thus be viewed in some lights as a failure. But after 1692, Puebloans emerged from their new submission to Spanish authority with crucial improvements in their way of life. Gone for good were the hated burdens of *encomienda* and *repartimiento*. Even more important, though new generations of Franciscan friars were as determined as ever to convert their charges to the True Church, the religion of the kachinas was allowed to exist, rather than being punished with the torture and even execution of shamans who refused to convert.

Such was the world that Escalante and Domínguez entered when they rode north from Mexico City to take up their new posts among the pueblos in 1774 and 1775, respectively. Francisco Atanasio Domínguez was about thirty-six years old when he set off on the expedition he would lead with Escalante (his birth date is uncertain). Unlike the younger padre, Domínguez was born in Mexico City rather than Spain. At the age of seventeen, he had been admitted to the Franciscan order.

Domínguez's charge in New Mexico was a demanding and important one: to visit all the pueblos and compile a detailed report of the condition of the church in each one, as well as a census of the Indian population. It was a mandate he would fulfill both before and after his daring journey into the unknown Southwest. The massive report he composed was filed, then forgotten, by the authorities for whom it was written. It was rediscovered only in the early twentieth century, among miscellaneous papers in the Biblioteca Nacional de México. Published in an English translation in 1956, it is now regarded as one of the most valuable primary sources on colonial New Mexico.

His eventual comrade, Silvestre Vélez de Escalante, arrived in New Mexico a year earlier than Domínguez, and was promptly assigned to the remote pueblo of Zuni. From that outpost in 1775, at his own initiative, he undertook the dangerous proselytizing journey to Hopi alluded to in the early pages of this chapter. Despite his youth, and poor health that would dog him throughout his short life, Escalante was regarded by his superiors as a friar of great talent and devotion.

Even before the Pueblo Revolt, the leaders of New Spain had been ambitious to explore and settle other regions of the vast continent that stretched indefinitely north from Sonora and Chihuahua. In the eighteenth century, a chief motivation was paranoia about rumored encroachments on that terra incognita by Russia from the north and France from the east. But rugged topography, hostile tribes, and the nightmarish difficulties of maintaining supply routes to regions so far from Mexico City thwarted one effort after another.

No one pursued these goals more zealously than the missionaries who hoped to bring the light of God to the natives stranded in spiritual darkness in those frontier regions. Father Eusebio Kino, an Italian Jesuit, pushed far into what is now southern Arizona, founding the mission of San Xavier del Bac, a few miles south of present-day Tucson, in 1692. He tried to make peace with the semi-nomadic tribes he encountered in that hinterland, including the Papago, Pima, Yuma, Yavapai, and Western Apache, but the truces he forged were fragile ones.

Meanwhile, the shores of the great Pacific Ocean north of the dangling peninsula of Baja California, reconnoitered by Spanish navigators, promised a huge, fertile ground for settlement and conversion. A mission at San Diego, the first in modern-day California, was established in 1769. Its founder was the Franciscan friar Junípero Serra, as charismatic and industrious a man as Kino. Eventually Serra would found twenty-one missions in California, but the one that galvanized New Spain's often desultory colonizing passion was Mission San Carlos Borromeo, planted at Monterey in 1770. Although it would take months for news—and orders—to travel from the Pacific coast south to Mexico City and then back north to Santa Fe, that foothold was what inspired the Domínguez–Escalante expedition of 1776. The viceroy in the capital, Antonio María de Bucareli, was seized with the bold idea of establishing a trading route directly from Spain's oldest northern colony in Santa Fe to its newest at Monterey. Yes, that route would cross a vast region utterly unknown to Europeans, but the blank on the map cried out for exploration. Serra himself was the project's most ardent booster, as he outlined the challenge that route would pose to its pioneers. "According to the best of my information," he wrote to Bucareli in 1773, "if they start straight west from Santa Fe, with a slight deviation to the south, they will strike Monterey." The opening of that route, he added, would assure "a harvest of many souls for heaven."

In an age before any accurate means of determining longitude had been devised, no one could say even approximately how far apart Santa Fe and Monterey lay. Animated, however, by the successes of Kino and Serra, Bucareli hatched his plan. To launch it on the ground, the viceroy turned not to conquistadors in the mold of Coronado, Oñate, and Vargas, but to Franciscan padres.

Young they might be, and new to New Mexico, but Domínguez and Escalante were the men for the job.

*　*　*

JUST BEFORE NOON on September 2, 2017, Sharon and I drove north out of Santa Fe. From Hertz at the Albuquerque airport, we had rented a dark gray Toyota RAV4 SUV with Texas plates. Throughout our trip, good old boys at gas stations would ask us, in their Lone Star drawls, "Where 'bouts in Texas y'all from?" "It's a rental," I would answer, hoping to forestall chat about great high-school football teams or the legacy of the presidents Bush.

Domínguez and Escalante had planned their own departure for July 4, 1776, with no inkling of the momentous colonial unrest that was reaching its boiling point in a Philadelphia hall thousands of miles to the east. But logistical snafus and last-minute parleys delayed their launch until July 29.

On that Monday morning, the expedition members celebrated mass in the *castrense*, or military chapel, on the Santa Fe plaza. With the kind of flourish explorers of the day lavished on official reports, Escalante begins his journal with a grand evocation of the solemnity of their mission: "On July 29 of the year 1776, under the patronage of the Virgin Mary Our Lady conceived without original sin, and of the thrice holy Joseph her most blessed spouse, we, Fray Francisco Atanasio Domínguez, current commissary visitor of the Custody of the Conversion of St. Paul in New Mexico, and Fray Francisco Silvestre Vélez de Escalante, minister and priest of the mission of Nuestra Señora de Guadalupe de Zuni—voluntarily accompanied by"—he then named the other members of the team, with short identifying tags for most of them—"after the aforementioned had implored the protection of our thrice-holy patron saints and received the Holy Eucharist, set out from La Villa de Santa Fe . . ."

More than two centuries later, the Santa Fe plaza, though still a cherished locus of New Mexico history, bears scant resemblance to the hub of the capital from which Domínguez and Escalante set out in 1776. Only the much-remodeled Palace of the Governors, on the porch of which every Sunday Puebloan jewelry-makers sit before displays of their handiwork, as tourists from all over the world snap photos and haggle over prices, still stands from that early era. Even Bishop Lamy's much-admired cathedral, at the southeast corner of the plaza, dates from only 1869. By the end of the twentieth century, the *castrense* was long gone; in its place stood a J. C. Penney store. In 2017, Penney's was gone as well, but a kindred establishment, the funky Five and Dime General Store, fronts the diminutive plaza. There you can buy postcards, T-shirts, and souvenir gewgaws, or sidle up to the snack bar to sample the "World Famous Frito Pie—as seen on TV."

For two years leading up to the 1976 bicentennial of Domínguez and Escalante's epic journey, a band of fifteen scholars and historians under the leadership of David E. Miller divided the 1,700-mile route of the expedition into ten segments, then fanned out in pairs and trios to pin down each day's path and campsite along the five-month itinerary. By vehicle, by foot, by horseback, and by airplane they cross-examined the countryside, trying to divine through travelers' intuition the exact mile-by-mile progress of the journey, about which Escalante's diary is often maddeningly vague. They also plumbed oral history by interviewing resident old-timers, both Anglo and Native American. Their report, *The Route of the Domínguez– Escalante Expedition, 1776–77*, is a masterpiece of exploratory rediscovery. Sadly, it was published only in a loose-leaf "edition" with a plastic binder, and remains a rare volume today. I bought a copy from Bookfinder, the cornucopia of old and out-of-print works, for

65 bucks. The manual, its cover spotted with food and wine stains, became Sharon's and my bible on the road.

As a companion volume, the bicentennial commission issued a massive *Domínguez–Escalante Trail Bicentennial Interpretive Master Plan and Final Report*, which likewise survives only in a loose-leaf plastic binder edition. It was the goal of the commission to spur local chambers of commerce, highway departments, and historical societies to erect plaques and markers all along the expedition route. The dream of the 1976 enthusiasts was to create a Domínguez–Escalante Trail that devotees would retrace, as Revolutionary War buffs pursue the Freedom Trail in and around Boston (or as through-hikers throng the Appalachian and Pacific Crest trails). One of the tasks Sharon and I assigned ourselves was to see how many of those wayside memorials had actually been erected.

Our first stop, then, was the DeVargas Center, a shopping mall on Guadalupe Street, not far north of Santa Fe plaza. In the hopeful words of the *Interpretive Master Plan*, "a free-standing historic information panel in the parking lot of the DeVargas Shopping Center would describe the beginnings of the Domínguez–Escalante expedition. . . . In addition the sketch 'Leaving Santa Fe' would be good." In the parking lot on September 2, I could find nothing resembling a free-standing information panel, so I entered the mall and wandered past Great Clips and Elegant Nails, Starbucks and Subway, Señor Murphy and Panda Express. The only wall-mounted plaques that I could find ordered visitors not to smoke and to keep their pets on a leash. Vargas himself may have hovered ephemerally above the center, but D & E were nowhere to be found.

Once out of Santa Fe, we hummed along at 60 mph on U.S. Highway 84. The road felt cozily familiar to me from so many jaunts in the past, as I had headed toward Los Alamos to climb at the White Rock crag, or along the Rio Grande to prowl among the basalt boulders looking for petroglyphs, or on a drive to Taos almost twenty years before to visit the grave of Kit Carson, about whom I was writing a book. More than a dozen times I had traveled Highway 84 on the way to Bandelier National Monument, whose canyons and mesas had been home to Puebloans for centuries before the Spanish arrived. My first visit to Bandelier had come on a family outing when I was about twelve. My brother Alan and I had made a happy game of scurrying through the cavates in Frijoles Canyon—houses carved out of the soft tufa rock left by massive volcanic eruptions in the past—although our sister Jennie was spooked by the place, convinced that ghosts lurked in the pebbly nooks of the escarpment.

Even in the padres' day, the road north out of Santa Fe was heavily trodden, and in his diary Escalante wastes no words on the first day's journey, noting only that "at the end of nine leagues [about 24 miles] arrived at El Pueblo de Santa Clara, where we spent the night." The Tewa-speaking natives of that ancient village called their home Kha'p'o, but Oñate, with a conqueror's zeal to rename the landscape he had subdued, bestowed upon the pueblo the thirteenth-century identity of Saint Clare of Assisi, one of Francis's protégées and the founder of an order called the Poor Clares. (In 1958, Pope Pius XII designated Clare the patron saint of television, based on a scrap of hagiography that claimed that when she was too ill to attend mass, she could see it broadcast on the walls of her convent cell.)

Domínguez and Escalante would emulate the practice of Oñate, naming virtually every one of their campsites after some Catholic saint dredged up from their encyclopedic knowledge of ecclesiastical history. The pueblo remains Santa Clara today, even among the Puebloans who live there, though as we drove through the dusty streets we saw "Kha'p'o" adorning signs and office buildings. In the 89° heat, no one was about, except the dogs lazing in the shade of trees and adobe walls. We stopped at the shop of Naranjo Pottery, where a husky young man wearing an MLB cap perched backward on his head and a T-shirt that read "Fist Pump All Summer Long" showed us his jars and bracelets. Sammy Naranjo turned out to be a relative of Tessie Naranjo, the sage Santa Clara writer and activist who had been one of my five articulate Puebloan informants for *The Pueblo Revolt*. I asked him if he knew of any memorial to D & E to be found in the pueblo. The 1976 commission had urged, "A trail marker near Highway 30 [today's 84] would be appropriate recognition of the pueblo as a campsite of the expedition. . . . The message on the panel would be a general outline of the D/E story with the date that the group visited here."

Sammy shook his head. But when the look on my face apparently betokened disappointment, he added, "There used to be a . . . a *thing* out on the highway." With his hands he sketched some kind of shelter, perhaps a *ramada*, the traditional Spanish refuge from summer heat. "But the construction crews tore it down this year." Sammy chuckled. "It's been there so long I never read the writing. I don't know what it was all about."

0 for 2 so far, I thought, on the D & E memorial trail.

Domínguez himself had not been favorably impressed by the denizens of Santa Clara. In his mission report, he wrote about the Tewa carpenters who in 1758 helped build the mission church, no trace of which survives today, "And since these workers were very gluttonous and spoiled (in this land, when there is work to be done in the convents, the workers want a thousand delicacies, and in their homes they eat filth), the gravy cost the father more than the meat (as the saying goes)." Domínguez counted 67 Indian families at Santa Clara, comprising 229 persons. And he added a gratuitous sneer against the pueblo, as he sized up the village: "They have no true home, because hunger and the enemy [Indians] pursue them from every side as a reward for their levity, weakness, etc."

From Sammy we bought a tiny black-on-black jar in the style reinvented and perfected in the 1920s by Maria Martinez, the legendary potter from the Tewa pueblo of San Ildefonso, 10 miles down the Rio Grande from Santa Clara, then headed back to our car, making a last pass through the streets. Nearly every house had an adobe *horno*, or beehive oven, standing in the corner of the yard. Brought to the New

World by the Spanish, who had taken it from the Moors, the *horno* today is a standard appurtenance of Puebloan homes. Young women must master the art of using the oven to bake piki, a tasty, delicate paper-thin bread made of cornmeal, before they are considered fit for marriage.

The Pueblo world today is woven through with syncretism, the often strange hybrids wrought by centuries of Franciscan efforts to Christianize the Indians. The church standing in the center of Santa Clara is a prime example, its courtyard filled with row upon row of headstones, an inordinate number of whose dead were surnamed Naranjo, a thoroughly Spanish appellation. During Vargas's reconquest of New Mexico, Lucas Naranjo, a warrior from Cochiti, was one of the boldest leaders of the last-ditch effort to resist the Spaniards. After his small band was defeated by Vargas, Naranjo's severed head was presented as a trophy to the pueblo of Pecos, which had joined the Spanish as an ally against its fellow Puebloans at Cochiti.

On this Saturday afternoon, the Santa Clara church was closed. I used the smelly porta-potty just outside the churchyard fence, wondering when services were held and just what kinds of sermons might reach the ears of today's half-acculturated Santa Clarans. As we headed out of town, I noted that the high school sports teams were named the Hawks.

We drove on north. In Española, we found the parking lot of the Richard L. Lucero Community Center. Here, the *Interpretive Master Plan* of the Bicentennial Commission had envisioned "a free-standing historic information panel and site . . . with a paved walk added for access. . . . A sketch of the padres would help." My search among the parked cars came up empty again. In one corner of the lot, a Latino family was gathered around a grill frying burgers. In their weekend joviality, they did not look like the opioid addicts conjured up by our Santa Fe friend's warning. Española is one of the most thoroughly Latino towns in the Southwest. For more than a century, Puebloans from Santa Clara, San Ildefonso, and Ohkay Owingeh (formerly San

Juan) have depended on the shopping plazas of Española to stock up on groceries and household goods, but the edginess of cultural clash persists. In 2003 Tessie Naranjo had told me, "When my mother, who is eighty-seven, and I drive into Española, and we're in the car after dark, she says to me in Tewa, 'Close the windows, the Spanish are all around!'"

The Commission's fond plans for a string of commemorative markers seem to have fallen on deaf local ears. With the Lucero Center, they were batting 0 for 3—0 for 4, if you counted the memorial in the Santa Fe plaza that did not exist.

From Española north we stayed on Highway 84, leaving behind the Rio Grande as we ascended its tributary, the Chama River. In 1776, Española was still a century away from being founded as a railroad depot, but 22 miles up the Chama lay Abiquiu, then a collection of adobe houses that stood at the northwestern frontier of the colony. Beyond was the half-known territory dominated by nomadic Utes. "Abiquiu" is a Spanish mangling of the Tewa name Phesu'u, meaning "timbered point of land." As a Spanish settlement, it dates from the 1740s, although it had been a Tewa pueblo long before that. By 1776, the trail to Abiquiu was already a regular run, and in his diary Escalante covers July 30 in a single long sentence, recording an eventless ride of "nine leagues, more or less" (about 24 miles).

In our RAV4, Sharon did most of the driving as I pored through my books and papers for clues to seeing the landscape through eighteenth-century eyes. Like me, she had become a cautious driver, almost never exceeding the speed limit, signaling diligently for turns and lane changes, keeping the headlights on day and night. (My Utah hiking buddy Vaughn Hadenfeldt liked to tease me for "driving like a Navajo," as he invoked the elders on the reservation who trundled their pickups along the highway in no particular hurry to get anywhere.) We almost never turned on the car radio, for this far from Santa Fe NPR seemed not to exist, the available stations ranging from country ballads to Hispanic pop to Christian evangelists. Our SUV was equipped with a "lane departure warning system" whose annoying chirps I never figured out how to disable. We chatted about friends back home in Boston, but more often about the day's logistics. I pointed out peaks and canyons I'd wandered among on other jaunts, and I read aloud from Escalante's diary and the Bicentennial Commission's route guide.

All the previous excursions by auto we had made over forty-nine years of marriage had been with the goal of getting somewhere— even the five mind- and body-numbing pilgrimages up the Alaska Highway in our baggage-crammed Saab on our way to unclimbed mountains. This journey, in contrast, felt more like a classic American road trip than any we had shared before. "I travel not to go anywhere, but to go," wrote Robert Louis Stevenson about his donkey ramble across the Cévennes in central France. But of course, I was indulging in an illusion. It was the ghosts of D & E that set our course.

In Abiquiu this late Saturday afternoon, the library and the community center were closed, but the church, Santo Tomas el Apostol, was open. Built in 1740, it is a gem of Catholic architecture softened by native ideas of harmony. The sinuous curves of its warm brown adobe walls that O'Keeffe so loved mute the sternness of the martyrs' portraits that line the walls of the nave, whose ceiling is supported by stout, carved beams of dark brown wood. But the house of worship that so many tourists photograph today is not the one in which Domínguez and Escalante celebrated a "solemn high mass" and "once more implored the aid of our thrice-holy patron saints" before setting off into the little-known north, for today's Santo Tomas was rebuilt from the ground up in 1935 after the old church burned down.

It would have been logical for the residents of Abiquiu to put up some kind of memorial to D & E, for the padres' mission embodied the boldness of Spanish exploration at its most energetic. So the Commission believed, urging that "an appropriate site in Abiquiu pueblo is recommended for placement of an Indian interpretive marker explaining the attitude and role of the pueblo with respect to Spanish exploration." I searched through the streets and managed to find two historic markers. One extolled the achievement of Georgia O'Keeffe; the other sang the wonders of the local geology—Chinle slate from the Triassic era. (0 for 5 for D & E along the trail.)

Domínguez had toured Abiquiu in 1775 as he took the measure of New Mexico's pueblos. His estimation of the character of the Indians living there was as dim as his verdict on the Santa Clarans. "The lands are extremely fertile," he wrote, "but their owners, the Indians, are sterile in their labor and cultivation, so that they do not yield what they might with attention, and as a result so little is harvested that the Indians are always dying. . . . There is little to be said about their customs, for in view of their great weakness, it will be understood that they are examples of what happens when idleness becomes the den of evils."

Whether or not the padres found themselves surrounded by lazy Puebloans sunk in a morass of sin, they recognized that Abiquiu was the last outpost of civilization before their small team plunged into the wild. They stayed over for a second day "due to various circumstances," as Escalante curtly records their delay. Annotating the 1976 edition of Escalante's journal in English, Ted Warner heightens the drama of that last step on the threshold of the unknown: "Abiquiu was on the frontier and was the last contact which the explorers had with a Spanish settlement for the duration of the journey, and one can readily imagine the final rush to complete provisions and send final messages, and the anticipation with which the group prepared to move on."

As the sun wheeled west toward a high forested ridge on September 2, Sharon and I drove dirt roads up toward our sublime campsite overlooking the waving grasses of the Abiquiu Land Grant on one side and the sharp square silhouette of Cerro Pedernal on the other. We hauled our gear out of the RAV4, set up our tent, cooked dinner on our stove, and built a small fire of ponderosa branches. In the wee hours my bad dream arrived. But when the sun pierced the horizon in the morning, I felt no trepidation about the long journey ahead of us—instead, a jittery impatience to get going, a hunger to move, a humming in the blood. During the two years before our trip, those were the emotions I had forgotten how to feel.

Chapter Two

WHERE ARE THE INDIANS?

FOR ABOUT TWO DECADES—ROUGHLY BETWEEN THE AGES of sixteen and thirty-six—mountain climbing was the most important thing in my life. For thirteen straight years, from 1963 to 1975, I went off on expeditions to mountains in Alaska or the Yukon. I was invited by others to join jaunts to the Andes and Himalaya, but I always declined, for in arctic and subarctic North America I had discovered my own limitless promised land.

Obsessed with Alaska, I felt little urge to explore the rest of the world. At the age of thirty-seven, I'd never been to Europe, let alone South America, Asia, or Africa. But by my late thirties, the climbing compulsion had dimmed. It was no longer so easy to convince myself that the latest close call in the mountains was a fair price to pay for the elusive glory of a first ascent. Now, when something started to go wrong on a cliff or a glacier, I tasted nausea rather than giddy thrill.

A certain traveler's curiosity must have lain dormant all those years beneath my mountaineer's skin. But it was only in 1981, at the age of thirty-eight, when I began to write for a living, that I learned to embrace other ways than climbing of probing the mysteries of the world, in other places than the Great North. Magazine assignments and book projects took me to New Guinea and Borneo, to China and Ladakh, to Mali and Ethiopia, to Svalbard and Antarctica. The best of those forays plunged me into genuine adventures. Still, through the first ten years of my life as a freelance writer, something was missing, something as vital as the urge to explore itself. No matter how deeply I immersed myself in the search for the incunabula that pulsed in the shadows of knowledge, nothing I wrote, nowhere I traveled, seized my soul as climbing in Alaska had.

All that changed in 1992, when I traveled to the Four Corners region of the Southwest to write about a small band of dedicated amateurs who were trying to solve a historical mystery. In the 1890s, a cowboy-archaeologist named Richard Wetherill dug thousands of prehistoric artifacts—works of the Anasazi, or Ancestral Puebloans—out of sandstone alcoves in southeast Utah. Most of his collections ended up in eastern museums, but during the century that ensued, virtually all knowledge of the provenience of those relics—the sites from which they had been excavated—was lost. Using Wetherill's own penciled notes, the amateurs, who knew and loved the canyon country, managed to reconnect all those pots and baskets and atlatls and mummies with the dwelling sites where the Anasazi had left them centuries or even millennia before.

I wrote the article and moved on to other assignments. But the Anasazi, who had flourished for eons on the Colorado Plateau before abandoning the region en masse just before 1300 AD, had wormed their way under my skin. Only a few months passed before I made some excuse to head back out to southeast Utah to search for other ruins and rock art panels in the backcountry. So began a new obsession, which eventually fueled several dozen magazine articles and four books. For twenty-five years after that Wetherill gig, I returned to Anasazi country nearly every spring and fall, whether or not I chose to write about what I discovered.

Gradually I realized that I had found a passion that spoke to my restless spirit as Alaska once had. But it was only after years of hiking in search of ruins and rock art that I reflected on the fundamental difference between the obsession of my twenties and early thirties and my new love of Anasazi country. Whatever its rewards (and they are deep and undeniable), mountaineering is in some sense an entirely selfish pursuit. A first ascent is a claim to ownership of a certain daunting piece of terrain. The bravest exploits of the men and women who flirt with disaster to probe the heights benefit no one but themselves. Nor do those deeds elucidate any better understanding of the world in which they unfurl.

The pursuit of the vestiges of the ancients, on the other hand, was only in a superficial sense a selfish quest. No one keeps records of who found the Clovis point on Lime Ridge or the pottery kiln on Cyclone Flat. But each time I spent a tranced hour stepping gingerly through a fragile ruin I had never before seen, or fingering painted potsherds on some grassy bench, my mind was preoccupied with the questions, Why here? Why this? What did this mean to the Anasazi? It was not myself I celebrated, as I had on reaching a virgin summit. It was Them.

The Southwest replaced Alaska as my favorite place on earth. So, in late August 2017, as Sharon and I headed out to Santa Fe to launch our journey along the trail of Domínguez and Escalante, I was returning to what had become my psychic homeland. Whether or not the Spaniards paid more than cursory notice to the ruins of the ancients, they were trying to solve a puzzle posed by the very landscape the Anasazi had mastered. The worldview embodied in the hallucinatory petroglyphs and inaccessible granaries left by the ancients all over the Southwest had often verged for me on the alien or the unfathomable. But as I would come to see in September 2017, the worldview of Domínguez and Escalante was equally strange to my way of thinking. The challenge of our journey—to comprehend an Otherness woven into the Franciscan maze of canyons, rivers, and mesas—would prove every bit as tangled and rewarding as the mystery of the Anasazi.

* * *

ONLY SIX MILES west of Abiquiu, a dam impounds the waters of the Chama River, creating the usual reservoir that serves as a magnet for speedboaters, fishermen, and RV campers. Sharon and I set out the warm Sunday morning of September 3 on Highway 84, determined to stick as close as we could to the vanished track up the Chama that Domínguez and Escalante had blazed on August 1, 1776. Almost at once the small party ran into trouble. Escalante complains about "bad going because there are some little mesas very much strewn with rocks," then later about a "wooded canyon" that proved "very bad going."

Modern highways iron out all the annoying wrinkles that topography throws across a traveler's path. The day before, Route 84 had sidled in cozy proximity to the Chama on its right bank as we climbed from Española toward Abiquiu. After crossing the stream within the town limits, however, the road veered far from the river on its east shoulder, as if striking out for gentler ground unscarred by the gouging power of water in flood. Only when we turned off the highway, parked at the visitor center for the Army Corps of Engineers recreation area, and walked back across the top of the dam could we gaze down at the boulder-strewn box canyon that so vexed the Spaniards.

The dam was built between 1956 and 1962, during the same Bureau of Reclamation spasm of turning reckless rivers into placid hydroelectric power plants that gave America Lake Powell as it obliterated Glen Canyon—"the place no one knew." Somewhere in the murky depths of Abiquiu Lake lies the obscure junction where on August 2 D & E gave up on the Chama and swung straight north up the dry arroyo of its tributary, the Rio Canjilon. Only the more vigilant motorists today, I suspect, notice that Highway 84 likewise bids farewell to the Chama here and opts for the shallower canyon of the Canjilon.

On August 1, the explorers camped early, after getting caught in "a good heavy downpour." The next day, they must have cursed the wilderness in which they found themselves entangled—though whatever curses the pious priests allowed themselves must have been full of invocations to the saints rather than imprecations against the devil.

After going barely a quarter league (less than a mile), the men stumbled through "a scruboak thicket so dense that in it four horses vanished from our sight while passing through, so that we had to make a halt in order to look for them."

Yet just as they burst free from this bushwhacking mess, the men came upon "a short plain of abundant pasturage and one very pleasant to see"—pleasant for Escalante, because "it produces certain rosettes having a tint between purple and white which if they are not carnations, are very much like those of the same color." Modern commentators seem uncertain about just what "rosettes" so enthralled the padre. Along Highway 84 on the morning of September 3, Sharon and I were flanked by dense thickets of chamisa, whose bursts of bright yellow blossoms danced in the late summer breeze. The plant, also known as rubber rabbitbrush, boasts the Latin name *Ericameria nauseosa*—"nauseous" because the flowers when crushed give off a smell "described as pineapple-like by some and as foul and rubbery by others," according to a USDA write-up. The indigenous natives of the Southwest made a medicinal tea out of chamisa and masticated it like chewing gum. Throughout our weeks of driving the highways across four states, blazing chamisa served as the default foliage injecting color into the often stark landscapes through which we careened in our SUV.

Escalante had an eye—and a tongue—for flowers. That same day, after thrashing with his team out of the scrub oak forest and rounding up the lost horses, he paused to admire not only the rosettes in the "abundant pasturage" but also "clumps of *lemita* [squawbush], which is a red bead the size of the blackthorn's, and its coolness and taste very similar to the lemon's, so that in this country it is regarded as its substitute for making cool drinks," as well as chokecherry (whose taste is "sharp bittersweet but agreeable") and the stiff reddish-brown thickets of manzanita (with a leaf "like that of celery"). Yet throughout the long journey, Escalante seems oblivious to the grander features of the landscape. As you rise along the sluggish green trickle of the Rio Canjilon, the gray precipice of the Brazos soars 30 miles away in the north. Two thousand vertical feet of ribbed quartzite, the Brazos is the biggest cliff in New Mexico. It offers a serious challenge to rock climbers today, though a coterie of Los Alamos–based alpinists led by George Bell, veteran of the tragic 1953 American K2 expedition, put up bold routes on the wall during the 1950s and '60s. Escalante makes no mention of this dramatic landmark, which must have frowned down on his team for three August days.

Having left the reliable torrent of the Chama, the party traveled for miles without a drop of water. This was the first of several such choices made by the Spaniards that puzzle the modern student of the journey: knowing how vital water was to their very existence, the team deliberately turned away from canyons through which flowed perennial streams to strike out blind across parched land. On the afternoon of August 2, they came to a small spring, but, Escalante observed, "for the horse herds to drink even a little of it, it will be necessary to dig waterholes."

Here Route 84 sails north across a lovely plateau on its beeline toward the town of Chama, a tourist mecca lined with cozy cabins for rent, and the depot of the Cumbres and Toltec Railroad, a narrow-gauge line that belches coal smoke into the mountain air as it trundles across a 10,000-foot pass into Colorado. The track was laid in 1880–81 as part of the wildly ambitious Denver & Rio Grande (D & RG) line linking Alamosa, Colorado, to Durango during the mining boom. The Toltec Canyon, through which the train chugs on its clever path, was one of a number of locations in the Southwest named by Anglos who were sure that the Indian ruins they found everywhere were proof that the advanced civilizations of Mexico had pushed their empires this far north. Thus also Aztec, New Mexico; Cortez, Colorado; Montezuma's Castle, Arizona; and the like.

Just off Highway 84, a cluster of Hispanic towns flourishes today. Aficionados of New Mexico's Spanish heritage have created a must-see drive along State Highway 76 through the old villages northeast of Santa Fe: Chimayo, Cordova, Truchas, Trampas, Peñasco. The towns between Abiquiu and Chama on either side of Route 84 are every bit as historic, but no tourist board has yet converted them into "authentic" museums of the past: El Rito, Canjilon, Tierra Amarilla, Los Ojos.

In Canjilon on Sunday morning, we couldn't find anyone to talk to. There seemed to be no such thing as a store or a gas station. I was eager to find a citizen, for the *WPA Guide to 1930s New Mexico* claimed that Diego de Vargas's descendants were supposed to have ended up in Canjilon. Like so many other conquistadors, Vargas fell hard from his sudden glory. Only a year after his bloody completion of the Bloodless Reconquest, he was kicked out of the governorship of the colony, held for three years under house arrest, then shipped back to Mexico City to face a formal investigation into his alleged misuse of royal funds. (Columbus himself was arrested on his return to Spain after his third voyage and spent six weeks in jail.) Vargas was exonerated in the capital and briefly restored as governor of New Mexico, but he fell ill on a raid against Apaches and died in 1704 at the age of sixty.

It would have been intriguing to meet a man or woman in the dusty streets of Canjilon and find out if in 2017 the name of Vargas even rang a bell. But the only humans we could discover at large were sitting inside the local church listening in rapt attention to a sermon being delivered in English. I poked my head in, but could not determine what denomination I was watching in their devotions. The name of the church, San Juan de Nepomuceno, hinted at Catholic rites, but later, when I learned that John of Nepomuk, from Bohemia (in today's Czech Republic), had been tortured and murdered in the fourteenth century by King Wenceslaus IV, I was left to wonder why the patron saint of those who perish by drowning in floods was so revered on the high-and-dry New Mexico plains.

We recrossed Highway 84 and drove down curving lanes into the town of Los Ojos. It looked prosperous, with freshly plowed fields gleaming with moist earth, stands of green alfalfa, and spirited horses trotting across the pastures. Here on August 3 the Spanish team had regained the Chama River 40 miles upstream from where they had abandoned it to follow the dry gully of the Canjilon. But as they forded the Chama, one of the men, Juan Pedro Cisneros (a colleague of Escalante's from the pueblo of Zuni), rode his mount into a hidden sinkhole and the waters rose over the horse's head (presumably giving Juan Pedro a good scare). Escalante does not waste words explaining how horse and rider were extricated from the riverine trap (perhaps John of Nepomuk came to their rescue). Instead, he waxes enthusiastic about what an excellent place this bend on the Chama would make for agriculture and livestock: "good land for farming with the help of irrigation; it produces a great deal of good flax and abundant pasturage. There are also the other prospects which a settlement requires for its founding and maintenance." The future site of Los Ojos was the first locale along the team's trail on which Escalante bestowed such praise.

One of the maddening aspects of the Franciscan's diary is that nowhere in its pages does he explicitly lay out the purpose of the journey. To be sure, establishing a trade route from Santa Fe to Monterey was paramount. But there were several other goals motivating the party. One was to scout for sites for future settlements—and along with prospects of good places to raise corn and wheat and cattle and sheep came the dream of establishing missions to bring the word of God to the Indians. Though the first mention of such a purpose would appear only many days farther along the trail, from the start Escalante (and we presume Domínguez) fully intended to return on a second voyage to build churches and staff them with clergy, as Kino had in southern Arizona and Serra in coastal California. That he never got a chance to do so, that there would be no second voyage, must have been the greatest disappointment of Escalante's life.

Sharon and I parked just off the road on the outskirts of Los Ojos to have lunch. We set up our Walmart folding chairs in a little pullout, as well as our collapsible aluminum table, on which we laid out our comestibles: brie cheese with Ritz crackers, carrots and celery stalks with hummus, cucumbers and baby tomatoes to dip in blue cheese dressing, a Snickers bar. I drank a Starbucks Frappuccino, Sharon a Diet Coke. A couple of locals in pickups waved as they drove by.

Behind our backs the scrub oak clung to a steep slope that culminated in a short cliff of dark basalt, seeping with ground water. In that miniature amphitheater someone had built a shrine. Before we packed up lunch, we climbed a short staircase built out of basalt blocks to stand beneath the diorama. A pair of statues of the Virgin Mary, one gazing up in beseechment, the other, hands clasped in prayer, staring at infinity in the west, composed a vignette of both hope and sorrow. Fresh flowers had been inserted in every cranny in the bedrock, and small figurines of the Virgin had been balanced on every available ledge, from which hung strings of rosary beads. The upward-pleading Virgin held a bouquet of wildflowers in her hands. The cliff dripped with nature's tears. A wooden bench dated 2017 urged pilgrims to sit and contemplate. The whole tableau was enclosed in a chapel made of mortared stones, topped with a sturdy cross.

It was only half a day later, when I woke abruptly at 3 AM, that the connection clicked in my brain. As they left Santa Fe on their uncertain journey through a wilderness known only to the natives, Domínguez and Escalante had prayed for the protection of "Our Lady conceived without original sin." Two hundred and forty-one years later, the descendants of the Spaniards who colonized New Mexico worshiped at a wayside shrine dedicated to the Madonna, and the flowers and rosary beads bespoke a passion that was alive and urgent in the hearts of farmers and herders who had fulfilled Escalante's vision of a thriving town beside the Chama.

As we drove through Tierra Amarilla, named for the yellow clay Puebloans turned into pots, I braked suddenly at a sign announcing the Escalante Mid–High School. Here was the first indication along the 1776 trail that locals had any idea that the Franciscan friars had passed this way. The sign hailed the school as "Home of the Lobos," who had won the state football championship in 2012. On Sunday the school was closed, but I found a janitor unloading vats of food who, when I asked about the name, invited me into the kitchen via a back door.

"It all happened way back when," he told me. "Escalante founded his first mission here. But they tore it down." The man did not clarify who "they" might have been. "They built the first school here right on top of where the mission was. Same place as the high school is now."

"Who were the natives Escalante ministered to?" I asked a bit disingenuously. "Jicarilla Apaches?" The border of today's Jicarilla reservation lies less than two miles from Tierra Amarilla.

"Yeah. Them, and also the Navajos. There's a big plaque in the auditorium telling all the history, but the door is locked. You could come back tomorrow . . ."

I didn't have the heart to tell the man that though Escalante had indeed passed through the site of the future town, he had never founded a mission here or anywhere else in the Southwest. Besides, the local legend was more interesting than the historical fact.

I was tempted to come back the next day, read the plaque in the auditorium, and speak to the other guardians of the Lobos' legacy. But in our first eight days in the Southwest, Sharon and I had retraced only the first six days of D & E's journey—six days out of the 159 it had taken the padres to complete their trip. The road lay long ahead of us.

* * *

Having regained the valley of the Chama on August 3, 1776, the Spaniards could simply have stayed with the river and followed it straight north upstream toward its headwaters in the San Juan Range. Highway 84 makes that sensible decision today. Instead, once more Domínguez and Escalante chose to strike off northwest through woods and hills rather than follow the stream. Another dam, creating Heron Lake on the edge of today's Jicarilla reservation, covers the shallow valley of Willow Creek where the team plunged into difficult terrain. In a dark pine forest, "a loaded mule strayed off and did not turn up until after sundown, so that we had to halt on broken brambly ground. . . . There was no water at this site." If the friars were dismayed by their balky progress, the name they gave the new campsite does not betray it. Taking their bearings on three mesas that rose as high as 1,500 feet ahead of them—Sawmill and Tecolote, as they are called today, and an unnamed neighbor—they designated the place of their bivouac La Santísima Trinidad, the Most Holy Trinity.

The country beyond Heron Lake remains roadless and difficult today. As the 1976 Commission surveyors wrote, "This portion of the route is inaccessible except on foot or by horse." Even those diligent researchers balked at retracing the Spaniards' trail through this outback, all of it on the Apache reservation decreed by President Grover Cleveland in 1887. They claimed that posted property thwarted their efforts to find the route, while confessing somewhat vaguely that "The country in this area is so complex that preliminary ideas were altered several times as the researchers made actual observations."

On the afternoon of September 3, Sharon and I likewise balked at pursuing the vanished trail through the Jicarilla uplands. Instead we drove up Highway 84 to the town of Chama, where the road makes a sharp turn to the west, offering us the easy squaring of the two sides of a right triangle whose hypotenuse would have been the jagged line pursued by the Spaniards long before us. We stopped at the town's visitor center. I hoped to learn if even the faintest memory of Domínguez and Escalante survived in Chama, as it did so beguilingly in Tierra Amarilla. At the desk I found a young woman with painted fingernails texting away on her iPhone. I was not surprised when the names of the Franciscan padres drew from her a blank look. I thought about asking directions to the library or the town hall, but on the Sunday before Labor Day both were sure to be closed. It was clear that our host was eager to get back to her iPhone. Striving for gentle sarcasm, I said, "I suppose we could find out on the Internet." "Oh, yes," she answered, beaming. "I am sure you can find out on the Internet."

We left Chama and headed toward the westering sun. The great cliff of the Brazos had receded behind us, but now another startling precipice, the south face of 11,323-foot Navajo Peak across the border in Colorado, loomed in the north. Twelve miles out of Chama, we left the pursuit of D & E for the morrow as we veered north, still on Highway 84, hoping to find a campsite in the San Juan National Forest.

Just before that northward veering, a sign beside Route 84 announced that the gentle crest we were crossing marked the Continental Divide, at only 7,766 feet above sea level. Indeed, all the waters we had skirted since Santa Fe eventually joined the Rio Grande, which flows relentlessly southeast until it empties into the Gulf of Mexico near Brownsville, Texas. Once we sailed at 60 mph across the highway crest west of Chama, all the waters that we would encounter for most of the next month ended up contributing their currents to the Colorado River, which dumps its mighty load into the Gulf of California—or used to dump, for the impact of Lake Powell and Lake Mead and the pipelines siphoning their waters to the golf courses of Arizona and the swimming pools of California is to cause the Colorado to dry up in the sands before it reaches the ocean.

In the big picture, that nondescript crest on the highway outside of Chama demarcated the Atlantic watershed from the Pacific. Domínguez and Escalante, of course, could never have recognized the divide, for the land that lay before them was an unmapped maze, and whatever rivers surged across that blankness might end up flowing almost anywhere within the northern frontier of New Spain. Not even the ocean coastlines had been fully navigated or charted.

I spent the first five years of my life in Climax, Colorado, where my astronomer father had built an observatory deploying the Western Hemisphere's first coronagraph, a telescope that artificially eclipses the sun. It happened that our house sat exactly on the Continental Divide, at about 11,300 feet above sea level. For the reporters who sometimes interviewed him in his cloister on the upper edge of a molybdenum mining town, Dad used to claim that each morning he read the paper to find out whether droughts were more sorely afflicting the American East or West before deciding on which side of the house to throw the dishwater.

At the one-ranch junction of Chromo, five miles inside Colorado, we turned east off Highway 84 to follow a county road up the banks of the Navajo River. On either side well-kept ranches, some dating from the early years of the twentieth century, anchored rich alfalfa pastures. The whole valley was lovely, a vignette of the West of the Marlboro Man, but half the homesteads sported "for sale" signs. Eight miles in, the road turned abruptly away from the river, as it climbed through dense pine and spruce up a series of switchbacks inside the national forest. Only in a few places did the trees relent enough to offer fugitive views of Navajo Peak, whose dark brown cliffs soared imposingly above. On Sunday afternoon of the three-day weekend, most of the pullouts were already occupied. Clouds had been gathering in the west, and for the first time since Santa Fe it looked as though it might rain. The temperature dropped from the mid-80s to the high 60s, which actually felt chilly to us at the end of a leonine summer.

About half the campers whom we passed were wearing camo gear, even though hunting season was still more than a week away. Strangers in camouflage tended to give Sharon the creeps, while I insisted that hunters were, on the whole, a harmless breed (except to their prey). We had argued the point for decades. But I too had grown alarmed by the rise in recent years of survivalists playing games in the wilderness, some of them fueled by rage against the government.

On an outing about six years earlier, Sharon and I were camped with a friend (call him Jack) on a blissful sandstone ledge on a mesa in southeast Utah. We had come back from a good hike to discover that the folding knife Jack had left out among the cooking gear was missing. We had dinner and sat in our lawn chairs watching the sun slide below the western horizon. At dusk, Jack hopped on his mountain bike to take a spin down the dirt road on which we'd driven in. Half a mile from camp, he ran into a man in full camo gear hiking toward him. At once, the man dived headlong into the bushes by the side of the road. Jack walked closer and said, "What the hell do you think you're doing?"

After a pause, Camo Guy said, "I just don't want to be seen."

By the time he got back to camp, Jack was in an agitated fury. He'd taken a photo of the footprints in the road. Now, on a hunch, he hiked into the piñons behind camp. He found the same footprints circling our camp in closer and closer arcs.

We packed up in the dark, Jack slamming his gear into the back of his pickup, then drove five miles to an obscure bend on another backcountry road, where we pitched our tents in an ugly patch of weeds surrounded by junipers. Jack was so angry he couldn't sleep. I felt philosophical—you can find crazies anywhere, I thought, even in the cities. But Sharon's latent unease about car camping in the West, the same malaise that had her Googling opioids and crime in Española the night before we left Santa Fe, was lastingly reinforced.

Now, in the San Juan National Forest, we found a pullout with a rocky platform on which we set up our camp. Dinner was beans and pea soup. I had a beer, Sharon a glass of red wine. I got a fire going inside an existing stone ring. Just before dusk, three guys in camo drove by on ATVs, peering intently into the trees on either side. I waved at them. Only one waved back, without really looking at me. An hour later, a gunshot rang out somewhere in the distance.

A breeze came up, sending a few sparks flying away from the fire—harmlessly, I thought. Sharon's discomfort escalated. At last she said, "We have to be really careful with the fire."

"I know. I am."

"Don't build it up any higher."

Ten minutes later, the breeze increased. Sharon shifted in her camp chair. "I don't think it's safe."

"Look, I've been making campfires for more than fifty years, and I've never come close to starting a forest fire."

She didn't answer. It was a quarrel we'd had countless times before. The camo guys, I knew, had darkened her mood.

I sighed. "What do you want to do with it, then?"

"Put rocks on top of it."

"All right, damn it."

Like Jack throwing his duffels into the pickup, I hauled stones and tossed them onto my campfire, which sizzled and smoked as the flames dwindled. Then the rain came, with thunder and lightning. We retreated to front seat of the SUV, where I wrote by headlamp in my notebook.

"You always have to be the expert about everything," Sharon complained.

"Look, dear." During the last twenty years or so, we had begun calling each other "dear." One more quirk, I thought, of old age. "The wind, the lightning, the fire—they're all just part of enjoying the evening. We're not at home watching CNN." Had we spoiled the evening with our spat? Or had it been the gloomy forest overgrown with deadfall and bushes, patrolled by ATVers in battle gear?

An hour later we crawled into the tent and got into our sleeping bags. We kissed goodnight. I slept, untroubled by the kind of dreams that had edged my mind with dread the night before, in our perfect campsite above Abiquiu.

At the place they called La Santísima Trinidad, Domínguez and Escalante camped after traveling only five miles beyond the Chama. The next day, August 4, the team faced more tough going, along a "sagebrush stretch without path or trail whatsoever." Still they pushed on toward the northwest, entering forest again, searching constantly for water. Some kind of falling out among the party must have occurred that day, for Escalante closes his journal entry with the cryptic remark that "We halted in a canyon which, on account of a certain incident, we named El Cañon del Engaño"—the Canyon of

Deceit. That same entry gives the first explicit clue to an arrangement within the team that helps explain their often quixotic route-finding.

Once they had traveled beyond Abiquiu, Domínguez and Escalante began naming features of the landscape, especially camp-sites, as they went. But other names, such as Canjilon and Nutrias (a small creek near today's town of Tierra Amarilla), were already in place by 1776. Ambitious traders who left no written records of their deeds had ventured beyond Abiquiu for decades before the Franciscans set out, as they bartered with the natives, even though such trade was forbidden by the authorities. On August 4, Escalante writes that it was "the guides" who chose the route toward the three mesas, away from the Chama. At least two mem-bers of the team had prior experience in the unmapped domain north of Abiquiu. One of them had actually accompanied another expedition sent out by the government in Santa Fe in 1765, a full eleven years before Domínguez and Escalante entered the field. That expedition, led by Juan María de Rivera, is so poorly docu-mented that by the twenty-first century it had almost passed into the realm of the aprocryphal. Decades of assiduous research by a single self-taught scholar, Steven G. Baker, have only recently res-cued it from oblivion.

The "guide" who had ridden with Rivera had spent enough time among Indians met along the way that he was passably fluent in Ute. He would serve as D & E's interpreter. His memory of the "trail" he had traveled more than a decade earlier was clear enough that for the first third of their long journey, the friars entrusted him to direct the way. About this man, Andrés Muñiz, almost no information has come down to us. He remains a cipher in the expedition record. One wonders whether Muñiz was the provocateur of the *engaño* on August 4 that Escalante so tersely records. Throughout the journal the "guides" are almost never singled out for praise, but only for scorn and criticism when their route-finding seems to lead the team astray.

About the Rivera expedition, whose precedent helps to elucidate the several motivations behind the 1776 voyage besides the quest to blaze a trail to Monterey, much more below.

* * *

IN JULY 2015, I was diagnosed with stage 4 throat cancer. At Dana–Farber Cancer Institute in Boston, I plunged at once into a rigorous regimen of chemotherapy and radiation that lasted for four months. During that summer and fall, I was hospitalized four times for side effects ranging from colitis to aspiration pneumonia. Twice I came close to dying, and the second time I was in so much pain and despair that I actually thought I wouldn't mind getting it all over with. In the middle of that ordeal, unable to eat, I had a feeding tube inserted in my stomach. It stayed there for seven months, as every day I poured cans of Osmolite or Ensure Plus straight to my digestive works.

Yet by January 2016 I dared hope that the brutal treatment had eradicated my cancer for good. Radiation had permanently ruined my salivary glands, and when I could eat by mouth again, my diet was limited to the softest and gooeyest and blandest of foods. For months on end I had no appetite at all, and every meal became a pleasureless chore. But these losses seemed a fair price to pay for staying alive. In May, Sharon and I took our first trip out West in a year, and feeble though my short hikes were, they filled me with the joy of rebirth.

In July 2016, however, a biopsy on nodules in my chest that had recently enlarged revealed that the cancer, rather than vanishing, had metastasized to my lungs. Cure was no longer possible: instead I would have to hope that drugs might "manage" the cancer that would never go away. During the following year, I endured two more hospitalizations and another seven-month feeding tube. After a collapse and dash to the ER and then ICU in June 2016, the doctors discovered that I was the victim of a fiendish imbalance called SIADH (syndrome of inappropriate antidiuretic hormone secretion), which had caused my sodium level to plunge to a nearly lethal 115 (normal being 135–145). Like the metastasized throat cancer that had probably caused it, SIADH is incurable. For the rest of my life, I would probably have to swallow 6,000 mg of salt pills every day, add electrolytes to all the water I drank, and get a blood draw to check my sodium level every few weeks.

As a last-ditch stab at treatment, my Dana–Farber oncologist decided to give me infusions every three weeks of Pembrolizumab, an immunotherapy drug virtually untested for throat cancer. Despite preliminary research estimates that Pembro worked for cases like mine in only 15–20 percent of patients, the nodules stopped growing. By March 2017, I was able to hike again, and Sharon and I started believing in a future.

In August, we traveled to Paris and Fontainebleau, where we got through eight days of sidewalk cafés and walks in the forest without mishap. We decided to go ahead in September with the most ambitious voyage I had dared to dream of during the twenty-seven months since cancer had become the ruling force in my abruptly circumscribed life.

For some twenty years I had pondered the idea of retracing the 1,700-mile loop that Domínguez and Escalante had inscribed across a Southwest that was a blank on the Spanish map. Their voyage had fascinated me ever since I first read Escalante's vivid but enigmatic journal. By 2017, I was acquainted in some sense with almost all of the country through which their small party had traveled. I had actually wondered whether retracing their route might prove too civilized, since so much of it lay along highways and back roads traveled by motor vehicles since the 1930s. Yet to see the world with their 1776 eyes, to reimagine the plunge into the unknown the padres had so boldly assigned themselves, to grasp the story whole . . . By the end of the summer, I was ready for an expedition as challenging in its own way as the journeys I had forged into the wilderness when I was young and afire with health and ambition.

* * *

ALONG THE DOMÍNGUEZ–ESCALANTE TRAIL, I wanted to camp out as much as we could, for nights in the forest or on the mesa would better connect us with the padres' experience in the wilderness than stays in soulless motels. But ever since cancer had changed my life, camping, even assisted by an SUV, with a Coleman stove, a folding table, and folding chairs, had become more arduous than it should have been. Having lost 30 pounds, I was hypersensitive to the cold, and mornings in the high 40s Fahrenheit set me shivering once I crawled out of the sleeping bag. We'd bought special inflatable mattresses twice as thick as our old Therm-a-Rests, but sleeping on the ground brought out the worst in my back pain. Even once easy chores like gathering firewood left me breathless.

Throughout our trip, food was a big problem. The pea soup and beans we'd had for dinner the night of September 3 represented the kind of fare that we could pour out of cans and flush through my dried-up, spice-aversive mouth and queasy esophagus. When we stopped in restaurants, I turned at once to the menu listings for soups and salads, flipping past the burgers and sandwiches that anchored those bills of fare. Smoothies and milk shakes were high-priority options. Time and again I'd ask the waitress, "Is your guacamole [chili, chowder, stew] spicy?" "Not really," she'd answer. "Hardly at all." "But I *mean* hardly at all," I'd grumpily fire back. "I can't take any spices, period. I'm suffering from a medical condition that . . ." Half the time, I'd have to push aside a bowl uneaten. More often on our journey than I'd like to admit, Sharon and I lunched at a McDonald's, where, oddly enough, I could manage a dozen superthin french fries with ketchup washed down with a vanilla shake or "frappé." Still, I was happy to put up with the aggravations and uncertainties of food on the road. Back home, after all, the preparation of meals I could enjoy and digest taxed Sharon's culinary creativity to the limit.

On Labor Day morning, as we packed up in a thin fog, the ATV trio rode by again, still wearing their splotchy brown-and-green uniforms, still staring into the trees on the lookout for—what? Deer they could legally plug in another ten days? Imaginary enemies? In our RAV4 we zigzagged down out of the national forest, rejoined the valley of the Navajo River, and backtracked until we were again on the D & E trail.

Early on August 5, 1776, the Spaniards descended from the maze of mesas and hills through which they had pushed their way rather than follow the Chama upstream, as they reached a watercourse that flowed westward—most likely today's Amargo Creek. Oddly, Escalante confidently identified that current as the Navajo River, of which Amargo is a minor tributary; what's significant is that "Navajo" was a name already in use, like Canjilon, testifying to the collective if unwritten experience of traders in the decade or two before 1776 who had explored this hinterland. The chronicler was puzzled by the fact that the so-called Navajo River "carried less water than the Chama." The team followed the creek downstream, "through canyons, over inclines, and through very troublesome tree growth." Still in a bad mood, probably because of the *engaño* that had vexed the padres the day before, Escalante records the first of his many complaints about the "guides" in the party who supposedly knew where they were going: "The experts lost the trail—and even the slight acquaintance they showed to have had with this terrain." (How can you lose the trail, I wondered, when you're following a creek downstream?)

Back in New Mexico on the morning of September 4, Sharon and I left Highway 84 for good as we turned left on U.S. 64, which follows Amargo Creek. The old Denver & Rio Grande tracks also descend this gentle canyon on their way to the gold fields of Durango and Silverton. On our left, tucked out of sight, stood the tiny settlement of Monero. We found a highway exit and followed cracked pavement up a side draw, and as we did so, it seemed that we drove back in time most of a century. Monero felt like a ghost town. We followed the road to where it dead-ended in the yard of what looked like the only inhabited dwelling, a place called the Carrillo Ranch. As we idled our car and looked around, two men came out of the house, accompanied by two big white dogs that padded along without barking.

"You guys get lost?" asked the older of the two Hispanic men. I explained that we were trying to figure out where the Spaniards had emerged from the roadless upland to the south. The names of Domínguez and Escalante rang no bells for the men who had greeted us. "That was way before my time," said the older fellow with a smile.

I mentioned a couple of place names as I pointed south. "Yep, that's over on the reservation," the man verified. "No roads from there."

I asked how old Monero was. The question seemed to baffle my host. "The coal mines," he said, pointing to the west. "That's why Monero's here. And the railroad used to come through."

"Say, about 1900?" I asked.

"Yes." The younger fellow had not uttered a word. The dogs stood patiently eyeing us. "Maybe even before that."

As we prepared to leave, I apologized for interrupting the pair's Labor Day morning. "That's all right," the older man said, then, "You be careful."

The difficult route the expedition had followed for two days through the hills to link up the Chama River with the Navajo ran smack across today's Jicarilla reservation. Yet nowhere in his journal does Escalante mention the Apaches. That omission, however, can be explained by a glance at New Mexico history.

As a subset of the great Apache domain, to be distinguished from the Faraon or Lipan or Mescalero Apaches, the Jicarilla first appear in the Spanish colonial record only around 1700. When they do so, the tribe is reported to reside along the upper Rio Grande as far east as Taos and Raton, along the Sangre de Cristo Range, and out into the plains stretching toward what would become Kansas. Yet aboriginal sites have been found by archaeologists as far west as the Chama valley. The reservation decreed by President Grover Cleveland, of course, was neither a Spanish nor a Mexican solution to the "problem" of Athapaskan Indians claiming their ancestral land but an American fiat concocted well after the United States appropriated New Mexico after the Mexican-American War ended in 1848 and the Gadsden Purchase added a buffer in 1853.

As such, the Jicarilla reservation followed the standard formula imposed by governments in Washington on the natives in the West, with the usual tragic results. The solution was not to settle tribes on their ancestral homelands, but to force them to move to arbitrary tracts of land deemed worthless for American settlement. Cleveland's parcel of 800,000 acres well to the west of the ancestral Jicarilla domain, tucked up in hill and mountain country against the Colorado border, was actually the third try at a "solution," following equally arbitrary reservation tracts laid out even farther west in 1874 and 1880. Only the accident of landscape and the flexibility of the Jicarilla people prevented the kind of outraged refusal to acquiesce that plunged the Chiricahua Apaches in Arizona into all-out war against the government during the same years.

The land Cleveland gave to the Jicarilla would prove rich in agricultural, mining, and recreational potential. That morning, as we drove into Dulce, the tribal headquarters, we stopped to ponder the Great Seal of the Jicarilla Apache Nation outside the big administration building. The winging arrow that bisects the center of the seal is surrounded by vignettes featuring wickiups that look like teepees, herds of cattle, and oil derricks. Nowadays Anglo hunters and fishermen pay the tribe to go after trout in the reservation's crystalline streams and deer and elk in its lordly forests.

No surprise, then, that the Spanish team failed to meet any Jicarilla Apaches between July 29 and August 5 as they wound their way northwest from Santa Fe. But another line in Escalante's August 5 entry only deepens the Indian puzzle. Late that day, as the team finally reached the banks of the San Juan River just downstream from its junction with the Navajo, Escalante comments, "Together they now form a river as plenteous as El Norte [the Rio Grande] in the month of July, and it is called Río Grande de Navajo for separating the province of this name from the Yuta nation."

On the map of the expedition's journey later drawn by its cartographer, the remarkable Bernardo Miera y Pacheco (of whom much more in the chapters to come), all the country across which the team marched after Abiquiu is inscribed with the label "Provincia de Nabajoo." The source of Escalante's judgment about tribal borders was the team's "guides," Andrés Muñiz, who had been with Rivera in 1765, and perhaps his brother Lucrecio, as well as the unwritten wisdom passed down by the illicit traders with the Utes. But by August 5, the ten-man party had encountered no Navajos, either. In fact, another eighteen days would pass before the Spaniards met their first Indian—a Ute who suddenly appeared on August 23, well to the northwest in what is today Colorado.

How is it possible that the team could have spent almost its first full month on the trail, passing through country that was home to hundreds, perhaps thousands, of Navajos and Utes, without running into a single Indian? This fact is all the more extraordinary in view of the team's unprecedented vulnerability. Escalante never records the kinds of armaments the men carried, but they cannot have been numerous. Nor was there a single soldier among their party. Other Spanish expeditions crossing Indian territory, such as the infamous Jornada del Muerto between El Paso and Santa Fe, traveled in hourly fear of attack by "savages." To plunge into the wilderness virtually unarmed and untrained for war would have seemed suicidal to most Spanish officials in New Mexico.

There is no possibility that the Navajos and Utes were unaware of the Domínguez–Escalante expedition. The ragtag crew led by friars in blue robes would have looked like sitting ducks. If the Spaniards carried no obvious treasure in the form of guns or provisions, surely their team of horses and mules would have made for a rich harvest of spoils. What kept the Indians not only from attacking the defenseless party but from slipping out of their covert observation posts to talk to the men, perhaps to engage in the kind of trade that had tempted settlers to venture northwest in the years before 1776?

Nowhere does Escalante express the slightest hint of wonderment, or even frustration, at the fact that, after twenty-three days en route beyond Abiquiu, the team had encountered not a single Indian. Yet that strange truth remains one of the mysteries surrounding the daring (and daringly naive) quest the padres launched in the same year that the American colonies declared their independence from a tyrannical king across the seas in England.

Chapter Three

ESCALANTE SLEPT HERE

IT WAS MIDMORNING ON SEPTEMBER 4 WHEN WE DROVE into Dulce, the headquarters of the Jicarilla Apache Nation. On Labor Day all of the government offices were closed, but the Wild Horse Casino was open, its parking lot mostly full. The day before, as we passed through Canjilon, Tierra Amarilla, and Los Ojos, the only houses of worship we had seen were Catholic ones, as was the wayside shrine in Los Ojos whose statues of the Virgin were bedecked with flowers and rosary beads. In Dulce (population 2,743 in 2010), on the other hand, I spotted a pair of Baptist churches. An Internet search later fleshed out the picture with the Jicarilla Apache Reformed Church, the Dulce Assembly of God Church, and a sole Catholic enclave dedicated, I thought appropriately, to Saint Francis.

I had also noticed the slender white spire of Dulce's Church of Jesus Christ of Latter-Day Saints. All over the West, Indian reservations embrace well-attended churches dedicated to the Mormon version of Christianity. Their presence always bemuses me, for the Doctrine of the Lamanites translated by Joseph Smith from the golden plates decrees that Indians are the descendants of the Lamanites, the bad guys among the believers who sailed to the New World from the Holy Land only to wipe out the Nephites (the good guys) in all-out war around 400 AD. For their perfidy, God cursed the Lamanites with dark skin. But if they converted to the church and led lives untainted by sin, the Lamanites might become in the afterlife "a white and delightsome people."

What could possibly be in it, I often wondered, for a Native American (or an African-American) to become a Mormon? I got one answer some years ago when I interviewed a Navajo man in Roosevelt, Utah, who was an elder in the church. As a kid growing up in Leupp, Arizona, on the Navajo reservation, he had watched a string of missionaries ranging from Seventh-Day Adventists to Jehovah's Witnesses fail to convert his father and mother. "The Mormon missionary was the only one who had taken the trouble to learn our Diné language," the man told me. "And then later I read the Book of Mormon, and it all sort of made sense."

From Dulce we headed west on Jicarilla Highway J44, still following Amargo Creek, barely a trickle as it entered the winding canyon. The old D & RG railroad tracks paralleled the paved road. Five and a half miles out of Dulce, Amargo Creek joins the Navajo River, and J44 expires in a junction. J9 pushes on northwest along the banks of the Navajo, while J39 veers southwest up an unpromising gulch called La Juita Creek. ("Amargo" is Spanish for "bitter." "La Juita" is a family name, original meaning unknown. Both appellations postdate D & E.)

Here, on August 5, 1776, the padres' party got very confused, then effectively lost. When they struck Amargo Creek the day before, somewhere near today's semi–ghost town of Monero, they mistook it for the Navajo River—whence their puzzlement that the streambed "carried less water than the Chama." Even so, as they followed Amargo downstream, they must have run smack into the true Navajo River, which had been the object of their day's itinerary from the start. (If only Escalante had bothered to explain the deceit—the *engaño*— that had divided the team the night before, we might better understand their perplexity on August 5.)

It is here that the chronicler grumbles about the "experts" losing the trail. Still, the obvious course ought to have been to follow the sizable current flowing downstream through the canyon toward the northwest, whether or not the team recognized it as the Navajo River. Sharon and I would have needed no map to make that obvious choice on September 4. But instead the Spaniards turned up La Juita Canyon.

The text of Escalante's journal covering the team's struggles in this dead-end canyon epitomizes confusion, and is impossible to correlate with today's maps with any certainty. The tone, though, betrays the exasperation that must have ruled a day of bashing through thickets and woods and climbing slopes in hopes of an orienting view. "And so," the friar records, "to avoid going farther down, we took to the northwest [actually southwest]. We traveled without a trail for about three leagues [eight miles], going up a high mount but without a steep grade, and we caught sight of the said arroyo's sunken channel [apparently the Navajo River, even though the team must have already skirted that stream for half a mile before turning up La Juita Canyon]. We went over to it down slopes which were rather rough but negotiable . . ." Then, at last, "we crossed it at a good ford and halted on the northern side."

Only, to the team's chagrin, the river they had just forded was not the Navajo. It was the San Juan. Thus they discovered that except for the half mile before the team headed up La Juita Creek, they had missed the Navajo River altogether. "The experts," Escalante writes, "said that these two rivers came together a little farther up"—meaning that the Navajo was a major tributary of the San Juan, but by following the advice of the "guides" the team had missed the confluence completely.

As Sharon and I drove along Highway J9, following the Navajo all the way, I wondered: Were the guides so incompetent as to choose a blunder through the hills over the obvious track along the river? Why did D & E not follow the lay of the land, instead of blindly taking a route urged by the guides—only to complain later about the poor advice given them by the "experts"?

In September 1975, two members of the Bicentennial Commission trying to rediscover the padres' route ran into "no trespassing" signs on J9 at the Colorado border. Instead of blithely motoring on into the Southern Ute reservation, as Sharon and I were able to do forty-two years later, W. L. Rusho and Brad Smith set themselves the challenge of finding the precise path of the errant detour the Spaniards had executed on August 5. Rusho and Smith headed up La Juita Creek in a four-wheel-drive vehicle, then parked at a three-way fork between the hills to the west. On foot they hiked west, then scaled the "steep, wooded mountain" they thought the padres' party must have climbed to get their reorienting view of "the said arroyo's sunken channel."

In the late 1990s, I got to know Bud Rusho as I researched a pair of articles and later a book about Everett Ruess, the romantic idealist and wanderer whose disappearance near the Escalante River in 1934 inspired a cult that shows no sign of attenuating today. It was Bud's compendium of Ruess's letters and journal entries joined to his own commentary, *Everett Ruess: A Vagabond for Beauty* (1983), that had launched the cult. Until his death in 2011, Bud and I exchanged friendly but contentious memoranda about our various theories as to how the twenty-year-old met his end. Bud was a relentless and diligent sleuth when it came to hunting down clues to the past on the ground. At his funeral service in Salt Lake City, fellow historian Steve Gallenson testified, "Bud Rusho knew as much history of every square foot of the West as any man who ever set foot on the planet."

Above La Juita Creek on September 26, 1975, Bud and his partner reached the summit of a nondescript hill at 7,753 feet above sea level, and declared it the mountain from which the Spaniards had gotten their bearings on August 5. Sharon and I didn't take the time or trouble to retrace Bud's scramble, but when I later studied the USGS topo map of the area, I wondered how my friend could have been so sure about Point 7753, versus points 7698, 7830, or any of another half-dozen rounded peaks in the area. The only primary source, after all, is Escalante's journal, which is quite vague about "going up a high mount without a steep grade," a description that could fit most of the hilltops in the area.

The urge to be more exact than is reasonable is a foible that afflicts all kinds of historical sleuthing, especially when it pertains to the wrinkles of topography. Schliemann was sure that he had dug up the one and only Troy. I thought for half a year in 2008 that I had found Everett Ruess's grave. (I was wrong.) Bud Rusho's certainty about Point 7753 was only the first of an inordinate number of over-positive declarations that Sharon and I would run into in the coming weeks along the Domínguez–Escalante trail.

As I imagined the 1776 party pushing their way through the forest on August 5, I realized that I tended to picture them only as a string of ten men on horseback. But of course the Spaniards were encumbered by a pack train carrying all their gear and food for a journey the leaders knew would last for a minimum of several months. Among the many omissions in Escalante's admirable journal is any record of gear, provisions, or beasts of burden. We are left to guess how much baggage the men brought with them, on how many and what kinds of animals, and what exactly their saddlebags contained.

A pair of photographers who, like Sharon and me, retraced the route by automobile published their own account in 2011, in a handsome coffee-table book titled *In Search of Domínguez and Escalante*. Greg MacGregor and Siegfried Halus tried to extrapolate the logistical details from comparisons with other Spanish colonial journeys. They write, "Based upon previous expeditions and adjusting for the size of their entourage, it is assumed that [D & E] started with thirty horses, ten mules, and twenty head of cattle." Steven G. Baker, the perspicacious historian of the two Rivera expeditions in 1765, is forced to guess the size and makeup of those parties themselves, for Rivera's journal, far more vague and cursory than Escalante's, does not even give a roster of his companions. Baker estimates a team of fifteen or twenty men, implying that "there could well have been upwards of sixty or more animals involved." MacGregor and Halus thus propose a ratio of four horses and mules per man, Baker a ratio of three to four beasts of burden per voyager. Since there is no mention anywhere in Escalante's journal of cattle, or of eating beef, even when the men were starving, I ended up doubting that D & E had brought any cattle at all.

Still, taking only the low-end ratio of three animals per man, I needed to recast my mental picture of the team as it thrashed its way through the forests and hills of such rugged country as their detour west of the Navajo River on August 5. Every man on horseback, and interspersed among them some twenty horses and mules, each with saddlebags and duffels strapped to its haunches and back. No wonder bushwhacking could turn into such an ordeal. It is a testimony to how tough the men were that on difficult terrain they could still cover distances as great as 15 to 25 miles a day.

As mentioned above, in Escalante's journal, there is likewise no record of the firearms or other weapons the men carried. In only a few passages does the friar report the firing of a musket to procure game—most notably, a pair of bison much farther along in their arduous journey. Not once does the chronicler indicate that a gun was brandished to confront a hostile native, much less fired. Yet MacGregor and Halus confidently assert, "Each person would have had one musket and possibly a lance." Baker is more skeptical. As many as four of D & E's ten men may have been *genízaros*, succinctly defined by Baker as "Indians who had been taken from their own peoples and reared among the Spanish settlements, where they served as slaves, servants, and herders." With their dual cultural backgrounds, *genízaros* were useful to expeditions in the roles of guides and interpreters. Andrés Muñiz was a *genízaro*, as were, in all likelihood, the last three members of the team named in Escalante's first entry on July 29: Lucrecio Muñiz, Juan de Aguilar, and Símon Lucero. (Indians raised by the Spaniards were invariably given Spanish names.) Escalante's constant use of "guides" and "experts" in the plural hints at the roles of those three men, otherwise faceless in the padre's record, in claiming a knowledge of the route through Indian country. And apropos of Rivera's teams, Baker states unequivocally that "The *genízaros* would have carried only bows and arrows as primary weapons."

About the food the men ate each day along the trail, Escalante is also mute. Passing allusions among scattered entries refer to corn, flour, sugar, and chocolate. Those items were indeed staples of all the Spanish expeditions, but it is hard to imagine the mules and horses carrying sufficient quantities of each to satisfy ten men for three or four months, or even longer. Yet for D & E, Franciscan purism dictated a policy never to trade with the Indians along the way, not even for food, and only extreme hunger would eventually force them to relax that resolve. The other staple, mentioned a number of times in the journal, was tobacco. All early expeditions swore by the essential value of nicotine, and many a rueful diary passage over the centuries curses the fate of men deprived of anything to smoke.

In Escalante's journal there is no record of the men's clothing, camping gear, or other equipment. Writing about Rivera's two expeditions eleven years earlier, whose baggage was most likely similar to D & E's, Baker dismisses any notion of armor, obsolete by 1765. The men's garb would have been "simple cotton or woollen clothing and some buckskin items," as well as "some woollen blankets or sarapes." Blankets would also have served as sleeping bags. We know that Rivera's teams carried a tent, as the padres' entourage almost certainly did, but as for such supplemental gear as cots and camp chairs, the spartan style favored by D & E probably precluded such luxuries. As early as September, Escalante complains about the cold, and we can be sure that compared to any modern expedition, the Spaniards were ill-equipped to deal with plunging temperatures or prolonged rain or snow. Cooking each morning and night would have been accomplished in pots and kettles over the campfire. Perhaps each man had his bowl, spoon, and knife.

It's evident that the padres carried with them a copy of Rivera's journals. If those documents are the same as the manuscripts that have come down to us—first translated into English by historian Rick Hendricks in 2015—they would have served only as the most cursory guide to the first leg of the wilderness journey Domínguez and Escalante undertook in 1776. (The translated journal occupies only thirteen pages of Baker's *Juan Rivera's Colorado, 1765*.) Though punctuated by occasional vivid episodes, as a trail guide Rivera's journals would have seemed maddeningly vague and unhelpful. Not once in his own journal does Escalante report that he chose his day's route from anything Rivera had written, as opposed to the advice of the "experts," whom the friar constantly castigates for leading the team astray. Yet as they traveled, D & E kept looking for signs of their Spanish predecessors. On November 20, 1765, at his point of farthest penetration into the unknown, on the banks of a river he mistakenly identified as the Tizón (the Colorado), Rivera carved a memorial in the trunk of a cottonwood tree: "a large cross with a 'Long Live Jesus' [*Viva Jesús*] at the top and my name and the date at the bottom, so that our arrival there may be verified at any time."

In 1776, the padres searched in vain for Rivera's memorial. Since cottonwoods seldom live longer than 150 years, we can assume that the explorer's inscription for eternity has long since crumbled into the soil—if the Indians did not cut it down before that for firewood.

*   *   *

UNCONSTRAINED BY "no trespassing" signs, Sharon and I sailed down Highway J9 into Colorado. A few miles beyond the state line, the road ended in a T junction with a state highway running east–west. Here was the junction, also, where the Navajo River flowed into the San Juan, the confluence so eagerly sought by Domínguez and Escalante. The place was occupied by a winsome ghost town called Juanita, named perhaps after the river. Even after the trip, I was unable to learn much at all about the history of this settlement. The wood-frame houses and stores had a gold-rush look, and an old rail car left stranded on a siding sported a faded D & RG logo. But there were indications that the town had harbored hangers-on until relatively recent times. The gates to one spread bore a tin plaque with the name Gallegos, above a family crest of two bears rampant. The little cemetery, enclosed in its wire fence, blazoned a titular signboard with the advice "For information call . . ." and a southwest Colorado phone number, as if still welcoming applicants who might choose this patch of ground for their eternal resting place. Bouquets of artificial flowers rested against gravestones, one of which memorialized Juanita Gallegos, born in 1931. Either she was still alive somewhere in her eighty-seventh year, or she lay buried elsewhere.

Juanita's architectural anomaly was a Catholic mission that overlooked the town from a hill to the north. The paint on the handsome wooden building—white for the walls and three-story bell tower, red for the metal roofs—had only just begun to peel. But when we headed up the driveway that leads to the church, we were stopped cold by a sign sternly forbidding access.

On August 5, having forded the San Juan River, the Spaniards called a halt and named their campsite Nuestra Señora de las Nieves (Our Lady of the Snows) in honor of the peaks thronging the horizon to the north, rising to 14,000 feet, still snowcapped toward the end of summer. Vexed by the lay of the land, Escalante set off solo that evening up the banks of the San Juan to find the confluence with the Navajo River. As far as we can tell, this was the first time on the journey that any of the men rode off alone. Were the others too tired to join him, after a day's march of 21 miles, including the strenuous detour through the wooded hills? The friar was back after a further jaunt of 16 miles, reporting that at the site of the river junction "there were good prospects for a moderate settlement."

Escalante was even more enthusiastic about the meadows surrounding Nuestra Señora de las Nieves, where "there was good land with prospects for irrigation and everything needed for three or four settlements, even if they be large ones." He noted the abundance of trees on both sides of the river: "leafy and extremely dense thickets of white poplar [aspen], scruboak, chokecherry, manzanita, *lemita,* and gooseberry." Sharon and I drove across the old bridge that spans the San Juan, only to be met by Ute reservation "no trespassing" signs and locked gates. Beyond lay another ghost town marked on the map as Carracas, about which later I could learn no more than I had about Juanita.

Throughout the journey, Escalante had a keen eye for places where future generations of Spaniards might build towns, and by implication where he might return to found missions. About the bend of the Chama where Juan Pedro Cisneros had plunged up to his neck when his horse stepped into an underwater sinkhole Escalante had been prescient, as the fertile fields and herds of livestock in Los Ojos testified. But here, along the San Juan, by 2017 his crystal ball had clouded up, for only the failed outposts of Juanita and Carracas bespoke the promise he had envisioned.

On August 6, the Spaniards traveled only six and a half miles down the San Juan, forging their way through "bad terrain," before halting for the day. It was not rough travel that stopped the team; instead, "Don Bernardo Miera had been having stomach trouble all along and this afternoon he got much worse."

Except for the roster on the opening page of his journal, which identifies Bernardo Miera y Pacheco as "retired captain of militia and citizen of La Villa de Santa Fe," this is Escalante's first mention of the man. Yet the "retired captain" cut a large enough figure in eighteenth-century New Mexico that today we know more about him than we do about Domínguez or Escalante—enough, in fact, about this gifted polymath that in 2013 historian John L. Kessell was able to write a full biography of Miera y Pacheco, a distinction that the two expedition leaders will probably never earn.

Born in 1713, Miera y Pacheco turned sixty-three during the first month of the expedition. Across the trajectory of his rich and varied life he was, in Kessell's pithy summation, " 'engineer and captain of militia' on Indian campaigns; explorer and cartographer of lands never before mapped; merchant; luckless silver miner; debtor and debt collector; district officer, or *alcalde mayor*; rancher; craftsman who worked in metal, stone, and wood; and prolific religious artist." As a member of the Domínguez–Escalante expedition he did not travel as a soldier, but he had trained as a military engineer and had fought in five Indian campaigns, three against the Comanches, one in an attempt to force the Navajos to settle near Mount Taylor in western New Mexico. Like Escalante, Miera y Pacheco was a native of Cantabria in northern Spain. When he emigrated to New Mexico is unknown, for despite tireless research Kessell was able to find no record of the man's existence between his baptism in 1713 and his marriage in 1741, which took place at the presidio of Janos in today's Mexican state of Chihuahua. According to Kessell, the Soldado Distinguido, as he was formally styled toward the end of his life, stood a smidgen under five feet, had blue eyes and "a straight nose."

Miera y Pacheco's lasting fame rests on his talents as a cartographer and religious artist. The map he drew after the 1776 expedition is a crowded masterpiece, on which he plotted not only the path of the team's wandering course through 1,700 miles of mostly terra incognita but indicated with little circles marked with crosses every single campsite (of the more than ninety) along the way. One ponders with astonishment just how the cartographer kept track of all the details of the landscape even as he rode his horse through storms and into cul-de-sacs. As a map of the American Southwest, Miera y Pacheco's was not superseded until well into the nineteenth century.

The altar screens and statues of saints, carved out of wood and stone, that the artist produced in the 1760s and '70s are likewise masterpieces. Many of them no longer survive, their glory captured only in faded drawings executed by Miera y Pacheco himself or his later admirers. Yet one altar screen, which Kessell calls "the most inspired religious icon of New Mexico's colonial period," has survived almost by accident into the twenty-first century despite being taken apart, moved, and reassembled twice by workers who probably had little idea of its value.

The altar screen rests today in Cristo Rey church on Upper Canyon Road in Santa Fe. Before we set out on our long drive, Sharon and I paid a visit one afternoon in August. The details of the densely configured composition are impossible to grasp on first viewing, but the power of the screen arrests anyone who pauses to look. Measuring 19 feet wide by 25 feet tall, it celebrates five saints, including Santiago (Saint James), who regularly appeared on battlefields to turn the tide against the enemy, as well as two "Our Lady"s, patrons of the colony's governor, who had commissioned the screen. The niches devoted to each figure are surrounded by ornate decorations in the form of vines, cords, grapes, and obelisks topped with human heads. All this carved out of a soft white volcanic stone and painted with colors (mostly blue and reddish brown) that have not entirely faded more than 250 years later. According to Kessell, the blocks of stone were most likely carved in place, at the quarry near Nambe pueblo north of Santa Fe from which they were dug out of bedrock.

As Sharon and I sat in the front pew in Cristo Rey that afternoon, churchgoers entered to pray. Without exception, they paused before the screen, bowed toward it slightly, and crossed themselves.

Escalante got to know Miera y Pacheco sometime after 1774, when the artist was commissioned to paint another altar screen for the mission at Zuni, where the Franciscan ministered to the natives. As Governor Pedro Fermín de Mendinueta began negotiating with Escalante (and, separately, with Domínguez) about the expedition to link Santa Fe with far-off Monterey, the young padre recommended his friend Miera y Pacheco as "someone clever enough for this affair." Apparently the governor mistook that remark as a nomination for the role of expedition leader. For some reason, Escalante got cold feet about his enthusiasm for Miera, clarifying in a letter to the governor that "he would be useful . . . not to command the expedition, but to make a map of the terrain explored. . . . [O]nly for this do I consider him useful."

Whether or not he was aware of this lukewarm vote of confidence, Miera y Pacheco signed on to the expedition without hesitation. From my first reading of Escalante's journal onward, I wondered about the imbalance this arrangement must have forced on the team. At thirty-six, Domínguez had only his journey up and down the Rio Grande as he compiled his survey of the colony's missions to qualify him as an explorer. At twenty-seven, Escalante had even less—only the jaunt from Zuni to Hopi and back in 1775. On both journeys the Franciscans had other men along in charge of logistics and route-finding. It's hard to avoid the conclusion that both Domínguez and Escalante were woefully underqualified to lead a grandly ambitious expedition into the unknown.

Miera y Pacheco, on the other hand, was vastly qualified not only as an Indian fighter but as an explorer of the plains east of Santa Fe and the mountains west of the capital. As we traveled the route of the 1776 expedition, I kept wondering how the sixty-three-year-old veteran had borne the often misguided orders of the two unworldly priests so much younger than he, and so much less wise when it came to traveling across difficult, unmapped terrain.

Like most journals written before the twentieth century, Escalante's is lamentably reticent about conflicts within the party. His account, moreover, was compiled as an official report to the governor and to the Franciscan custodian of New Mexico, and was intended to convince them that an overland route to Monterey was still worth pursuing, not to mention to promote the establishment of towns and the founding of missions along the way. Strife within the party would hardly boost the officials' faith in the ultimate value of such an ambitious campaign.

So I was keen to read between the lines of the journal, to sniff out episodes in which it seemed likely that Miera y Pacheco simply got fed up with taking orders from his green and hopelessly naive juniors.

The *engaño* of August 4, for instance: who deceived whom, and what was it all about? Miera's stomachache would trouble him throughout the expedition, and two and a half months from that first upset, with the team in dire straits, his decision to take into his own hands an unusual cure for the malady would provoke from Escalante the most indignant outburst against a teammate in the whole journal—a tirade of righteous fury that must have riven the depleted party to its core. But of that debacle, more in good time.

At the campsite of Nuestra Señora de las Nieves, for the first time the Spaniards made a celestial observation to determine their latitude. The instrument they carried for the purpose was an astrolabe. The device, whose origins date back to the second century BC, is used to measure the angle between the horizon and some heavenly body— in D & E's case, usually the sun—thereby determining latitude. The observer (probably Miera y Pacheco) took his reading at noon, when the sun reached its highest point in the southern sky. The only problem, in an era before accurate clocks had been invented, was knowing exactly when noon arrived.

At Nuestra Señora de las Nieves, the team came up with a latitude of 37° 51' N. The actual latitude of today's ghost town of Carracas is 37° 01' N, so the Spaniards were off by a matter of 50', or 57 miles. Nowhere does Escalante state the latitude of Monterey, which is 36° 36' N. But implicit in the whole idea of the journey was the plan to push north from Santa Fe to a latitude roughly equal to that of the new colony in California, then head straight west to close the gap.

We should not assume, however, that Escalante knew the latitude of Monterey with any precision. To appreciate just how hard it was for news from the California coast to reach New Mexico, consider the following facts. The resupply wagons that traveled the 1,200 miles from Mexico City to Santa Fe, even along a well-beaten trail, routinely took six months to arrive. Even the fastest couriers on horseback required one to three months. The lag between Monterey and Mexico City was of comparable duration. (By 1776 New Spain still took its ultimate orders from the king in Castile; the communication of a single question and response between the New World and the Old could take three years to complete.)

Even if Domínguez and Escalante knew the exact latitude of Monterey, they had no idea of how far away it was, for the simple reason that by 1776 no accurate means of gauging longitude had been perfected. In 1714, the British parliament had passed the famous Longitude Act, offering a reward of £20,000 for the solution of a problem that had vexed navigators since antiquity. Although John Harrison claimed the prize in 1773 after inventing a chronometer precise enough to solve the problem, no practical knowledge of the answer to the conundrum had reached the remote colony of New Mexico by the time D & E set out. That crucial unknown—how far away was the phantom colony of Monterey?—would hang over the expedition throughout its wandering course.

By August 5 the party had covered, by their own reckoning, 145 miles on the ground since leaving Santa Fe. If the men had any idea of how small a portion of the journey they would ultimately make that stretch represented—not even one-tenth of the distance—Escalante's journal gives no hint of that gloomy truth.

On the morning of August 7, Miera y Pacheco's stomachache had relented—or, as the chronicler put it, "God willed that he got better . . . so that we could continue on our way." And here, at last, the landscape opened up before the men on horseback. That day they came in sight of La Piedra Parada, or Standing Rock, the striking pair of pinnacles near today's Pagosa Springs that Anglos would name Chimney Rock. There, in the eleventh century AD, the Anasazi built a small but important village whose alignment with the towers was tied up with Chacoan priests' mastery of the arcane astronomical phenomenon called the lunar standstill. No Europeans, however, would discover the ancient ruin beneath the pinnacles for another century and a half. But the twin towers were a landmark so well known to Spaniards that, three days earlier, Escalante had vowed that the team was following "the said trail of La Piedra Parada." (Why Standing Rock as a marker, I wondered, and not the Brazos?)

Now it seemed as though the party, so bewildered as it had sought to follow the Chama and Navajo rivers, knew at last where it was going. Through that day and the next, the men crossed, successively, rivers whose names they already knew—the Piedra, the Pinos, the Florida, and at last the Animas—names first bestowed by Rivera in 1765. Here, as we drove across cultivated plateaus on back roads linking the towns of Arboles and Ignacio, Sharon and I gave up trying to follow D & E mile by mile. For one thing, the first part of their route on August 7 had been obliterated by the Navajo Reservoir, another dam-building boondoggle from the glory days of the Bureau of Reclamation. It was the third place on our drive where artificial lakes drowned the lost trail of the pioneers. And there was no point trying to suss out exactly where the Spaniards had bisected the corn fields and alfalfa pastures of today's Ute and Hispanic farmers and ranchers. As the Bicentennial surveyors had confessed about this stretch, "they could have camped anywhere," and "they probably would have gone" somewhere, while "in all probability, they paralleled" such-and-such latter-day road.

Yet as if to compensate for this fuzziness, the surveyors decided that they knew exactly where the team had crossed the Animas and camped on the evening of August 8: "four miles south of the city limits of Durango." As if even that specification were too vague, R. W. Delaney and Robert McDaniel fixed the spot for eternity as "a level place directly west of the livestock sale barn." Of course the livestock barn of 1976 is no more, while the banks of the Animas south of downtown Durango swarm today with Walmart and Home Depot and Target and half a dozen motels.

Once again, the vagueness of Escalante's journal goads modern-day scholars to claim a certainty they cannot justify. All the chronicler says is, "We crossed [the Animas] and halted on the opposite side." Throughout the previous two days' travel, Escalante had waxed enthusiastic about "very good land for farming" and "extensive and good lands . . . with all that may be desired for a goodly settlement." But on the banks of the Animas, he was not impressed: "There is no good pasturage here," where the river "runs through a box channel." Poor Escalante! He had envisioned thriving settlements along the San Juan where today Juanita and Carracas crumble toward oblivion, but on the site of Durango, population 18,503 in 2016, by far the largest town we had visited since leaving Santa Fe, he saw only an indifferent bivouac site.

Instead of camping out on the night of September 4, Sharon and I stayed in a motel. The next day we met John Kessell for lunch at his favorite Durango restaurant, Ken and Sue's, where I grilled the historian, who knows as much about colonial New Mexico as any man or woman alive, for his insights into the Domínguez–Escalante expedition. It seemed, however, that he had drawn the same blanks that had stumped me. "Where were the Indians?" I asked, referring to the strange fact that all the way from Abiquiu to Durango (and beyond), the Spaniards had met not a single Navajo, Apache, or Ute. Kessell could only shrug. How much did D & E know about the country before they set out? "The key to all this," said the historian, "is Andrés Muñiz, who had been with Rivera. But we know almost nothing about Muñiz."

I praised Kessell for the tenacity of his research into the life of Miera y Pacheco: traveling to Spain to hunt down obscure documents in parochial archives just to find, buried in the mountains of paper about long-forgotten lives, the barest mention of Miera's family, or infiltrating the musty vaults of the Biblioteca Nacional in Mexico City to sort out Franciscan hierarchies. (The list of archives plumbed in Kessell's bibliography runs to twenty-six institutions in four countries.)

As always in the company of a true scholar, I felt both admiration and—what? Something halfway between envy and pity? A book like Kessell's *Miera y Pacheco* might sell a thousand copies, a fair portion of them going to libraries. The university press that published the book would pay the author zero dollars as an advance, subjecting him instead to the often nasty process of peer review. You couldn't make a living writing such books, so you became a professor for your day job, as Kessell had at the University of New Mexico. I had decided, at age thirty-six, that if I wanted to make a living as a writer, I had to *quit* teaching. Yet all of my books and articles that touched on history or archaeology depended critically on the deep arcana I'd gleaned from the Kessells in their fields. I could only be glad that they had done so much of my homework for me.

If lunch at Ken and Sue's was Sharon's and my Durango pleasure, we also had a Durango chore to perform. The forty days we planned to spend on the D & E trail were a span almost three times as long as any trip away from home I had taken since July 2015, when I learned I had cancer. Among those five or six shorter forays, two had ended in medical crises, when I collapsed and had to be rushed to emergency rooms. It was sheer luck that I had been stricken only a few miles away from excellent hospitals in Hanover, New Hampshire, and Mammoth Lakes, California, rather than off in the boonies or camped in the wilderness.

It was Sharon who had borne the burden of getting me to safety in every one of the ten or so hospitalizations I had needed to stay alive in the last two years, either when she called 911 for an ambulance or drove me groaning in the back seat to the emergency room. She had agreed to our D & E extravaganza only on two conditions: that we buy Global Rescue insurance, which would cover the cost of an airlift, if necessary, all the way from some trail in Colorado or Arizona to Brigham and Women's Hospital in Boston; and that we rent a satellite phone.

On all my Alaskan expeditions, I had relished the purism of cutting ourselves off from any prospect of outside rescue. There was a bracing freedom in the realization that if we got in trouble on a big wall or a remote glacier, we would have to get ourselves out of it. Toward the end of the twentieth century and the beginning of the twenty-first, adventure had been corrupted by the pathetic need of climbers on Everest or sledgers in Antarctica to be in almost hourly contact with the outside world by sat phone, radio, and Internet, and to count on rescue by plane or helicopter if things went wrong. But now, because of the cancer, I agreed to the sat phone Sharon demanded, which we carried in the back seat of our SUV every mile of the way. I could only hope that we never had to take it out of its plastic case except to charge the batteries.

There was also the matter of the Pembrolizumab I was taking every three weeks, which was all that stood between me and death by metastasis. At the last minute, my oncologist at Dana–Farber had decided it was safe to go six weeks without Pembro, since its carry-over effect seemed to have worked wonders already. But on the eve of our flight from Boston to Albuquerque at the end of August, my latest blood draw gave a sodium level of 125—dangerously low. Sharon wondered whether we should cancel or postpone the whole D & E trip. I couldn't bear the thought. I agreed to swallow my 6,000 mg of salt pills a day and to sprinkle salt on all my food and drink salty V8 juice and put drops of electrolyte in all the water I drank, but we had to arrange for a blood draw in the first decent facility we came to on the road. That turned out to be the Mercy Regional Medical Center in Durango.

For some reason, the center refused to tell Sharon and me the results of the test. That classified information would have to be relayed through Dana–Farber. (What was the risk? That I would, metaphorically speaking, rip out all my tubes and stomp out of the hospital to get back on the road?) We waited through an anxious day and night until we got the news from my oncologist's assistant. Somehow, as we had camped in the national forest and sorted out the bends of the Chama and Navajo rivers during the previous week, I had jacked my sodium level up to 130. That still wasn't in the "normal" range of 135–145 but it was good enough for me—and for my wardens back in Boston.

Not that it had ever been hard for us to hang out in Durango. It was Sharon's and my usual gateway to Cedar Mesa, where we bought groceries for as much as three weeks, camp chairs and coolers, beer and wine. There are no liquor stores in Bluff or Blanding, the towns closest to my favorite Anasazi wilderness; you can buy 3.2% Bud Lite at the K & C convenience store in Bluff, while Blanding is as dry as the staunchest Mormon could desire. I had always been told that it was illegal to import more than a six-pack of beer and a single bottle of wine from Colorado to Utah, and had heard many a tale of college boys on spring break busted on their way to their Lake Powell house-boats, so we always stashed our Tecates and cabernets under piles of foodstuffs from City Market or Albertsons as we drove west on the McElmo road. Sometimes in Durango we stayed at the Strater, a gem of a gold-rush hotel, which looks much the same as it did in 1887.

In town we'd always had our choice of five or six really good restaurants and a dozen serviceable ones, a perk that meant a lot more to me before radiation killed access to all my favorite foods. Maria's Bookstore is one of the best in the Southwest, and up on the mesa east of town, Fort Lewis College has a strong anthropology department and library. Four or five times I'd ridden the old coal-chugging narrow gauge train up spectacular Animas Canyon to Silverton, and way back in 1963, six of us had hiked down the tracks from Silverton on the day before Christmas on our way to making the first winter ascents of five sharp peaks in Colorado's most serious range, the Grenadiers.

Before the trip, I'd casually noticed Dominguez and Escalante Roads, a pair of intersecting streets south of downtown Durango, not far from where the Bicentennial folks insist the expedition camped in 1776. Now I made local inquiries. None of the clerks I talked to whose businesses stood on Dominguez Road had ever heard of the Franciscan, and the Toyota dealer even denied that his address was on a street named after the explorer. But on Escalante Road, I had better luck. There proudly stands the Escalante Middle School, founded in

1995, and inside a glass case in the foyer I read that the school's name had been chosen by a vote of students, teachers, and unspecified community members. The brief résumé of the expedition even got the essential details right. (The school's team name, the Eagles, reflected a constituency that "identifies with endangered animals.")

Durango was founded in 1880 as a shipping depot by the D & RG Railroad, as if snubbing the company nose at hard-drinking Animas City two miles up the valley. The Colorado governor named the town after Durango, Mexico, though nobody seems to remember why. If the Eagles had their way, though, Escalante would be recognized as the town's founding father.

On the morning of September 6 we headed out of town on U.S. Highway 160 and after two miles turned left up Wildcat Canyon. The Spaniards took something like this route on August 9, and though Escalante grumbled about the climb out of the Animas canyon as "quite difficult, consisting of plenty of rock and being very steep in places," soon he was pleased with Wildcat's "narrow valley of abundant pastures." About 10 miles on, after cresting a low divide, the party came to another river that they identified as the La Plata.

For the first time in his journal, Escalante explicitly tips his cap to Rivera. The river, he writes, "rises at some western point of La Sierra de la Plata and descends through the same canyon in which there are said to be veins and outcroppings of metallic ore. However, although years ago certain individuals from New Mexico came to inspect them by order of the governor, who at the time was Don Tomás Vélez Cachupín, and carried back metal-bearing rocks, it was not ascertained for sure what kind of metal they consisted of. The opinion that some formed previously, from the accounts of various Indians and from some citizens of the kingdom, that they were silver ore, furnished the sierra with this name." *Plata*, of course, is Spanish for "silver."

The great disappointment of Coronado's massive *entrada* was that in two years of dogged searching and cross-examining the natives, the Spaniards never discovered workable deposits of gold and silver in the Southwest. Inca and Aztec gold had so dazzled Pizarro and Cortés that they laid waste the two greatest empires in the New World to seize the precious metals. Even as late as 1776, the quest for treasure in the ground still stirred Spanish blood.

According to Steven G. Baker, Rivera's twin thrusts into the Southwest were launched as much as anything by the arrival in Abiquiu sometime in the early 1760s of a Moache Ute man bearing a single piece of rock he had dug out of the ground in a mountain range in his homeland far to the northwest. The Abiquiu blacksmith smelted the stone, from which he extracted enough pure silver to cast a pair of rosaries and a crucifix.

In 1765, guided by a pair of Utes, Rivera spent much time panning the La Plata up to its headwaters in the mountains where, he reported, "We saw such a variety of veins of different colors that they are innumerable. It can be said without exaggeration that the whole sierra is pure ore and there is much to see." Alas, Rivera's men had no picks or shovels for mining, but they carved enough ore out of the ground with their knives to carry it back to Santa Fe, where the precious stuff further whetted the appetite of the governor.

Eleven years later, under a different governor, the two Franciscans looking for a route to California, forbidding their men to trade with the Indians (none of whom they had yet encountered), and scouting for the sites of future towns and missions, nonetheless caught silver fever on La Plata Creek. Their ardor was dampened when it rained heavily for two days and the temperature plunged. Escalante concluded that the whole region was always "excessively cold even in the months of July and August." Here Domínguez caught a bad cold, with "a rheumy flow in his face and head." The journal for August 10 and 11 is a litany of misery: the ill-fed horses grew weak, the "trail" turned to mud, the cold depleted everyone, and at last Domínguez "got worse, the trail became impossible, and so, after very painful traveling another two leagues to the west, we found ourselves obliged to halt."

When Domínguez awoke on August 11 exhausted, with a high fever, the team gave up all hopes of mining silver. Escalante's regret is palpable: "For this reason we could not go over to see the sierra's metallic veins and rocks mentioned, even though they were a short distance away, as one companion who had seen them on another occasion assured us." A little more than a century later, the La Platas and the San Juans would become the center of a frenzy of fortune-building in gold and silver matched by only a handful of bonanzas anywhere in the American West.

At the small village of Hesperus, we regained Highway 160, which I had driven countless times before. More or less on the D & E trail, we headed west. Six miles along, we pulled over at the Escalante Wayside, a memorial I had often perused, but never as carefully as we did now. Here was the first tangible fruit of the Bicentennial Commission's ambitious campaign to install commemorative markers all along the 1776 loop, the only salute to the daring expedition we had found in the 240-odd miles we had driven since Santa Fe.

It was handsomely done, a bronze plaque mounted on a conglomerate boulder that happened to have come to rest at this place sometime after the last ice age. The scene depicts Domínguez and Escalante walking in their robes, rather than riding. One of them holds a small cross in one hand, a string of rosary beads in the other. Behind them in the distance, three teammates feed and adjust the loads on four horses, while another four men look on. The text pins down the date of the expedition's passage as August 10, and explains their goal as "seeking a route to link the long established missions of New Mexico with Monterey, the recently founded capital of California." An adjoining panel hails the party as proto-peaceniks: "Throughout their journey they encountered a dozen native tribes, yet they never resorted to violence against their fellow men."

A separate panel commemorates the Spanish Trail, which became a trading route only some fifty years later, and singles out the French mountain man Antoine Robidoux as one of the pioneer traders to the

Utes. Some passerby had gouged a vicious "X" with a knife across an 1843 painting of Robidoux. I wondered what particular deed or character flaw had so angered the slasher, who spared the gentle Franciscans. Perhaps it was Robidoux's penchant for buying Ute pelts and blankets with bottles of rotgut and firewater.

We drove another ten miles west to the town of Mancos. I'd spent time here twenty-five years before, when I first got interested in the Anasazi, for this was the home of Richard Wetherill, who with his four brothers and assorted cronies was credited with the Anglo discovery of the ruins of Mesa Verde, and who dug antiquities out of the ground all over southeast Utah. Back in 1992, I had come to Mancos with Tom Wetherill, Richard's great-nephew, to visit the family's Alamo Ranch, with its stately Pennsylvania Dutch barns (zinc-plated roofs, wooden-pegged joints, ventilator cupolas) still intact. In the 1880s, from a frontier settlement living in daily fear of a Ute attack, the Wetherill brothers rode unarmed into the canyons west of the ranch, won the friendship of Ute chief Acowitz, and began to unlock the prehistoric secrets of the great mesa that looms over Mancos.

On August 10, after their miserable ride through rain and mud, with Domínguez plagued by his "rheumy" head, the expedition camped on the east fork of yet another river, which they referred to as both the San Lázaro and the Mancos. Rivera had called the small stream the Rio del Lucero, but it was Mancos—apparently D & E's coinage—that stuck. It is a very curious appellation, for in Spanish it means "one-armed" or "one-handed." No one today seems to know what the name referred to. One source, vaguely citing "unverified lore," would have it that the party's horses, crippled by their "traverse" of the San Juan mountains, regained their health by chowing down on the lush green grass along the river. This is nonsense, for by August 10 the team had barely skirted the southern foothills of the San Juans, and for all his complaining, Escalante makes no mention of crippled horses or of lush streamside grasses.

At Mancos we left Highway 160 to take state road 184, which

trundles northwest for 17 miles to reach the Dolores River and the town of the same name. In 1976 the Bicentennial Commission, not content with proposing the Escalante Wayside, urged renaming Route 184 "the Domínguez–Escalante Memorial Highway," for "the highway approximates the route of the expedition through this area." Forty-one years later, the blacktop is still known only as Colorado Highway 184. As on our jaunt through Arboles and Ignacio two days earlier, Sharon and I made no attempt to divine the precise path the Spaniards had taken through this gently tilted plain, sectioned into fields and pastures today. About the ride on August 12, Escalante specifies only a 22-mile ramble through "leafy tree-growth" and "a sagebrush stretch." Delaney and McDaniel, the surveyors responsible for this passage in 1975, concluded only that "the expedition probably took a more direct route than does Colorado Highway 184."

Throughout the whole of our own retracing journey, Sharon did most of the driving, as I shuffled maps and reread (usually out loud) the day's entry from Escalante's journal, as well as the commentary in the Bicentennial report. In recent years, Sharon has become a devotee of Google Maps on her iPhone for unearthing driving directions. In unfamiliar cities, as we try to find a restaurant or a medical center, I have to admit that the system works pretty well, though when the smirking disembodied voice orders, "In two hundred feet, turn right on Narragansett Street," I have to resist the urge to argue back, "Yeah? How do you know?" Always, though, even in the most convoluted urban mazes, I'm not happy unless I have some kind of paper map in hand as backup. All my life I've needed to know, every waking moment, no matter where I am or how far indoors, which way is north. Every day on our D & E pilgrimage, I had a map in my head that precisely marked where we were on the long circuit the padres had imprinted on the land. Sometimes, as Sharon was driving switchbacks up a mountain road, I would ask, out of the blue, "Okay, which way is Santa Fe from here?," and when she pointed 130 degrees in the wrong direction, I would cruelly snicker.

I like to think that my sense of direction was honed on my Alaska expeditions, when in a blinding snowstorm it was vital to know where the col leading to the next cirque must lie, but I'm pretty sure I had maps in my head from the age of six or eight onward. I know that by now I'm a hopeless reactionary, pining for the good old days when you could pick up a free highway map at every gas station, or, to hark back to childhood, when you could figure out just by looking around that if you took the alley between Columbine and Mariposa Avenues and then cut across the vacant lot, you could save thirty steps on the hike home from Uni Hill School.

Reactionary or not, I actually feel a thrum of low-level anxiety each time I surrender to the GPS in Sharon's iPhone, relieved only by the miraculous arrival at the intended destination. Whenever I read one of those stories about some hapless boob blindly following a GPS into disaster, I feel a surge of righteous amusement. The woman in Brussels, for instance, who went to pick up her friend at the train station and ended up in Zagreb. ("I was distracted," she claimed.) Or the Japanese tourists trying to drive to a destination east of Brisbane, Australia, who had to abandon their car, stuck up to the windows in water, because they didn't realize that nine miles of ocean intervened between the mainland and North Stradbroke Island. Or, closer to my home, the woman in Massachusetts who got her car stuck in a sand trap on a golf course when she followed the GPS order to turn left into an apparent cornfield. (The investigating officer reported, "Mrs. Maione stated that she did not even like golf.")

I'd like to think that Magellan had some kind of map in his head as he tried to circumnavigate the globe in 1519–22, even before any real map existed. And that Domínguez and Escalante had a mental chart of where they were, even when they wondered if they were lost, and that surely Miera y Pacheco was drawing a comprehensisve map in his head every mile along the way, from which a year later he would sit down with his quills and inks and draw the astonishing map that would remove so much of the incognita from the terra the expedition had explored.

In 2016 I read a remarkable article in the *New York Times Magazine* about how for centuries before first contact, the native canoers of the Marshall Islands had perfected the arcane art of "wave-piloting" to navigate vast ocean distances between tiny islands. In the article, Kim Tingley referenced a neuroscientific study that found that people who navigate only by GPS never activate the hippocampus, causing that part of the brain to shrink, whereas those who eschew GPS, like London taxi drivers who memorize the labyrinth of the city streets, have their hippocampuses enlarge. Some researchers were trying to figure out "what effect, if any, the repeated bypassing of this region of the brain might be having on us." The hippocampus, after all, is, in Tingley's words, "an evolutionarily primitive region largely responsible for our emotional lives."

So far, though, on the D & E trail I wasn't worried about Sharon's hippocampus. I just wished she could point a little more accurately across the mesas and mountains toward Santa Fe.

* * *

On August 12 the Spaniards reached the Dolores River, crossed it, and camped on its northern shore. Most students of the journey think that their campsite was about where today's town of Dolores stands (2016 population: 997). The padres knew the name of the river from Rivera's expedition eleven years before. Their predecessor must have been in a gloomy mood as he traversed this lovely corner of Colorado, for the full name he gave the stream is Rio de Nuestra Señora de los Dolores, or River of Our Lady of the Sorrows, and the full name of the Animas is Rio de las Animas Perdidas, or River of Lost Souls.

To give Domínguez a chance to recover from his cold, the team stayed in camp all day on August 13. They took their second reading by astrolabe, coming up with a latitude of 38° 13 ½' N—once again too far north, this time by 44½', or 51 miles. The friars were pleased with the site, finding "everything that a good settlement needs for its establishment and maintenance as regards irrigable lands, pasturage, timber, and firewood." Founded in 1891 as yet another railhead of the D & RG, Dolores soon became a ranching town. The *WPA Guide to 1930s Colorado* remarks that the town "periodically lives and dies with the cattle industry."

Not many readers of Vladimir Nabokov's *Lolita* realize that his heroine is named after the town, which the author fell in love with on one of his butterfly-hunting excursions in the late 1940s. Lolita's given name is Dolores Haze, and her other nickname is Dolly. In the climactic scene, when Humbert Humbert confronts Claire Quilty before shooting him, he taunts his rival with a line that embeds one of Nabokov's many secret clues to the origins of his fable. "Do you recall a little girl called Dolores Haze, Dolly Haze?" Humbert demands. "Dolly called Dolores, Colo.?"

In his August 13 entry, Escalante further notes, "Upon an elevation on the river's south side, there was in ancient times a small settlement of the same type as those of the Indians of New Mexico, as the ruins we purposely inspected show." When the Bicentennial retracers came through in 1975, a team from the University of Colorado was in the process of excavating an Anasazi ruin on a hilltop two miles west of town. Since it lay on the south side of the river, the archaeologists decided to call it Escalante Ruin. At the time, a museum near the site was under construction. Founded only in 1988, the Anasazi Heritage Center is today one of the finest small archaeological museums in the West, with vibrant changing exhibits and a hands-on approach to making prehistory accessible to students and children.

By 2017, the Heritage Center had taken full possession of Escalante Ruin, with a zigzag half-mile trail leading from the museum to the fully restored grid of roomblocks surrounding a large central kiva. From the ruin you get a lordly view down to the Dolores River, though yet another dam, creating McPhee Reservoir, has turned the current into a placid lake. In 1975 the surveyors reserved their judgment about the excavators' claim to have found the ruin Escalante visited, for a sketch map drawn by two longtime residents located two other ruins that could have fit the bill, since bulldozed out of existence by local ranchers. The museum's proud hilltop ruin, wrote Delaney and McDaniel, "may or may not be the one mentioned by Escalante."

The Heritage Center's brochure also claims that Escalante's observation was "the first record of an archaeological site in present-day Colorado." This claim, unfortunately, is not true. On the Los Pinos River in 1765, Rivera stumbled upon other Anasazi roomblocks, and he showed a keener curiosity about those relics of antiquity than Escalante would about his—though for all the wrong reasons. Wrote Rivera in his journal,

> We began to see along [the river's] banks the ruins of old buildings that provided evidence of having been a pueblo. There are still many burnt adobes as though from the bottom of a smelter. Carrying out the necessary investigations with greater reflection and care, we found among the ruins of the pueblo something like a smelter in which they smelt ore, which appeared to be gold. We gathered some burnt adobes from it to show them to the governor.

Since the museum brochure was so certain about Escalante Ruin, I sought out the chief ranger for further elucidation. After all, Escalante's entry is pretty generic about the ruin's location: "upon an elevation on the river's south side."

"How do you know the ruin CU excavated is Escalante's?" I asked the man.

"We're 99.9 percent sure it's the one he discovered," the ranger answered. I waited for further clarification, but in the time-honored tradition of scholars confronted by skeptics, the ranger merely alluded to "further researches" and "documents" that he unfortunately didn't have right at hand.

It was the pattern Sharon and I had already come to expect along the D & E trail. Most of the way, the 1776 expedition drew a blank in locals' memories. But where it lit a bulb instead, our informants appealed to deep insider knowledge, to a connection with the past that transcended the narrow margins of the padre's diary. At the Anasazi Heritage Center, at that moment the whole museum resembled a country inn on some hallowed historic roadway. I could almost see the shingle hung above the front door: "Escalante slept here."

Chapter Four

SEARCHING FOR YUTAS

Where *WERE* the Indians?

On August 12, 1776, as they arrived at the Dolores River, the Domínguez–Escalante expedition was fifteen days out of Santa Fe. The team would ride north and west for another thirteen days before encountering their first Native American (not counting the Puebloans at Santa Clara and Abiquiu). Across 234 miles of travel, through canyons and over mountains, as they traversed northern New Mexico and southwestern Colorado, the Spaniards had not even discovered a Navajo hogan or a Ute wickiup—unless Escalante failed to mention such an event, which seems unlikely.

On his first expedition in 1765, Rivera had made contact with *his* first Indian near the site of present-day Durango. Bizarrely enough, that meeting with a Moache Ute named Cuero de Lobo (Wolf Hide) had been prearranged. Earlier that year, the Ute had shown up in Abiquiu, where he met with Governor Vélez Cachupín. Ever since another Ute had brought his *clavo de plata*, or silver nail, to the Spanish outpost, the old colonial dream of mining fortunes in precious metals had been reawakened in Nuevo México. By 1765, the bearer of the lump of ore from the La Plata Mountains had died, but Cuero de Lobo agreed to guide Rivera to the deposits among the high peaks. The chief motivation for Rivera's expedition, in fact, was to discover the vast treasure of gold and silver that Coronado and his successors were sure the land of Cíbola must be hiding.

Like Domínguez and Escalante, Rivera traveled during high summer. And like them, in all the country between Abiquiu and the Animas River Rivera met no Indians, not even Navajos. On the map Miera y Pacheco drew after the D & E expedition, he unequivocally labeled the terrain between Abiquiu and the San Juan River "Provincia de Nabajoo." In 1775, on his way back to Zuni from his failed mission to convert the Hopi, Escalante had been warned that a party of Navajos was planning to ambush him and kill his whole party. Why, then, in 1776 did Domínguez and Escalante run into not a single Navajo during the whole five-month span of the voyage?

There seem to me to be three possible explanations. One was suggested to me by my friend Matt Liebmann, a Harvard anthropology professor whose specialty is the Southwest. Matt wondered whether the Indians might have been busy with the annual transhumance. The Navajos, of all the region's tribes, had become the master sheepherders, driving their flocks each summer into the mountains at and above timberline. Perhaps when D & E passed through (and Rivera before them), they missed the Navajos altogether because they never climbed higher than about 7,500 feet above sea level, well below timberline.

Another possibility is that both Navajos and Utes were fully aware of the advent of the strange caravan led by the two men wearing robes. The natives could easily have watched the procession pass by from lookout posts behind rocks or trees. Deciding neither to attack the Spaniards nor trade with them could have been dictated by uncertainty as to how well armed the men were, or how fierce in battle— or, conversely, how poorly equipped and provisioned, so that it would not have been worth the risk of casualties to launch a raid. Parties that rode through the Jornada del Muerto from El Paso to Santa Fe usually hauled wagons with them, and wagons were sure to carry the kinds of valuables that Spaniards with only horses and mules could not afford.

The third explanation is the one Escalante would have affirmed without a qualm—that God watched over his team, protecting it from harm. As he had bragged to the Hopi informants in 1775, "I was not worried . . . because I trusted in God who is infinitely more powerful than all the men there ever were, are, or will be."

By the morning of August 14, Domínguez had recovered from his bad cold, so the team set off again, following the Dolores downstream. Escalante's journal entry for that day is confusing, as he complains about "a rather troublesome stretch of sagebrush" followed by "a tall and craggy canyon." What canyon could that be except the one carved by the river? Yet after riding for 18 miles, "we arrived a second time at El Rio de Dolores." Twice thereafter the men were forced to wade the river, before making camp on its west bank, in "a brief meadow of good pasturage" they named La Asunción de Nuestra Señora or the Ascension of Our Lady. No matter how troubling their difficulties, the team had made a good day's march, covering 22 miles.

In 1975 Delaney and McDaniel, the Bicentennial retracers, drove a county road along the east bank of the Dolores on a straightforward jaunt to the D & E campsite, which they located as the clearing where Narraguinnep Creek comes in from the east. Yet they too puzzled over Escalante's journal entry, concluding that the "tall and craggy canyon" the team entered around midday was not that of the Dolores itself, but rather of a minor tributary to the northwest. The team would then have had to cross a dry mesa and plunge down a steep hillside to regain the bed of the Dolores.

If Delaney and McDaniel are right, as I think they are, how do we account for Domínguez and Escalante's perverse route-finding? Throughout their long journey, the padres seem to have suffered from a kind of canyon phobia. Already they had veered away from the easy course of the Chama to blunder through brush and forest and over high hills in search of the Navajo River. Now they seem deliberately to have left the canyon of the Dolores, only to have rediscovered it downstream, after a ride up a side canyon that went nowhere and across a dry mesa. At each campsite, the team needed abundant water for both men and mounts. Why not simply stick close to the perennial flow of the Dolores?

Sharon and I would have been happy to drive Delaney and McDaniel's county road, but it has long since vanished under McPhee Reservoir. By September 8, we had been out from Santa Fe a mere seven days, yet now for the fourth time we could not follow the D & E route because a reservoir had been plunked down on top of it. Instead we followed back roads on the plateau west of the Dolores, past fenced-off fields belonging to ranchers based in the hamlets of Prairie View and Cahone, as we searched for the obscure byway that meandered back down to the Dolores. At last we parked in a pullout next to the spacious clearing of the Virgin Mary entering heaven, celebrated by Catholics today, not coincidentally, on August 15, the morning after the padres had arrived there 241 years earlier.

Construction of McPhee Reservoir, a gleam in the eye of the Bureau of Reclamation as early as 1961, began in 1977. The purpose of the dam and impounded lake, then as now, was to provide irrigation for two Colorado counties, Dolores and Montezuma, and for the Ute Mountain Indian Reservation. It's a small reservoir compared to such monsters as Lake Powell and Lake Mead—barely seven miles long, with an average entrapment of a mere 381,000 acre-feet of water. (What's an acre-foot of water, I wondered as I first came across that stat. For perspective, Lake Powell holds an average of 2,235,000 acre-feet of the wet stuff.)

Oh, yes—McPhee is also a mecca for recreationists, who gun their motorboats and water-ski across its friendly surface, hook their RVs up to electric outlets, and camp in the seventy-one sites equipped with picnic tables and "barrier-free flush toilets." Not to mention a few volleyball courts, horseshoe pits, and a softball field. Fishermen dangle their lures here in hopes of snagging all kinds of non-indigenous species such as black crappie, Kokanee salmon, and yellow perch.

Like all the reservoirs in the West, though, McPhee is an

archaeological tragedy. The canyon of the Dolores downstream from today's town of the same name may have vexed the Spaniards in 1776, but from 500 to 900 AD it was an elysium for the Anasazi. The building of Glen Canyon Dam on the Colorado, begun in 1960, came too early for the archaeologists to accomplish more than a frantic and incomplete survey of the thousands of prehistoric sites the lake would swallow. But in 1977 a well-organized team, under the leadership of Dave Breternitz, prowled and probed so diligently through the seven miles of canyon the McPhee waters would flood that the Dolores Archaeological Program (DAP), as the effort was titled, stands today as one of the last and probably the finest of the large-scale archaeological salvage missions in the West.

In their five months on the trail, one of only two or three Ancestral Puebloan sites the padres recorded was the hilltop village beside the Dolores later identified as Escalante Ruin, excavated by the CU team and curated at the Anasazi Heritage Center. Preoccupied with getting to California and worried about encounters with living Indians, Domínguez and Escalante can be forgiven for paying scant attention to the vestiges of the ancients they must have come across along the way. It's not surprising that in his journal entry for August 14, Escalante grumbles about troublesome sagebrush and craggy canyons without noticing that other visitors had found the Dolores far more congenial twelve centuries before the Spaniards came through.

The DAP worked in the field for six seasons between 1978 and 1983, employing no fewer than 540 archaeologists, students, and volunteers. During that time, the teams discovered 1,626 Anasazi sites and partially excavated 101 of them. Those loci ranged from fugitive lithic scatters to villages that were once home to several hundred men, women, and children apiece. After the end of their fieldwork, as the water level rose south of the McPhee dam, the DAP published thirteen scholarly volumes devoted to their discoveries. Thousands of artifacts from their work are preserved in the Anasazi Heritage Center.

But do the water skiers care? Do the farmers and ranchers in Cahone and Prairie View give a damn? In 1986 Breternitz and others published their culminating opus, *The Dolores Archaeological Program: Final Synthetic Report.* By 1993 the book was out of print.

Dave Breternitz, who died in 2002, was a legendary figure in Southwestern archaeology. I met him only once, very briefly, at the informal gathering of scholars and passionate amateurs called the Pecos Conference. A few months after Sharon's and my trip, I asked archaeologist Steve Lekson, who for twenty-five years has been my friend and mentor in the prehistory of the Southwest, for his take on the man who spearheaded the DAP's heroic effort to save the Dolores's past. Himself a legend in the field, and its preeminent exploder of received ideas, as in his radical and provocative book *The Chaco Meridian,* Steve promptly emailed me back:

> A local boy who landed at the University of Colorado, David Breternitz was the ultimate field archaeologist. He excavated everywhere, always with university students whom he trained very well and worked very hard. When Breternitz drove the college kids nuts, his wonderful wife, Barbara, would restore balance. Barbara and David were a team that many of today's leading Southwestern archaeologists recall with much fondness and more than a little awe.
>
> Giants walked the earth in those days. F'rinstance: a frantic student's admission to graduate school lacked a last-minute medical exam. Professor Breternitz filled out the required form with plausible blood pressures and pulse rates, and signed it "Dr. Ben Dover, M.D." The student went on to a long, healthy career in archaeology. Who now, in these puny times, would do this?

About the archaeological significance of the DAP discoveries dating between 500 and 900 AD, Steve added:

One of the nagging questions in the Mesa Verde region was, where was Pueblo I? The Pueblo I time period too often was missing at sites that had the rest of the chronological sequence: Basketmaker III, [no Pueblo I], Pueblo II, and Pueblo III. Nobody had looked in the Dolores Valley. Breternitz and DAP found them there, huge Pueblo I sites that marked the origins of the social stratification that ultimately built Chaco Canyon, far to the south.

There's another reason why D & E might have been too distracted on August 14 to notice any signs of habitation. Sometime during that day an event took place that must have been the most monumental occurrence to befall the expedition since leaving Santa Fe. It's maddening that Escalante narrates it in a single paragraph in his journal, and never again refers to what it signified for the team. And even more maddening is the tone in which he recounts the event, reverberating with annoyance shading into disgust. Here's the passage:

> This afternoon we were overtaken by a *coyote* and a *genízaro* from Abiquiu, the first Felipe and the second Juan Domingo by name. So as to wander among the heathens, they had run away without the permission of their masters of that pueblo, with the desire of accompanying us as their excuse. We had no use for them, but, to forestall the mischief which either through their ignorance or through their malice they might do by wandering further among the Yutas if we insisted on their going back, we took them on as companions.

A *coyote* was what in frontier culture would later be called a half-breed, looked down on as inferior by citizens with "pure" Spanish blood in their veins. But in view of Escalante's implication that both Felipe and Juan Domingo were effectively slaves, or at best servants indentured to their "masters" in Abiquiu, both men must have been *genízaros,* Indians captured in infancy or childhood and raised in the colony by Spanish families. The contempt embedded in Escalante's phrase "so as to wander among the heathens" obscures the possibility that both fugitives might have been Utes, who wanted only to return to the people among whom they had been born and brought up.

Throughout the rest of his journal, Escalante almost never again mentions Felipe or Juan Domingo by name, though by reading between the lines one can guess at a couple of junctures where they played critical roles. One wonders, too, just what sort of "mischief" D & E were afraid the two new arrivals might perform if they were ordered to return to Abiquiu. The phrase "by wandering further among the Yutas" seems ludicrous, given that the team had met not a single Ute (or Navajo) during the first fifteen days of the expedition.

What blew my mind when I first read that journal paragraph, though, was how matter-of-factly Escalante recounted what must have been a spectacular feat of travel and tracking by the two *genízaros.* As slaves or servants escaped from their "masters," Felipe and Juan Domingo almost certainly had neither horses to ride nor mules to transport their gear. And on foot, how could they have carried enough food to sustain them for two weeks on an arduous trail? It's not likely, either, that they had guns, so how could they have hunted along the way?

If the men's goal was simply to join the D & E expedition, why did they wait fifteen days to make their presence known? I tried to imagine the skill it must have taken for the two *genízaros* to follow the caravan through little-known country, keeping enough distance so as not to be detected, yet never losing track of the team ahead of them, for 234 miles.

What the real motive for Felipe and Juan Domingo's truant flight may have been remains a mystery. Escalante's sneering line, "so as to wander among the heathens," betrays his Franciscan myopia—as if reveling in idolatrous ignorance were some kind of sinful pleasure to be expected from half-breeds and captives. The sheer virtuosity of Felipe's and Juan Domingo's expeditionary deed—pulling off without apparent hardship a major journey that had already taxed a well-equipped and fully provisioned team to near the breaking point—deserves the kind of salute that Escalante could never have imagined offering the hitchhikers who now became the eleventh and twelfth members of the party.

If Felipe and Juan Domingo were Utes born in Colorado, they may well have been useful to the padres from here on out as interpreters or guides, or simply as men who had been born to the roving life of the frontier. At the very least, they supplied two more able bodies to contribute to the daily chores of camping, gathering water, cooking, and packing the horses and mules.

* * *

THE BACK ROAD that took Sharon and me down to the Dolores River again, at the campsite they named for the Ascension of the Virgin, is marked today by a sign proclaiming the Lone Dome State Wildlife Area. Just before the road crosses the Dolores on an old concrete bridge, another sign sketches the history of the Bradfield Ranch, first homesteaded in 1900. As many as 650 cows used to roam the banks, in the heyday of one of the last "big valley" ranches of the sort familiar to us from John Ford westerns. It must have been a grand place, but nothing of it remains. In 1978 the heirs to the cattle barons sold the spread to the Bureau of Reclamation as part of the deal that made the McPhee Reservoir possible.

In the clearing here the Bradfield Recreation Area caretakes a complex of campsite pullouts complete with fire pits and concrete picnic tables, screened from the sun by ramada-like shelters. But it looked as though no one had camped here for a while, and the register box was empty. Here, too, is the put-in for river trips on the Dolores, rumored to be one of the finest low-profile floats in a West dominated by commercial outfits running the Grand Canyon. But because the flow of the Dolores is regulated by each year's release from the McPhee Reservoir,

whose logic seems to be known only to Bureau of Reclamation staff-
ers, many a year went by when there wasn't enough flow downstream
from here to carry a raft. After our trip, I inquired about a float trip
for the spring of 2018, but no outfitter could guarantee a launch.

For all the effort to turn this genial bend on the Dolores, where
two side streams join the river, into a recreation mecca, the clearing where the Spaniards camped on August 14 had a forlorn, even a
desolate feel about it. And among all the signage, not a word about
Domínguez and Escalante.

I knew that a few miles downstream, the Dolores entered a canyon
whose walls rose higher as the current cascaded north until the distant rims loomed 2,300 feet above the river. That roadless gorge was
touted as the pièce de résistance of every Dolores float trip. But it was
one corner of my native Colorado that I had never seen.

I also judged that D & E had no knowledge of the abyss that lay
ahead of them, for here, at the Bradfield bridge, the river flows gently
through broad-shouldered hills that tumble only a couple of hundred
feet above the stream. Yet as the expedition set out on August 15, the
men again chose to leave the canyon, climbing a slope on its western
side, parting from the Dolores less than a mile beyond the campsite
of the Virgin's Ascension. As usual, Escalante offers no explanation
for the team's escape, except that, after another 20 miles of riding
through sagebrush and scrub forest on the plateau west of the river,
"we paused to rest in a small arroyo which the guides thought had
water, but we found it completely dry."

The padre's gripe about one more mistake on the part of the team's
feckless "guides" is par for the course, but reading between the journal's lines one senses that a growing malaise had gripped the party.
The surprise arrival of Felipe and Juan Domingo had put Escalante
in a bad mood, and now the team seemed to move on, always vaguely
to the northwest, in a fog of uncertainty. They weren't lost, since
they knew the Dolores flowed nearby, a few miles to the east, but
they seemed baffled by the lay of the land. Toward late afternoon on

the 15th, the search for water dictated a halt while part of the team scouted ahead.

Those scouts found water not too far away, but the source was "so scanty that it sufficed for the people only and not for the horse herds." Yet it was a momentous discovery, for the spring or pool had been deliberately covered with rocks and wood to forestall evaporation. The men realized that on the eighteenth day of the expedition, some 280 miles from Santa Fe, they had at last discovered signs of Indians. Utes, in fact, for "according to some of the companions who have traveled among them," this was what those Numic nomads did when "some misfortune overtook them"—the obvious misfortune being running out of water. Despite the inadequacy of the source to quench the thirst of the horses and mules, the Spaniards camped at the spot. They called it La Agua Tapada, the Covered Water.

It was a bad night. In the morning more than half the horses were missing, driven by thirst to break whatever hobbles restrained them and search for water. Whether some of the team tracked them down or the horses returned on their own is unclear, though Escalante swears the animals had gone halfway back to the previous camp. Despite the late start, the Spaniards hoped to work their way back to the Dolores by nightfall. But the "little-used trail" they followed "played out on us because the ground was very loose and it had been obliterated by the rains." Instead the team stumbled on toward the northwest, at last entering a shallow canyon. A little way down that defile, the men found a better water source and stopped to quench their thirst. After drinking their fill, they improved the source by digging a pair of water holes that the depleted horses and mules promptly drained. And now, in late afternoon, Domínguez and Escalante dithered. Where was the Dolores? Somewhere to the east, of course, but did this shallow canyon lead into it, or toward somewhere else? And in this "dense wood of piñon and juniper," could the canyon be traversed at all?

It was too much for Bernardo Miera y Pacheco. Without a word to the others, he set off down-canyon alone on horseback, forcing his way through the trees. Searching the hillsides for a trail, Domínguez and Escalante did not even see him leave. Waterless once more, the team set up camp, then sent one man ahead to track Miera down "before he could get lost."

*　*　*

FROM THE DESOLATE campground at the Bradfield bridge, Sharon and I drove up onto the plateau west of the Dolores. There we set out on back roads toward a dead-end point on the map, 13 miles farther north, labeled "Dolores Canyon Overlook." Fences again sectioned off well-plowed fields. The main crop here was neither alfalfa nor corn but pinto beans. As the pavement turned to dirt, we snaked through the junipers with no other cars in sight. The road ended in a small parking lot. We hiked the short trail beyond and all at once emerged on a sandstone shelf that thrust like a stern injunction over a great void. Far below us, the Dolores twisted through bends the river had carved eons before. For the first time since leaving Santa Fe, we stood on the rim of a true canyon. The promontory had a bit of the feel of one of the overlooks fenced off for tourists on the South Rim of the Grand Canyon. And though the scale was smaller, here, instead of the selfie-snapping mobs that throng the South Rim, we had the place to ourselves.

I scanned the river with my binoculars, trying to gauge the scale of its rapids, then trained the lenses on the bands of ruddy sandstone on either slope that probably hid Anasazi granaries. At that moment, I would have given much to ride a raft through the deep gorge, leisurely inspecting the banks for prehistoric presence.

Escalante's journal gives no hint that his team knew this canyon lay downstream from the campsite of the Ascension, but it was obvious that the Spaniards could never have gotten their horses and mules through this lordly cataract. Perhaps Andrés Muñiz had learned the hard way about this obstacle on the Dolores when he'd come through with Rivera in 1765. In any event, the detour the team took up on the western plateau on August 16 saved them from the nasty trap that would have enfolded them had they stayed close to the river. If the team indeed suffered from canyon phobia, for once their evasion served a useful purpose.

We ate a picnic lunch at the overlook, basking in a silence broken only by the soft breeze rippling the piñons. Reluctant to leave, I trained my binocs on the forested slopes on either side of the distant thread of the Dolores, trying to patch together a hiking route from rim to river. Before cancer, I would have contemplated that 2,300-foot descent and climb back up as a good day's outing. Now it signified an impossible challenge.

We drove back into the grid of roads that bordered the pinto bean fields until we arrived at Dove Creek, the last Colorado town on U.S. Highway 491 before the Utah border. Here for decades the Adobe Milling Company has advertised "Anasazi beans," supposedly the same strain that fortified the ancients a thousand years ago. On a previous trip we had bought a sackful of these legumes. Back home Sharon boiled them for hours. When we ate the beans, they were still crunchy, though the taste was blandness epitomized.

Dove Creek is a dreary-looking highway stop today, with the Adobe Milling Company providing its only hint of a touristic come-on. But I had read in the *WPA Guide* that not only had Zane Grey resided here "in his younger days," but that he had written most of *Riders of the Purple Sage* in Dove Creek. In fact, claimed the guide in 1941, "There are several elderly townsfolk who identify themselves with characters in the book."

Somewhere I had read that in the 1920s Grey was the best-selling author of all in English, outstripping Hemingway and Fitzgerald and H. G. Wells by a good margin. But does anyone under forty today even recall his name?

At Adobe Milling, I chatted with the woman behind the counter. She'd never heard of Domínguez and Escalante, and she seriously doubted that Zane Grey had ever lived in Dove Creek, even though her mom, a history teacher who had died at age ninety-three only three years before, "had all of Zane Grey's books." A tough claim to back up, for among the more than ninety works in Grey's oeuvre were three baseball novels and eight books about fishing.

I mentioned our trials cooking the Anasazi beans. Another local woman piped up, an edge in her voice, "Not for me. Five hours in the crock pot, that's all." From beans our conversation drifted to the ancients themselves. Said the woman behind the counter, "Every time my dad dug up a field, he came across their stuff. That's how he got interested in the Anasazi." In Dove Creek we weren't far from the Mormon strongholds of Blanding and Monticello over in Utah, bastions of a time-honored legacy of illegal pothunting of Anasazi relics. "Dad would trade some of the stuff he dug up," my informant went on, "because folks were too poor to buy them. He was real interested in what all those things he found were used for. But nobody else cared about that old junk."

Then she added a detail that made me wince. "Dad said that some of the fellows would dig up Anasazi pots, then set 'em out in the field and shoot at 'em for target practice."

From Dove Creek we headed north on the vector of Colorado Highway 141 toward a place marked on the map as Slick Rock, where the road switchbacked off the plateau to cross the Dolores once more, before wandering east into the broad basin of Disappointment Valley. The only town along its 20 miles of blacktop was a cluster of houses called Egnar. Not a soul was abroad there, and the tiny post office was closed. Intrigued by the name, I wondered if Egnar had been some pioneer Mormon homesteader sent out from Salt Lake City in the 1880s to forestall the Gentiles, as the Hole-in-the-Rock party that founded Bluff and Blanding had done. Later I learned that Egnar was simply "Range" spelled backward.

At the Slick Rock bridge over the Dolores, we were back in cactus and sagebrush country. Along the banks stretched cliffs of grayish-red sandstone darkened by centuries of patina. It was the canvas favored

by the Old Ones for their petroglyphs, but as we scanned the cliffs
for rock art we found only bullet holes: target practice decades earlier
for bored cowboys, who would have preferred to see their scars gouging the heads and genitals of Anasazi shamans. We drove north two
miles along the east bank of the Dolores until we faced the mouth
of Summit Canyon, which joined the Dolores from the southwest.
No road or trail today traverses that narrow, well-forested tributary,
and as I studied its bends with my binoculars, I wondered how many
travelers had ever hiked its length. Years ago, John Kessell, Miera y
Pacheco's biographer, had looked up Summit Canyon from the spot
where we stood. He had come determined to explore its secrets, but
for reasons he failed to explain over lunch in Durango, he thought
better of the excursion. Nor had the Bicentennial retracers in 1975
ventured into Summit Canyon. Having stopped at a café then operating near the bridge to probe local knowledge of the rocky valley, they
were "advised not to try it."

Late on August 16, when Domínguez and Escalante realized that
their cartographer was missing from camp, they sent a "companion"
down the unnamed canyon to look for him. Then they waited, vex-
ation mingled with worry, long into the night. Only after midnight
did the scout return with Miera y Pacheco, who crowed over his solo
reconnaissance. "They said," wrote Escalante, "that they had arrived
through the canyon at El Río de Dolores, and that in the intervening
space there was no more than a difficult but improvable stretch for
getting through. This made us decide to continue through here the
next day."

It was clear to me that the veteran of so many Indian campaigns
in New Mexico had gotten fed up with the indecisive friars who led
the expedition. It must have been obvious to Miera y Pacheco that the
brush-choked canyon would lead back to the Dolores. Yet as far as we
can tell from Escalante's journal, this was the first time on the expedition that any member had willfully set out on his own. Had the team
been organized along military lines, Miera's flight might have been

condemned as treasonous. Instead, thanks to its happy outcome, it was the decisive thrust the whole team badly needed.

In the next day's journal entry, Escalante not only forgives his cartographer's rash deed—he seems to congratulate him for it. Among the relentlessly humorless pages of the journal, is there here the slightest hint of good-natured joshing within the weary team? "The canyon we named El Laberinto de Miera," writes the Franciscan, "because of the varied and pleasing scenery of rock cliffs which it has on either side and which, for being so lofty and craggy at the turns, makes the exit seem all the more difficult the farther one advances—and because Don Bernardo Miera was the first one to go through it."

Before cancer, a hike the length of Summit Canyon would have been just the sort of outing I would have loved to tackle. How intriguing it would have been to explore the "pleasing scenery" and rocky walls of Miera's Labyrinth! But now, as I gazed wistfully up toward the secret canyon bends swathed with evergreens, that trek, like so much else in my new world of recovery, stretched out of reach.

Where Summit Canyon opened into the Dolores, the team made a startling discovery. In the mud of the riverbank they found "quite recent" footprints. The Yutas must be near at hand.

Domínguez and Escalante had set out from Santa Fe twenty days earlier with altruistic intentions about any encounters they might have with Indians along the way. The men were forbidden to trade with Utes or Navajos. Ideally, the party would live throughout their long and uncertain journey on the provisions they carried with them, supplemented by whatever food they could wring from the wilderness by hunting and gathering. Their only goal among the natives was to bring the word of God to savages who had lived from one generation to the next in benighted ignorance. That was a purpose so pure and noble that it justified any risk of life to bring it about.

So far, however, the voyage had been one grinding lesson in hardship after another, with California still unimaginably far away. Although it was humiliating for Domínguez and Escalante to admit, by now the whole team needed help. And for help, they would turn to the very infidels whose souls they intended to save. The length of the single sentence in the journal entry for August 17, in which Escalante confesses to that need, encumbered by one qualifying phrase piled on top of the next, as if the friars were apologizing to God Himself, captures the abject surrender that the footprints in the mud on the banks of the Dolores betokened. As Escalante wrote, "Weighing the fact that if [the Yutas] had seen us and we did not make advances toward them they might suspect some mischief on our part, the fear of which would alarm them, and that one of them might be able to guide us or furnish us with some hints for continuing our journey with less difficulty and hardship than the one we were now experiencing—for none of our companions knew the water sources and terrain ahead— we decided to seek them out."

Easier said than done. Once the team had reached the Dolores, a three-man party went ahead—Domínguez himself, accompanied by Andrés Muñiz as interpreter and Juan Pedro Cisneros—to try to make contact with the Utes. For eight miles they followed the tracks upstream without scaring up a single Indian. Escalante's account of that futile errand piles more mysteries onto the predicament in which the Spaniards felt they had become ensnared. The scouting party following the footprints "ascertained that they were Tabehuachi Yutas but could not find them, after having gone as far as the point where the little Río de las Paraliticas (so named because the first of our own to see it found in an encampment by its edge three female Yutas with the infirmity of this name) separates the Tabehuachi Yutas from the Muhuachi ones, the latter living to the south and the others to the north."

The various subtribes named by Escalante require some ethnographic unscrambling today. The different bands distinguished by the Spaniards have some basis in cultural reality, but they were so fluid that intermarriage and migration blurred boundaries and ethnicities. The Muache (Muhuachi) Utes anthropologists identify today lived along the Front Range all the way between Santa Fe and Denver. It seems unlikely that D & E would have found them as far west as the Dolores River. The Tabehuachi, known today as the Uncompahgres, occupied the Elk Mountains and Gunnison River country as far west as present-day Montrose, Colorado. That Muñiz could have identified the tribe by footprints alone defies credibility.

But what strange encounter lies behind the reference to the three paralyzed Ute women that some Spanish wanderer—not, apparently, Muñiz—had seen on some previous journey? The specificity of that side creek somewhere in today's Disappointment Valley seems to imply that, thanks to Muñiz, the expedition was far from lost, for not only did the *genízaro* recognize the River of the Paralitics, but he knew the story behind it. So why did D & E need Utes to guide them and to offer "some hints for continuing our journey"?

As it turned out, despite the fresh footprints, six more days would pass before the expedition met its first Ute.

* * *

At this point in our journey, Sharon and I took a weeklong break, as we drove west to Bluff for some hiking and camping on Cedar Mesa and the Navajo reservation. We also stopped in Moab and Telluride to catch up with old friends. Yet during that week, I could not get our interrupted journey out of my mind. In fact, some punitive imp in my conscience castigated me for being unfaithful to Domínguez and Escalante.

Three episodes during that week reconnected me, however tangentially, to the Spaniards' quest. Outside of Telluride, on a trail up Deep Creek, off Last Dollar Road, Sharon and I hiked through glades of aspen trees I had first visited almost thirty years before. Here Basque sheepherders hired to tend flocks through the subalpine summer as early as the turn of the twentieth century had whiled away their idle hours carving their names and comments into the aspens. The bark of that soft, deciduous tree "bleeds" over such scars relatively quickly.

Inscriptions I had first read around 1988 had blurred into meaning-less black scabs. Other trees must have fallen in the interim, since the life span of aspens is no longer than that of cottonwoods. But I found other messages that I had first noticed on any of seven or eight hikes over the years, still singing the loneliness of those long-gone men displaced from their homes on the border of France and Spain. The oldest date I could now make out was 1930, most of a century in the past. "Last day workin sheep," opined one veteran, whose name was reduced to a blob. Another signed his tree "G J B and his doog Ponte." I found one diorama I'd never seen before. The herder had carved a pornographic cartoon of a naked woman in the bark, with gaping vagina, and left a pithy message, "P. K. lost his prick here," in single words stacked top to bottom below the portrait.

I thought of course of Rivera carving his cross and *"Viva Jesús,"* along with his name and the date, in the cottonwood tree at the point of his farthest penetration in 1765. And of D & E looking for the inscription in vain. How much more humble were the Basque graf-fiti, and yet the impulse of the sheepherders was really the same as Rivera's: to leave some record of their passing, some boast to face down the indifference of eternity. Once only, as far as we know, months hence, at the turning point of their direst predicament, Domínguez and Escalante would carve their own record of their passing, not in ephemeral cottonwood bark but on a sandstone wall overlooking the Colorado River—a proclamation that would not be rediscovered until 2006, and then by the sheerest of accidents.

Speaking of cottonwoods: in Bluff Jim Hook, the owner of Recap-ture Lodge and my friend since 1992, told me about the tree ring study carried out along the San Juan River by a USGS team out of Flagstaff as part of a survey to reconcile the Navajo Reservation boundary of today with that promised by the 1868 treaty that had returned the Diné to their homeland after the genocidal nightmare of the Long Walk and Bosque Redondo. Although cottonwoods rarely live as long as 150 years, the Flagstaff team had found a clump of

trees that cored out to a date of 1776, plus or minus 30 years. When
he'd first heard about the anomalous dates, Jim had been excited, for
he knew his Four Corners history. The year 1776 was synonymous
with Domínguez and Escalante, even though the padres' expedition
came nowhere near Bluff. "Just the thought that those trees might
have started to grow when those guys explored the Southwest," said
Jim, not bothering to finish the sentence.

Sharon and I drove out Highway 162 a few miles east of town to
visit the cottonwood grove. The trees looked no bigger in girth than
any of hundreds of others lining the banks of the San Juan, though
perhaps they had a certain stately, withered air that bespoke their
great antiquity. Standing beside them, listening to the faint tremor of
their still-green leaves as they twisted in the warm breeze, I too could
feel the connection with the explorers whose closest approach on their
long loop passed 50 miles to the east.

The next day Sharon and I hiked beneath the cliff that rises on the
south bank of the San Juan at Upper Sand Island, just west of Bluff.
A rich mélange of rock art—Anasazi, Ute, and Navajo—ranged
across the sandstone wall. I'd perused the petroglyphs several times
before, but now a single set of carvings seized my attention. Three
beautifully rendered horses stood in profile, one facing the other two.
Atop one horse and standing beside another, two stick-figure humans
in silhouette commanded the beasts. Both wore on their heads the
tall-peaked, broad-brimmed hats favored by Spanish and Mexican
vaqueros, so unlike the ten-gallon hat of the American cowboy.

History records no expedition of Spanish or Mexican explorers
that came anywhere near Bluff or Cedar Mesa. I wondered if this
single panel could have been etched in sandstone to commemorate
the news—or perhaps years later, the legend—of the advent of the
Domínguez–Escalante team far to the east. The padres themselves
would not have worn the steepled Spanish hats, but all the other men
in the party might have. The San Juan River, after all, had been a
well-worn passageway through the ages for the Anasazi, then for

Detail from Miera y Pacheco's altar screen masterpiece, in Cristo Rey church, Santa Fe. *Photograph by David Roberts.*

Back road above Abiquiu, on the way to the first campsite. *Photograph by David Roberts.*

The author pondering the day's events, first campsite above Abiquiu. *Photograph by Sharon Roberts.*

In Tierra Amarilla, New Mexico, the high school named after Escalante, supposedly built on the site of his first mission—though Escalante never founded any missions. *Photograph by David Roberts.*

The Virgin praying in a wayside grotto near Los Ojos, New Mexico. *Photograph by David Roberts.*

Plaque commemorating the expedition at Escalante Wayside, between Durango and Cortez. *Photograph by David Roberts.*

Escalante Ruin, excavated and restored by a University of Colorado team in 1975. *Photograph by David Roberts.*

Detail from Miera y Pacheco's map of the expedition route, showing the great bend of the Dolores River. Near here the team met its first Indians ("Yutas tabeguachis"). *By permission of the British Library; Cartographic Items Add. MS. 17,661.d.*

The Dolores Canyon overlook. The expedition turned east rather than penetrate this abyss.
Photograph by David Roberts.

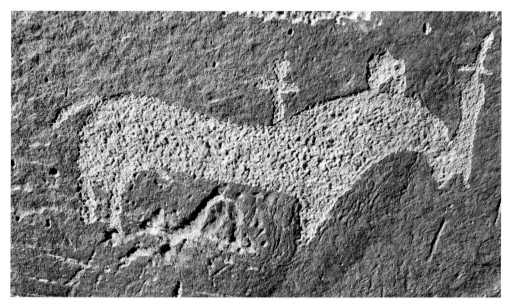

Navajo petroglyph on the San Juan River near Bluff, Utah. Could this depict the D & E team?
Photograph by Emmett Lyman.

Bedrock Store in Paradox Valley, where Clark from Brooklyn fumed about the McPhee Reservoir release. *Photograph by David Roberts.*

Sharon at blissful camp on the Uncompahgre Plateau. *Photograph by David Roberts.*

Detail in bas-relief from commemorative ramada, Montrose, Colorado. *Photograph by David Roberts.*

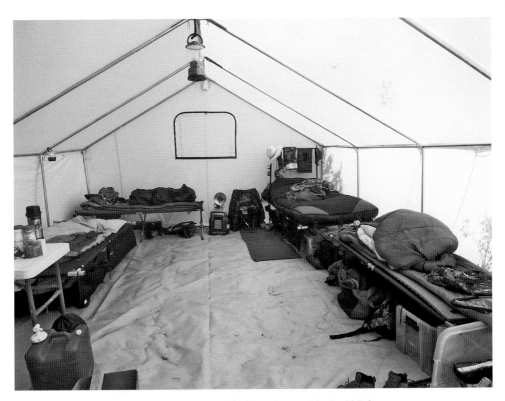

Hunting camp of Rich, the bow hunter on Grand Mesa. *Photograph by David Roberts.*

Escalante eagerly greets the Utes on the Gateway to the Canyons mural, Delta, Colorado. *Photograph by David Roberts.*

And the Utes eagerly greet the padres. *Photograph by David Roberts.*

Navajos and Utes. On August 5 and 6, 1776, the Spaniards had camped beside the San Juan, albeit some 140 miles upstream from the petroglyph panel at Sand Island. It was an idle thought, a wishful linkage, but all the sweeter in my brain since no scholar could ever prove or disprove it.

During our week off the D & E trail, I also thought a lot about the kind of journey Sharon and I had assigned ourselves. It was essentially a version of that quintessentially American concoction, the road trip. During my decades of adventure, I'd made quite a few long drives by car, especially up the Alaska Highway on the way to my beloved ranges. For other books, I'd retraced parts of the journeys of Carson and Frémont across Wyoming, Colorado, and California; of the doomed Mormon handcart teams in western Wyoming in 1856; and in search of Chiricahua Apache hideouts in the Mexican states of Sonora and Chihuahua. In arctic Svalbard, I'd hunted down the desolate island where from 1743 to 1749 four Russian walrus hunters had pulled off the most astounding feat of survival I'd ever heard of. And in Iceland I'd driven the Ring Road, stopping to explore each empty meadow or thundering waterfall where some cardinal deed hymned in the medieval sagas had taken place. But I'd never spent a month on the road, driving short distances each day, letting the chance encounters and curious finds along the way shape the experience.

Before I latched on to Domínguez and Escalante, I'd suggested to Sharon that we take a road trip all across the West in late summer and early autumn 2017, just because it seemed like the kind of *Wanderreise* I could handle with the limitations cancer had imposed on me, now that I could no longer backpack into the wilderness or climb big walls. I wasn't even sure it was a journey I'd write about, but I reread several classic road trip narratives just to get ideas. John Steinbeck's *Travels with Charley* beguiled me all over again. A key to the success of that deceptively slight memoir is the way Steinbeck's avowed goal—to reconnect with average Americans, as he prided himself on having done in his youth—falls apart, and he gets fed up with talking to strangers and eating in truck stops and sleeping in generic motels. Steinbeck has the courage to admit that he's homesick, that he just wants the whole trip over with—and that's when the book hits its stride.

On the other hand, I gave up for the second time on William Least Heat-Moon's *Blue Highways*. The endless, protracted set scenes with characters met along the way started to smell fishy to me. Without a tape recorder, how could the man have captured verbatim so much picturesque regional dialogue? And I started to resent the feint by which an out-of-work English professor took on a gratuitous persona as a Native American soothsayer—which, if I remembered right, was the semi-scam that had turned the book into a bestseller in 1983.

There was Kerouac's *On the Road*, but I just didn't have the heart to plow again through that stream-of-consciousness rant, which, uncharacteristically for my generation, had left me cold when I read it as a teenager.

Once I decided to retrace D & E, and to write about it, I worried whether the best road trip narratives documented solitary journeys. Steinbeck's dog made a handy foil for the author's soliloquies behind the wheel, but Charley, thank God, couldn't really keep up a conversation. D. H. Lawrence's *Sea and Sardinia* offered a possible solution to how you might write about travel with your wife, which was to treat her as an entitled bitch and mock her under the sobriquet of the Queen Bee. I had no intention of abusing Sharon that way, no matter how well it served Lawrence. On the other hand, Margaret Murie's *Two in the Far North*, which I had relished as an account of pioneer days in the Brooks Range, stuck in my craw on rereading, for somehow the first time round I had failed to notice how slavishly Murie worships her biologist husband (a genuine Alaska hero), and thus how soft and domestic the whole journey becomes, no matter what real hardships the couple mastered.

So as we set out from Santa Fe at the beginning of September, I had no good model for the kind of book I wanted to write. Domínguez and Escalante themselves, along with their faceless cronies, would have to set the pace. My job was not to worry about how I wrote about Sharon, or about the road, but to read always between the lines of Escalante's maddening journal, at once so suggestive and so opaque, as blind to cultural bias as it was curious about the Other, as the young Franciscan, by turns confident and despairing, recorded a journey the likes of which the American Southwest has seen only once in history.

One thing I knew: by the morning of September 18, I was dying to get back on the trail.

*   *   *

WE DROVE INTO COLORADO from the west on County Road 46, which becomes 90 at the border. Switchbacks lowered us into timeless Paradox Valley, where a wide basin was filled with fields both plowed and fallow between distant rims of pale red sandstone. On the two-block main street of Paradox, where the only store looked as though it had been closed for at least a decade, there was no one about. But the schoolyard a block away was thronged with kids on this balmy morning. We puttered on to Bedrock, where we crossed the Dolores River once more.

I was reading *One Man's West*, David Lavender's blithe memoir of a young adulthood working in the Camp Bird mine near Ouray during the Great Depression and caretaking the family homestead in Paradox Valley. Back then the ranching life was hard, the roads unreliable, with machines and men regularly breaking down, the cattle dying in storms, but the characters the author worked with and the beauty of the landscape turned ordeal into idyll. In the valley, Lavender absorbed the local lore. And on one page I read the following: "the Rio Dolores—River of Sorrows, so named by the Spaniard, Escalante, in 1776, when a Negro favorite of his exploring expedition fell into the stream from a bluff near the present town of Dolores and was drowned."

Lavender would become an excellent historian, and even in 1943 he could have learned the true story of the naming of the Dolores. But in a place like Paradox Valley, oral traditions were sovereign. As at Tierra Amarilla, where the locals swore the middle school was built on the very site of Escalante's first mission to the Indians, I was beguiled by the enduring myth. A favorite Negro? Drowning? From what faint echo of some other journey, some half-forgotten tragedy, did Lavender's version derive?

In Bedrock, the funky wood-and-stone general store was open. The proprietor, a man named Clark, was ready to talk our ears off. The place, he claimed, was the oldest continuously operating general store in Colorado, founded in 1881. But just as I started to hope the man had deep roots in this outback, Clark revealed that he was from Brooklyn and had moved to Bedrock only five years before. He'd never heard of David Lavender, so I didn't bother to ask about Domínguez and Escalante.

Clark was pissed about the McPhee Reservoir. "Last spring they released it for the first time in ten years," he fumed. "It was terrible for us in Bedrock. There was mud everywhere. They just don't give a crap about us."

Though Clark didn't mention it, I later learned that scenes from *Thelma and Louise* were filmed at the general store. The man was handy, however, with statistics. Two hundred thousand people a year, he claimed, "used" the Dolores. (For rafting? Fishing? Where were they all?) The combined population of Paradox and Bedrock was a solid 286.

As the Spaniards searched for the Yutas after August 17, they prolonged their love-hate affair with the Dolores River. From the mouth of Summit Canyon, they tried to head downstream, but the broad meanders of the river kept sweeping against the vertical cliffs on either side. As Escalante complained, "No way was found by which to get out without going through the river's box channel, in which, because of so much rock and the necessity of having to cross it many times, we feared that our mounts would wear out their hooves." The discouraged team accomplished less than three miles' progress on the 18th before stopping to camp again. The next day, D & E determined to escape the canyon of the Dolores once more, preferably to the northwest, but the scouts the leaders sent out came back with gloomy forebodings of "high mesas and canyons . . . where we could again hem ourselves in and find ourselves forced to backtrack," as well as a scarcity of water holes on the plateau.

The unease that had settled on the team seemed to deepen into a state of controlled panic. The journal entry for August 19 records the team's confusion. "Paths" of some kind branched out from various points along the Dolores to the northwest, the southwest, and the northeast. "We conferred," wrote the friar, "with the companions who had journeyed through this region as to which direction we should take in order to forestall so many difficulties, and each one had a different opinion." Which "companions" besides Andrés Muñiz did the leaders consult? Who had been there before? Felipe and Juan Domingo, the *genízaros* who had trailed the team until they joined up on August 14? The trail that led to the northeast, one of the "guides" divined, must lead to the Sabuaganas, yet another band of Yutas apparently distinguishable by their footprints.

Twentieth-century ethnographers could barely find any historical references to the Sabuagana Utes after 1760. They are tentatively identified as the Taguaganas, about whom little is known except that they lived near the Dolores River. Whether or not the "companions" had traveled through this region on previous jaunts, the whole team by now was desperate to find some Yutas to help them figure out where to go. And so, late on August 19, the men made a momentous decision.

Escalante underscores the gravity of the "quandary" (his word): "We put our trust in God and our will in that of His most holy Majesty; then, after begging the intercession of our thrice-holy patron saints that God might direct us through where it would be more conducive to His most holy service, we cast lots . . ." The casting of lots, or cleromancy, was a time-honored Catholic procedure by which critical decisions were left up to the divine will, or what we in an agnostic age would call chance. The padres may well have put markers representing the three trails into a hat and asked a teammate to draw one. On August 19, God apparently favored the path that ought to lead to the Sabuaganas. "This one we decided to follow until we reached them."

Miera y Pacheco got out the astrolabe and took another reading of the party's latitude. His calculation of 39° 6' N was more than a full degree and a half too far north. Is this a further sign that the men were lost? On the morning of August 20, the team headed northeast—almost directly opposite, as they had to know, any route that would take them closer to California. In doing so, they left the troublesome Dolores River behind for good.

It was a miserable day's march. Miera vociferously disagreed with the padres' route-finding, so the team put Andrés Muñiz in the lead. "The interpreter took us over a high rough incline, so rocky that we expected to find ourselves forced to backtrack from halfway up, for the mounts were being so much abused that many of them were marking the spoor on the stones with the blood which these were drawing from their hind and fore feet." On the crest of some divide, the men rode on through aggravating swaths of prickly pear cactus, then into another "box channel" of a dry arroyo. The grueling long day's effort gained the team a scant 10 miles, and not a single Sabuagana came in sight. At the end of the day, however, just when tempers must have been stretched to the breaking point, the men stumbled upon a generous pool of water fed by a small spring. And not only were there abundant footprints around the spring, but also "the ruins of huts"—Ute wickiups. The Sabuaganas had camped here, though how long before, no one could say.

Two more days would pass without success. The short entries in Escalante's journal numbly record only the travails of travel: sagebrush, "steep inclines," waterless stretches, "bad canyons." If they were still following the path on which they had left the Dolores, it's hard to tell, so aimless seems their wandering. And during August 21 and 22, the padre makes no more mention of Ute footprints, much less wickiups. Yet a single slope off a mesa down which the team rode on the 22nd Escalante identifies as "the one which Don Juan María Ribera in his diary dwells on as very trying." This passage offers the clearest evidence that D & E carried a copy of Rivera's journal with them. Yet so topographically vague is that diary that it's hard to imagine even the cleverest of navigators using it as a trail guide

On the evening of the 21st, the team camped beside a new river called the San Pedro. It's not a name chosen by Domínguez and Escalante, yet neither does it appear in Rivera's journal. The only likely stream on today's map is the San Miguel, a sizable waterway that heads in the San Juan Range near Telluride, then flows west and north until it joins the Dolores near the uranium ghost town of Uravan, only about 20 miles north of the place where D & E abandoned the Dolores. (Outfitters today offer the San Miguel as a float trip alternative to the Dolores when the latter river is too shallow for rafts.)

On the morning of August 23, the team left the banks of the San Pedro to climb yet another hill. They were still heading east, still convinced that the Yutas must be nearby, though the journal implies that now the team anticipates Tabehuachis rather than Sabuaganas. The tone of the diary is dogged pessimism. *Where are the Indians?* the men must have asked themselves every hour. On a low ridge they found "good pasturage" and stopped to let the horses feed. It was a blessing, for ever since leaving the Dolores, they had found almost no grasses for their mounts to graze, as "the earth was scorched and dry enough to show that no rain had fallen all summer."

Here the men also found a cluster of curious structures, which Escalante describes as "the ruins of a small and ancient pueblo, the houses of which seem to have been made of the stone with which the Tabehuachi Yutas had fashioned a weak and crude rampart." The friar's conclusion that these were Ute buildings must have been wishful thinking, as the "ancient pueblo" was almost certainly an Anasazi ruin, or perhaps the work of their northern contemporaries, the Fremont. Whatever it was, the ruin has never been rediscovered in modern times.

*   *   *

FROM BEDROCK, Sharon and I headed east on Route 90 toward Naturita. Out of the blue, at the junction with Highway 141 coming out of Uravan, we ran into a roadside marker commemorating the D & E expedition. The billboard sported a route diagram and a pair of vignettes from Miera y Pacheco's map. The sign bore much of the same language that we'd read at the Escalante Wayside west of Durango, including the slightly hyperbolic claim that "throughout their journey, they encountered a dozen native tribes but never resorted to violence toward their fellow men." This was the spot, we were informed, where the Spaniards had camped on August 21, 1776.

Yes, here at the road junction we had come to the banks of the San Miguel River. But the precise site of the D & E campsite was only the Bicentennial Commission's best guess. In 1975 Delaney and McDaniel wrote, "We talked to several people in Naturita who showed us on the map their ideas for the travel of this date and the best campsite." To be sure, local knowledge can be useful, but 199 years after the Spaniards had passed by, how could even the savviest graybeard in Naturita (founded ca. 1882) know anything about where the demoralized explorers had pitched their tents on the evening of August 21, 1776?

After Paradox and Bedrock, Naturita (2016 population 530, with a loss of 100 residents since 2000) looked like a happening place. At the visitor center the young docent spilled out the story of her German grandmother, still alive at ninety, who'd come to the U.S. in 1948 and ended up serving in the Eisenhower administration—as what, we never learned. She too had never heard of David Lavender, but "You know, I did learn a little bit about Domínguez and Escalante growing up here." I didn't push for specifics.

Naturita boasts a gas station, a grocery store, a hotel of sorts, and even a drive-in theater, or at least the old sign from one. We stopped at the city park on the banks of the San Miguel for a picnic lunch. I ate one of my standard post-radiation meals that a mouth bereft of salivary glands could handle: brie cheese on Ritz crackers, sweet green peppers, Starbuck's Frappuccino, and a fresh local peach. As we dined, a fellow drove up in a pickup, emerged with a metal detector, and started sweeping the ground near the kids' swings and jungle gym. "What are you looking for?" I called out.

"Money," the man answered. "I found a diamond ring here once."

We drove north on County Road 97 five miles to Nucla, roughly following the route of the Spaniards during their dispirited search for Utes. In *One Man's West*, Lavender vividly recounts a Christmas party and dance in Nucla that gathered all the ranchers and hermits from the farthest corners of Paradox Valley. A sample:

> The orchestra is a four-piece affair—piano, fiddle, banjo, and saxophone. It is very bad. But it can keep time, and that is enough. There are foxtrots and waltzes for the younger folk, but many of the pieces are quadrilles, square dances, and Virginia reels. Pete Hubbard does the calling. He stands on a table, his shirt sleeves rolled to his elbows, the sweat pouring down his round, wrinkled face. By midnight his stentorian bellow has sunk to a croak.
>
> About one o'clock the arrival of old Jeff Grable causes a flurry. One of his charges is howling and will not be comforted. Jeff can't tell whose baby it is . . .

In the middle of get-rich-quick, every-man-for-himself Colorado, Nucla (originally called Piñon) was founded in the wake of the financial disaster called the Panic of 1893 as a communal, socialist response to the horrors of capitalism. Lavender gently teases the way Nucla's idealism had clashed with reality by the end of the 1930s:

The founders of the town had decided that lawyers, churches, and saloons were equal evils and had banned them all. Everything was to be run on a share-all, cooperative basis. The first problem had been an irrigating ditch. A considerable job it was, too, seventeen miles long, including a mammoth log trestle supporting a flume. Each colonist received for his labor on it credit at the commissary for food and supplies, plus water credits toward the purchase of ditch rights. The canal succeeded, and several prosperous farms sprang up. But the beautiful mist of socialism had soon faded under the hot sun of private ownership. Except in one or two minor respects Nucla today is like any other remote farming town. Even the lawyers, churches, and saloons came creeping back.

Indeed, Nucla looked very much like Naturita. On its eastern edge, we drove past its signature eyesore, a gigantic generating station, originally a coal-burning power plant. So far has Nucla evolved from its utopian origins that in 2013 it became the only town in Colorado to pass a law making gun ownership mandatory.

Somewhere near here, once again on the banks of the San Pedro (San Miguel), the Spaniards camped on the night of August 22. The next day, on the low ridge, they discovered the ruined pueblo they mistook for a Ute habitation site. After the horses had eaten their fill of the "good pasturage," the team moved on, still headed east. By now they were 30 miles as the crow flies east of the bend on the Dolores where they had made their fateful decision to proceed in a direction away from their goal of California.

Suddenly that afternoon, twenty-three days and 307 miles beyond Abiquiu, the expedition met its first Indian. Escalante's account of that event has an almost hallucinatory aura:

After one league of travel to the northeast and another to the east, we were overtaken by a Tabehuachi Yuta, who was the first one we had seen in all that we had traveled until now. . . . In order to talk with him at leisure, we halted near the beginning of the water source where we had rested, and here we named it La Fuente de la Guia [The Guide's Fountain]. We gave him something to eat and to smoke, and afterward through the interpreter we asked him various questions about the land ahead, the rivers, and their course. We also asked him where the Tabehuachis, Muhuachis, and Sabuaganas were.

At first he denied knowing anything, even the country where he lived.

Escalante assumes that it is fear that prevents the Ute from answering the interpreter's questions. But if so, why had the man deliberately "overtaken" the Spanish party? Throughout the 1,700-mile journey the expedition would complete, the men's interactions with natives seem riddled with misunderstandings. How well did Andrés Muñiz speak Ute? How different were the dialects spoken by the various bands? More than two centuries after the fact, the answers are unknowable.

In the early 1990s, when I researched a book about the war between the Chiricahua Apaches and the governments of the United States and Mexico between 1861 and 1886, I was struck by how many pivotal exchanges had gone wrong because of what must have been botched translations by interpreters. Yet previous historians of the conflict seemed to have ignored that epistemological dilemma.

Throughout Escalante's journal, the reader can never take what he says various Indians say at face value. Sometimes the padre's bias is nakedly on display; at other times, we can detect only confusion. No matter what went on that midday near the San Miguel River, the consequences for the expedition would be profound. Escalante continues:

After [the Ute] had lost some of the fear and suspicion with which he conversed with us, he said that the Sabuaganas were

all in their own country and that soon we would be meeting
them; that the Tabehuachis wandered scattered about throughout this sierra and its surroundings. . . . We suggested to him
that he might want to guide us as far as the encampment of a
Sabuagana chieftan who our interpreter and others said was
very fond of the Spaniards and knew much of the country. He
consented on condition that we wait for him until the next day
in the afternoon; we agreed to wait for him, both to acquire
him as a guide and lest he came to suspect something of us
which would disturb him and the rest.

The Spaniards had indeed "acquired a guide." The great question about the expedition during the next month becomes, just whose
needs and purposes was the ragtag procession of explorers now
fulfilling?

Chapter Five

FINDING THE RÍO TIZÓN

IT WAS WORTH THE WAIT. THE NEXT DAY, SHORTLY BEFORE noon, the Yuta returned, bringing with him two women and five children, "two of those at the breast . . . all of good features and very friendly." Unfortunately, the family plainly expected to trade with the Spaniards, for they brought with them manzanita berries, a delicacy the men had already sampled as they rode up the Chama on August 2, finding them "like grapes, and very tasty." Now the friars had to explain that they weren't interested in trade, a claim that bewildered the Ute.

But after a preliminary parley, the family sat down with the Spaniards, and when the wife offered the travelers jerked venison to go with the berries they accepted, offering flour in exchange. In due time, the Ute man proposed a price for his services as a guide, to which the Spaniards agreed, handing over "two big all-purpose knives and sixteen strings of white glass beads." What was this barter all about, if not trade?

Some uneasiness must still have lingered about the meeting, for Escalante was concerned "lest they took us for scouts intending to conquer their land." To allay the Ute's fears, the friar told him a story that must have turned the man's confusion to utter bafflement. He explained that "a certain padre, a brother of ours," had recently made

a trip of his own into the vast territory on the New Mexican frontier, during which he came into contact with quite another tribe of
Indians, the Cosninas, know today as the Havasupai. The homeland
of these natives lay on the downstream end of the Grand Canyon,
at least 500 miles to the west and south of the present conversation.
It's entirely likely that the man the Spaniards had just hired to guide
them was completely unaware of the existence of the Cosninas.

Escalante babbled on. News of the journey of this brother, this
fellow padre, might have passed on to the Payuchi Utes (the Southern Paiutes, still hundreds of miles away), and thence perhaps to the
Tabehuachis and the Sabuaganas. To make matters more urgent,
Escalante was worried about his far-off brother. Had he come
to harm? Had the Ute sitting here with his family, kids and all,
heard any news?

Reading this bizarre entry in Escalante's journal, one wonders just
what sort of answer the Ute tendered. Whatever it was, no matter
how thoroughly Escalante misunderstood, his words put the padre at
ease. No, the man hadn't seen the long-lost brother, but "fully sharing
our worry," he was reassured thereby that this strange Spanish team
was not bent on conquest.

In this journal entry on August 24, for the first time we hear
about Fray Francisco Hermenegildo Tomás Garcés. And therein
hangs a tale.

Father Garcés, a Franciscan born in Aragón in Spain, had been
posted to the mission at San Xavier del Bac in what is now southern Arizona in 1768. From that base he ministered to the Pima and
Papago as he tried to bring them into the Christian fold, and a restless
spirit drove him to an extraordinary career as an explorer.

It is unlikely that Escalante and Garcés ever met. But from Hopi
on July 3, 1776, the thirty-eight-year-old Garcés wrote a letter to
his fellow Franciscan, as the missionary posted to the nearest other
pueblo, at Zuni, detailing his most recent expedition. In January
1776, Garcés had set out from San Xavier del Bac on a far-ranging

reconnaissance that would last eleven months, taking him all the way to California, then back beyond San Xavier to Hopi. It was a mark of Garcés's courage and adaptability that he traveled with only two Indian companions. Along the way, he survived meetings with several tribes considered to be deeply hostile to Spaniards, and rumored to be cannibals—including the Cosninas, or Havasupai.

As he traveled, Garcés developed the conviction that a northern route through the homeland of the Yutas would best link Santa Fe with Monterey. Writing to Escalante on July 3, still in mid-journey, he was addressing a fellow believer in the northern route, on which the younger Franciscan would set out with Domínguez before the month was out.

By traveling in roundabout fashion from California to Hopi, Garcés might have demonstrated a southern alternative to the northern route directly from Santa Fe to Monterey that D & E hoped to discover, and in which Governor Mendinueta had put his faith. But Garcés's own encounters with the many hostile tribes he passed among in southern Arizona and California, not to mention at equally hostile Hopi, made that itinerary a shaky proposition. Only a few years later, Father Garcés would pay with his life for his trust in those southern natives. The fact that in his letter to Escalante, Garcés voiced his belief that a northern route would be faster and safer than the meandering path he had so bravely pioneered underscores the danger and impracticality of the southern route. Almost fifty years later, the Spanish Trail that would finally link Santa Fe to Monterey followed D & E's reconnaisance far more closely than Garcés's zigzagging route.

By early July, Escalante was no longer at Zuni, having traveled to Santa Fe to prepare for the great expedition. Somehow Garcés's letter caught up to him just before he left on July 29. Throughout the long journey into the unknown land of the Yutas, Garcés's remarkable feat was very much on the younger friar's mind. As to why Escalante apparently believed that by late August, when he met his first Ute near the San Miguel River, Garcés might still be in the wilderness, much less far enough north for the Tabehuachis or Sabuaganas to have gotten wind of him, let alone perhaps lost or in harm's way—all that is yet another of the many mysteries that haunt Escalante's journal.

So on August 24, the padres signed up their Tabehuachi Yuta guide to lead the party onward. If he and his family were to accompany the Spaniards, he needed a name. His Ute name, perhaps unpronounceable, would never do. So D & E dubbed him Atanasio, after Domínguez himself. As Atanasio, the new guide became more than another misnamed native. He emerged, in effect, as the team mascot.

Musing upon this enigmatic passage in Escalante's diary, I fantasized about the exchange, as the padre heard what he wanted to hear.

Escalante: "We're worried about Brother Garcés. Have you seen him hereabouts? Or heard any word about what he's up to?"

Atanasio: "No, my friend. Not a word. But we'll keep an eye out."

Escalante: "The last we heard from him he was hanging out with the Cosninas. And as you know, they are a very dangerous bunch."

Atanasio (to himself): *In the name of Sinauf and all the other gods, who are these Cosninas? I think this fellow wearing his blue blanket is a little crazy.* (Out loud): "Yes, very dangerous. That's why we have nothing to do with them. And now, should we get on our way?"

* * *

ON THE AFTERNOON of September 18, Sharon and I left Nucla and drove east on Highway 90. We knew that the Spaniards, guided now by Atanasio, had crossed the Uncompahgre Plateau, taking four days to complete the rugged traverse. There's no telling today just where the party traveled on that trackless upland, but the Bicentennial Commission, relying as usual on their tendentious judgments about "likely" campsites and water sources, concluded that the expedition had more or less paralleled present-day Route 90. That road, rising through a badlands of scrub oak, was Sharon's and my only choice. In his journal Escalante complains about the "encumbered terrain" as the team ascended through "dense clumps of scruboak."

We were checking the pullouts along the highway, hoping to find a campsite with a view to the western horizon. It was still a day or two before bow hunting season opened and the pullouts were all empty. Somewhere along the road we passed the site of a ghost town called Ute without recognizing it. It's marked on the AAA "Indian Country" map (everybody's cartographic bible to the Southwest), but even after the trip I could find no information about that fugitive settlement.

In my teens and twenties, I'd climbed a lot in the Elk Range and the San Juans, but I'd never visited the somber and summitless Uncompahgre Plateau, named after the same Ute band that Escalante referred to as the Tabehuachis. We took the drive slowly, with Sharon at the wheel of our RAV4. It was another warm afternoon with clear skies and a gentle breeze, and I relished every bend in the curving highway.

Exactly thirteen years before, on September 18, 2004, with my fellow devotees of all things Anasazi Greg Child and Vaughn Hadenfeldt, I'd come to the end of our eighteen-day, 125-mile traverse of the Comb Ridge in Arizona and Utah. The Comb is a massive monocline created by the cataclysmic slippage of tectonic plates 65 million years ago. We decided to try that marathon backpack partly because, as far as we could learn, no one else had ever done it, but mainly because the Comb was riddled with hidden sites that had once been numinous places for the Anasazi, then for both Navajos and Utes. That September we blundered into a heat wave, and nearly every day we sweated and suffered under loads as heavy as 80 pounds in temperatures above 90° Fahrenheit. But it had been a rich and gratifying mini-expedition. Now, in 2017, I looked back on our Comb traverse as the last major backpacking trip I would ever undertake. Forty days along the Domínguez–Escalante trail, almost entirely by auto, would hardly be the equivalent. But on this thirteen-year anniversary, I was supremely happy to be exploring with Sharon, and to be still in quest of some kind of discovery in the limitless Southwest.

We found an ideal pullout at about 7,000 feet of elevation, where a dirt track trickled 50 yards off the highway to an abrupt end in a shelf of sandstone thrusting clear of the scrub oak. We parked our folding chairs on that perch, settled in for dinner, and spent an hour watching the sun slide toward the rim of the world. A solitary piñon defied the bedrock, climbing in tortured asymmetry toward the sky like one of the cypresses in Everett Ruess's woodcuts from the Monterey coast. Far to the south, the graceful pyramid of 12,618-foot Lone Cone stood as Colorado's last sentinel before the Utah desert, and even farther to the west, beyond the La Sals, we glimpsed the thin blue silhouettes of the Henry Mountains. After dark we built a small fire of piñon branches and stayed up late.

Even blissful car camping had become something of a trial for me, thanks not so much to cancer as to its side effects and to the nuisances of advancing age. Since January I'd been afflicted by lower back pain on the left side. The best guess of a parade of doctors was spinal arthritis; on the X-rays I could see where a couple of vertebrae had given up the struggle and hung slumped in wobbly defeat. Over the months I'd been dosed with physical therapy, massage, acupuncture, trigger point and lidocaine injections, painkillers ranging from morphine to fentanyl patches to Oxycontin, and an electric gizmo that sent a zapping shiver through my back, all to no avail. In the car I kept a small Therm-a-Rest pillow tucked between my back and the seat, and I carried the pillow into restaurants to mitigate the assaults of plastic and wooden chairs. Bending over and picking up things turned the pain up a notch, so pitching our tent, gathering firewood, and even tending the fire increased my discomfort.

The SIADH I've lived with since June 2016 meant that I had to pee many times each day. Crawling out of my sleeping bag, slipping on boots or sandals, unzipping the tent, getting to my feet, and going out in the night amounted to a routine a lot more aggravating than padding from bed to bathroom at home. That night I had to get up and go five times, but at least each trip outside the tent gave me another chance to survey the sky full of stars. Yet mornings were rough. The worst my back hurt during the whole trip was in the early hours after a camping night, and I was so sensitive to cold that a 50° morning, like ours on September 19, felt arctic.

Yet those nights in the tent and by the fire put us in closer communion with Domínguez and Escalante, and the pleasures of *camping sauvage* in the dry but aromatic Southwest had been for decades one of my chief joys in life. The silence of those nights, pierced at dusk by the whirr of bats, or in the morning by birdsong, or at any hour by the distant yips of coyotes, put me back in touch with the wanderlust that had driven me to Alaska so long before, and that had given my year its vernal and autumnal azimuths with every trip into Anasazi country for the last quarter century.

As the fire dwindled, I asked Sharon why this trip had so pleased her thus far, for it was clear that despite all her apprehensions about my illness flaring into crisis, she was savoring each day as keenly as I was. She thought for a moment, then said, "It's wonderful to drive all these back roads. To go slowly, and not have any place we have to get to. And to read Escalante's journal, and see what they saw, and search for the things he writes about that don't make any sense." She took my hand in the dark. "And you know," she went on, "I could never go on those hard climbs with you. And when I was working full-time, and you were off on assignments . . ." She left the sentence unfinished. "This is the best thing we've done together in a long time. I feel that I'm as important a part of it as you are, even if you'll end up doing the writing. That the way I see the country matters, that I can help you rediscover whatever we're looking for."

As far as I could tell, not a single car drove by in the night. The next morning we pushed on up Route 90, finally cresting the divide at around 9,000 feet. Here, though it was unmarked on the map, some sort of ghost town was fading gracefully into ruin: the bleached wood of barns and buildings, old wagons and ranch tools rusting among the tall grasses. The San Juan Range stood boldly against the southern horizon. We saw Mount Sneffels, already touched with autumn snows, a proud fourteener that Sharon and I had climbed in dead winter in 1971. On Route 90, we had left behind not only the scrub oak thickets but the piñons and junipers. Here the open forest was dominated by dark spruce and willowy aspen, the leaves just starting to turn yellow. I read in *The WPA Guide to 1930s Colorado*, "According to a Ute legend, the continuous quivering of aspen leaves, even when there is no appreciable breeze, is due to the Great Spirit who once visited earth during a full moon. All living things awaited him, trembling with anticipation—all save the proud aspen, which stood still, refusing to pay homage. The deity, angered, decreed that in the future its leaves should tremble whenever eye looked upon them." Well, maybe. In the WPA telling, the legend smacked of Edwardian pieties—Sara Teasdale out of Sir James Frazer?—as much as Numic cosmogony. As we stopped to take photos, I laid aside my literary baggage and absorbed the still, sharp clarity of the place.

Domínguez and Escalante topped the Uncompahgre Plateau near midday on August 25. They too were taken with the loveliness of their surroundings, as Escalante salutes the "very good pastures and pleasing scenery" he credited to "beautiful poplar [aspen] groves briefly spaced from one another." (*Briefly spaced*, I thought—a nice observation.) Nearby they stopped to camp at a copious spring they named El Ojo de Lain, after one of the well-born members of the team, Don Joaquín Lain, identified in the July 29 roster simply as a citizen of Santa Fe. It's one of only a handful of mentions of Lain in the whole journal.

Here the men reached the highest elevation so far on their long, wandering circuit. If the August night was cold, Escalante never complains about it, even though just before camping the men had gotten soaked in a heavy downpour. The next day they rode down from the high divide, still headed northeast. Sharon and I drove the winding road, losing 3,000 feet in an hour, and met the Uncompahgre River on the main street of Montrose.

Escalante identified the team's campsite along that river, which they called the San Francisco, as "next to a big marsh greatly abounding in pasturage." Montrose is a town that cares about its history, so I was hopeful that here we might scare up some local knowledge about D & E. My first stop was a washout, however, for I discovered that the promisingly named Museum of the Mountain West was a reconstructed frontier town from about 1885, no doubt authentic in all its details but a monument to Western kitsch. Among the buildings were the Miner's Delight Saloon, a scary-looking dentist's office, and a "Tonsorial Emporium." I didn't stay for the reenacted shootout with cowpokes biting the dust in front of the saloon.

I had better luck at the Montrose County Historical Museum. There, when I asked about Domínguez and Escalante, the docent on duty beamed and said, "I can tell you exactly where they camped."

"Where?" I asked.

"Right there at Target." I must have done a double-take before I realized she meant the Target store, at 3530 Wolverine Drive on the south side of town.

"How do we know that?" I wondered.

"Because that's where Chief Ouray's lodge was." If anything, the woman's confidence had soared another notch. Ouray was her QED. I didn't have the heart to remind her that the Ute chief had been born some fifty-seven years after D & E had come through this country, and then in far-off Taos, New Mexico, rather than Colorado. Instead I parried, "But they were here for one night only—"

"Yes, but there were so many of them."

"They were only twelve." That seemed to slow her down. I thanked the woman, then Sharon and I got back in the car and drove south on U.S. Highway 550 past a shopping mall or two to the bridge over the Uncompahgre River. The Bicentennial Commission had concluded that the campsite of August 26 was very near this bridge. Sure enough, bordering the river on the far side was a small swamp, thick with cattails and tall grasses. Mentally I cut the Historical Museum woman some slack. The Target store, after all, stood only about a third of a mile north of the swamp. Chief Ouray notwithstanding, some echo of the Spaniards' passing must still be pulsing in the streets of Montrose.

I was curious how the town, founded in 1882, got its name. The *WPA Guide* came to my rescue. It turns out that the founder, one Joseph Selig, had plucked the name from Sir Walter Scott's novel *A Legend of Montrose* "because the country resembled that in Scotland where Montrose fought." Selig? Zelig? I mused. Highland chieftans on the Uncompahgre? It was too much to take in.

Just across the Highway 550 bridge stands the Ute Indian Museum. It's a handsome building, with tall exhibits cased in glass scattered like islands through the ample interior, and massive painted teepees (rather than wickiups) strewn across the front lawn. Here, I thought, at last the threads that stitched the padres to the Tabehuachis and Sabuaganas would be sewn together. But I was disappointed. The backward reach of the institution's history seemed to end with the nineteenth century. The place was all about Chief Ouray (1833–80), who tried to broker peace with the U.S. government, foreseeing doom for his people as the only alternative, but who ended up signing away the rich mining lands of Colorado for a reservation in desolate Utah. To this day, Ouray is sneered at by Native American activists as a sell-out. I was bemused to learn that Ouray was only half Ute, his father having been a Jicarilla Apache. The museum also celebrated Ouray's wife, Chipeta, who lived until 1924.

But the museum had nothing to tell me about Utes in 1776, when Atanasio guided the Spaniards through western Colorado. A volunteer named Maureen apologized for the oversight, but she was eager to let me know that the small spring out back, marked by a mortared well on top of which a teepee had been pitched (its charm diminished, alas, by a large "keep off" sign), was the very water source the Domínguez–Escalante party had used on August 26. I nodded wearily, reminded of the ranger at the Anasazi Heritage Center insisting

that Escalante Ruin was verifiably the one the padres had so offhandedly noticed as the team first rode along the banks of the Dolores. In
the journal on August 26, Escalante says nothing about the spring,
mentioning instead only the swamp that served as a campsite, which
the party named La Ciénega de San Francisco.

Just across the street from the museum, however, the Bicentennial
Commission had finally achieved its ambitions, with the elaborate
"commemorative ramada" envisioned in the 1976 *Interpretive Master
Plan and Final Report*. Four tall plinths in white stone held up the
bare wooden beams of the ramada. A skillful bas-relief portrayed the
expedition as a rather desperate stumble through the wilderness, but
the motifs of the four panels sang an anthem of uplift: "In Behalf of
the Light" ("The Franciscans' mission to spread Christianity and care
for the people"), "So Bold, So Beautiful a Land" ("It took bold men
to ride into a bold land"), "Building an Empire," and "Pageant in the
Wilderness" (the last a crib from the valedictory 1951 tome of the great
historian Herbert E. Bolton, the first chronicler fully to engage the
saga of Domínguez and Escalante and the first to retrace their route).

For all my skepticism, I had to admit that the memorial was very
well done, even though the despair etched in the bas-relief clashed
with the march-of-progress tone of the texts. The ramada, in fact,
would turn out to be the most impressive memorial to the expedition
that Sharon and I came across on the whole 1,700-mile loop. It made
me wonder, though, why the woman at the Historical Museum had
been so adamant about her Target campsite. All she needed to do on
her lunch break was drive a couple of miles down Route 550 to visit
the ramada and get the local chapter of the D & E story straight.

The complete blank about eighteenth-century Ute history in the
Ute Indian Museum could be attributed in large part to the wholesale resettlement of the Colorado tribe under Chief Ouray to an arbitrary reservation 100 miles away in northeastern Utah in the early
1880s. Since the first time I read Escalante's journal, I'd realized
what a gold mine it would be to get stories from living Utes about

the strange expedition led by the blue-robed padres that had passed through their homeland in 1776. Those explorers (along with Rivera) were surely the first Europeans the Utes had ever seen. In the early 1990s, when I researched the Chiricahua Apache war against the U.S. Army from 1861 to 1886, I had met with the direct descendants of Cochise and Naiche, who shared with me priceless stories about the Apache tragedy.

But the Spanish disruption of the Ute heartland had occurred a century before the Chiricahua war. And my experience at Jemez, when I had failed utterly to gain any Puebloan testimony about the great revolt of 1680, left me pessimistic about a kindred mission to the Uintah and Ouray Reservation. In the end, though, it was cancer that won out. In 2017, I just didn't have the energy to set off on what I feared would be another cultural wild goose chase.

* * *

SINCE HIRING THE no doubt perplexed Atanasio on August 24, Escalante hadn't said a word about their Ute guide in his journal. On the 27th, the team packed up camp and followed the Uncompahgre downstream on its west bank, crossing the river somewhere north of where Selig and friends would found their Scottish-looking settlement a century later. Near the river the Spaniards ran into another Ute, whose name translated as "Left-Handed." (I thought again of Mancos. Was left-handedness—in Spanish *zurdo*—as sinister as one-handedness?) The long powwow with this other Indian ended up, in the padres' view, a waste of time: "We tarried a good while with him, and after a lengthy conversation drew forth nothing more useful than that we had suffered from the heat, which was indeed very fiery . . ."

At the end of a day's ride of 16 miles, the party camped on the east bank of the Uncompahgre, where Escalante again reported excellent pasturage. The Commission locates this camp as about two miles north of the small town of Olathe.

On Highway 550, Sharon and I headed northwest out of Montrose, following the Uncompahgre. At Olathe, we turned west on a small street that dead-ended shortly after recrossing the river. Sharon pulled over while I studied the map. A man came out of the small clapboard house with a stone chimney in front of which we were parked. He wore a cut-off T-shirt bearing the message "Seasons After." I guessed that he was at least part Ute. I rolled down the window as he squinted in the sun. "You folks okay?" he asked. I launched into my recital of D & E, short version. Nothing registered on the man's face. "Just wanted to make sure you folks were okay," he repeated. I thanked him as Sharon prepared to make a U-turn. "You have a nice day," Seasons After said as he waved goodbye.

It was obvious that few of the travelers bombing along 550 between Montrose and Grand Junction bothered to check out the streets of Olathe (population 1,573 in 2000). So far from the norm was our little detour, it seemed, that it might have signaled that we were in trouble. A couple of weeks earlier, when we had turned off the highway at Monero, New Mexico, the fellow at the Carrillo Ranch had voiced the same sort of concern. All through the West, as I'd learned often before, though never so vividly as on the trail of D & E, small-town life just beyond the U.S. highways and the "destination" cities ran on its own hermetic track.

I wondered about the name Olathe (pronounced "Oh-layth"). Later I learned that the Colorado hamlet was named after Olathe, Kansas, a suburb of Kansas City that likes to tout itself as the fourth-largest city in the Sunflower State. It was named by *its* founder, one Dr. John T. Barton, in 1857, after he asked his Shawnee interpreter what his people's word for "beautiful" was. Barton and his cronies were abolitionists, and only five years later Quantrill's raiders came by, killed a half dozen citizens, and laid waste to the fledgling town. What all this had to do with Olathe, Colorado, I never found out.

Eleven miles farther north along Route 550 we came to Delta, where the Gunnison River joins the Uncompahgre. The stone wall of a two-story building beside the highway had been painted with an arresting tableau under the Chamber of Commerce rubric "Gateway to the Canyons." The scene depicted the meeting of Domínguez and Escalante with the Utes. On the right, one padre rode his horse as he held a small white cross thrust forward in his right hand. Behind him the other friar walked as he led his horse by the reins. The faces of both men beamed in joyful greeting. On the left, three Utes, wearing only leggings and headbands, rode toward the strangers. Four teepees behind the riders adumbrated their camp. The Utes, too, were beaming. One stretched out his left hand in greeting. Signed by the artist, one Seth Weber, in 2012, the composition blazoned the fevered dream of missionaries in all times and all places—of natives overjoyed to emerge from heathen darkness to embrace the Word.

On August 28 the expedition left the Uncompahgre River to cut across relatively level land, taking a bearing slightly east of north. After 10 miles, the men came to the new river running east to west across their path. Atanasio told them that his people called it the Tomichi, but D & E already knew it as the San Xavier. The team halted at a bend in the river to decide what to do next. The San Xavier was a powerful waterway, bigger than the San Francisco (the Uncompahgre), comparable in size, Escalante claimed, to the Rio Grande as it flowed from north to south through the Spanish colony centered around Santa Fe.

Ever since August 24, when the expedition decided to forgo for a while its western push and submit to the guidance of Atanasio, it would seem that the men were entering terra still incognita to the Spanish. But Andrés Muñiz swore that this was precisely the way he'd come with Rivera on the second expedition in 1765—which was why he knew the river already as the Río de San Xavier. And here, on the south bank, Muñiz further swore, Rivera had carved his name and date and a cross with the motto "*Viva Jesús*" in the cottonwood tree. Domínguez and Escalante searched for the tree but never found it.

Before Steven Baker devoted decades of careful research to the Rivera expedition, that earlier Spanish reconnaissance of the greater Southwest lingered in a kind of historical limbo. Baker eventually proved that Rivera had reached the Tomichi (or San Xavier, or Gunnison) not where D & E halted and searched for the engraved cottonwood, but some 10 or 11 miles farther west. Rivera had followed not the Uncompahgre River to reach the Gunnison but the much smaller Robideaux Creek, which flows almost due north off the Uncompahgre Plateau. And in a tour de force of confirmation, some 15 miles up Robideaux Creek, in a remote canyon accessible only by foot or horseback today, he had discovered an inscription carved in the ruddy sandstone wall by Rivera's team on October 15, 1765.

My friend Fred Blackburn, who first introduced me to the Anasazi country in 1992, and who is the finest decipherer of all-but-illegible historical inscriptions I've ever met, made the definitive reading of the badly faded script. All that could be positively identified was the name Juan María Rivera. Four undecipherable lines of characters etched below the signature might well have given the date (later determined to be October 15 from Rivera's journal), perhaps the team's home base of Santa Fe, and maybe the formulaic *"paso por aqui"*—"passed by here." Blackburn, Baker, and the rest of the sleuthing team made their analysis on September 5, 2004. That very day Greg Child, Vaughn Hadenfeldt, and I were on the fifth day of our Comb Ridge traverse, camped in a beautiful oasis of wildflowers and prickly pear just below the ridge crest on the west. The day before, a violent wind and rain storm had swept across our corner of Arizona, filling the potholes on the Comb with drinking water that supplied all our needs for the following week of parched cloudless days under the 90° sun.

The Tomichi–San Xavier–Gunnison marked the end of exploration for Rivera. He did ford the river, albeit anxiously, for the water came up to his horse's saddle, and scouted a little beyond (Baker could not ascertain exactly where), before deciding it was time to head back to Santa Fe. In his sketchy diary, Rivera covers the return journey in a single sentence. The voyage home, across a distance he estimated at 395 miles, took him only fourteen and a half days.

So from their camp on the Gunnison on August 28 onward, Domínguez and Escalante would finally be exploring a wilderness completely unknown to Europeans. There was still time enough and will enough to find a way to California.

As Sharon and I studied the big painting on the wall of the building in Delta, the Gateway to the Canyons indeed beckoned ahead. I knew the map, of course, but the route looked obvious. The combined waters of the Uncompahgre and Gunnison surged northwest. Fifty miles on they joined the mighty Colorado at Grand Junction. And the Colorado carved its way west across Utah, linking one canyon after another. Standing there, I could feel the tug of the Gateway ahead.

But Domínguez and Escalante had other ideas. The whole agenda of the expedition seemed to have shifted. On August 28, after fording the river, the party headed not northwest but northeast, along the banks of the Gunnison. In the journal Escalante explains the team's "intention of . . . continuing upstream until we came upon some encampments of the Sabuaganas, which yesterday we heard were around here, and in them some Indians from among the Timpanogotzis, or Lagunas, into whose country we were already planning to go."

Why did the Spaniards now want to find the camps of the Sabuaganas? And who were the Timpanogotzis, or Lagunas? Why did the team need to forge on to the homeland of that even more distant band of Utes? How long had this been the plan, since this is the first time Escalante mentions it?

What, indeed, was going on?

* * *

VIRTUALLY EVERY HISTORIAN who writes about the Domínguez–Escalante saga, even if only glancingly, assumes that the whole purpose of the expedition was to blaze a trading route from Santa Fe to the new colony in California at Monterey. On the very day the team left Santa Fe, Domínguez wrote to his boss, Fray Isidro Murillo, the Provincial, or head, of the Franciscan Custody in New Mexico, confirming that the journey to Monterey had been ordered by Murillo himself. Getting the approval of the colony's governor as well was merely a bonus, and both D & E were delighted when Governor Pedro Fermín de Mendinueta "not only applauded our plan but also opened his heart and his hands, giving us supplies and everything we might need for the journey."

Of course, as Escalante's frequent observations that such-and-such a campsite might be a good place for a Spanish settlement make clear, the idea of building towns along the way and thus expanding the New Mexico colony across the wilderness occupied by Navajos and Utes had a strong secondary appeal. And where there would be towns, there would be missions to the Indians. Later during the journey, Escalante would promise the natives he befriended that he would come back the next year and build churches to minister to their souls.

Yet there were several other primary purposes embodied in the great voyage, and teasing them out of Escalante's journal, with all its vexing lacunae and blink-and-you've-missed-them asides, becomes a tricky exercise in historiography. These secondary goals help explain the mystifying detours and changes of course the padres took, starting with their abandonment of the Dolores River on August 19.

To unravel this tangled skein, one must reexamine the two 1765 expeditions of Rivera. Establishing a trading route to California played no part in those earlier trips' goals, for the founding of Monterey still lay five years in the future. Rivera was no Franciscan, and he took orders not from Governor Mendinueta but from his predecessor, Governor Tomás Vélez Cachupín, an ambitious expansionist who nonetheless believed in making peace with the colony's Indian enemies.

Cachupín sent out Rivera in June 1765 primarily to look for silver deposits in the La Plata Mountains, after the Ute trader had brought his "silver nail" to Abiquiu, reigniting the old conquistadorial dream of bonanzas of gold and silver that must lie hidden in all the Indian lands of the New World. But Cachupín was just as curious about the legendary Río Tizón, a waterway whose size reportedly dwarfed even that of the Rio Grande. The Tizón was supposed to lie many leagues to the northwest of Santa Fe, way up in Yuta country.

On his first expedition, Rivera got as far as the big bend of the Dolores River, somewhere near where the University of Colorado archaeologists would later excavate and restore Escalante Ruin. But when he asked his Ute informant, a certain Chief Chino, about the Tizón, he got a pretty discouraging reply. As Rivera recorded in his journal on July 16, Chief Chino told him that

> the Spaniards should not be stupid because that river was very far away and in bad land without pasturage or water. There are many sand dunes that would tire our horses, and the sun that shines on this route would burn us, for it is very strong and insufferable. Not knowing the route, we would suffer much hardship or we would die of hunger, and if not, one of the many nations there are before we arrived at that river would kill us. We should return to our land.

As if that were not warning enough, Chino went on to describe the kind of treatment intruders might suffer at the hands of the strange tribes in the badlands between the Dolores and the Tizón.

> Among these nations there is one that kills people with just the smoke they make, but they do not know what it is made with. It is so strong that as soon as it is smelled, a person dies without lingering. Beyond this, there is on the route a very deep cellar in the care of a man. In it is a great variety of animals, one in particular that tears to pieces those who come or go without giving a pelt when they pass by.

That was enough for Rivera. He turned back to the La Platas to hunt down Cuero de Lobo (Wolf Hide), the Ute who had promised to show him the limitless deposits of silver that had evaded all previous Spanish explorers of New Mexico. But when he got back to Santa Fe at the end of July, Governor Cachupín, infatuated by the mystery of the Río Tizón, sent Rivera back out on a second expedition. It was on this journey that Andrés Muñiz served as interpreter, establishing his credentials for the Domínguez–Escalante expedition eleven years later.

By mid-October, Rivera had pushed far beyond the Dolores and reached the Gunnison, where he would carve his *"Viva Jesús"* in the cottonwood tree. The Utes he had fallen in with told him that this river was indeed the Tizón. Initially skeptical, for the current flowing east to west across his path looked no bigger than that of the Rio Grande near Santa Fe, Rivera eventually gave in, recording in his journal that he had indeed discovered the mighty Tizón. But his private doubts outweighed his token acquiescence. From the Indians he learned that there was yet another great river ahead—the "real" Tizón, perhaps. So Rivera was still of a mind to push farther north and west, but once again his guides warned him about the disasters that would engulf the party should they persist:

> A short distance from having crossed the river, about a day's walk, there was a kind of people who, when the hunting is poor, eat their children for sustenance. At another day's journey, one finds other people who are very white with hair the color of straw. These are very much enemies of all the other nations. One must travel two days among them, but it must be only one at a time and at night. Then one goes to the foot of a small sierra where there is a very large lake. There are people who live there like rocks and more than rocks. . . . When we arrived at the red people, as a sign of peace they would take each one by the hand. We would never meet again or return

to our land, and they would kill [the guides] because they brought us.

So, once again, Rivera turned back.

Puzzling over these strange passages in Rivera's account, I toyed with four possible explanations. The most likely seemed to be that the Utes had their own good reasons for not wanting Spaniards to thrust their way into a territory as yet unspoiled by Europeans, and so the guides made up their scary stories to dissuade the pushy Spaniard. The second was that there were indeed several tribes between the Gunnison and the Tizón, all at war with one another. The tales of Indians living like rocks and of a beast demanding pelts could well be rumors passed from one valley to the next, like the warnings Ulysses's sailors heard on their way home from Troy.

The third explanation sprang from the usual confusion introduced by interpreters. Perhaps what Rivera heard was only a badly garbled version of what the guides reported. And the fourth explanation laid all the blame on Rivera. It may be that by October 1765 the man had had enough of the Yuta country and wanted only to go home, and so, to save face with Governor Cachupín, he made up horror stories to justify his prudence in not pushing beyond the river that the Yutas, after all, swore was the Tizón. Of course, in doing so he would risk contradiction by his own men, by Andrés Muñiz in particular. But no governor in Santa Fe was going to take the word of a *genízaro* over that of the stalwart Spaniard he had entrusted to lead two expeditions into the unknown.

At a distance of 253 years, there's no sorting out these alternate theories. The whole business becomes even more complex when we plumb the origins of the Spanish obsession with the Tizón. How, in fact, by 1765 did Rivera—or Cachupín himself—even know that a massive river by that name lay somewhere off in the incognita of the northwest?

Tizón is a Spanish word meaning "burnt stick" or "firebrand." Way back in 1540, an explorer name Melchior Diaz, a lieutenant of Coronado's on the grand expedition in quest of the Seven Cities of Cíbola, was dispatched westward somewhere near today's border between Arizona and Sonora to try to make contact with a Spanish fleet sent north along the Pacific coast, ostensibly to add a naval wing to Coronado's campaign of conquest and empire. Diaz never rendezvoused with the mariners, but as he sought the ships he became the first European to discover the Colorado River, at a place well south of the Grand Canyon, where it flowed in its sluggish course down to the Gulf of California. Diaz named the river the Tizón because the natives in the vicinity used burning sticks to ward off the cold of winter.

How could it be that 225 years after Diaz, another Spanish explorer would search for the same great river, under the same name, some 900 miles upstream, across titanic stretches of unexplored land? Given that the Colorado River runs from north-central Colorado to the Gulf of California through a series of rugged canyons, none of which had yet been traversed by Europeans—Glenwood, Cataract, Glen, and Grand, to name only the most spectacular—how could Rivera have known that the Tizón lay somewhere beyond his carved cottonwood tree to the northwest?

Did the Indians themselves know the full course of the great river? What communication might the Utes of western Colorado have had with the Yumas who roamed near the delta where the river emptied into the Gulf of California? And even if we could divine the answers to these questions, we would still need to understand why reaching the Tizón was so important to Rivera and to his governor, as well as, a decade later, to Domínguez and Escalante and their governor.

The August 28 entry in Escalante's journal, announcing the team's intention to find the main encampment of the Sabuaganas and then to push north and west to reach another tribe, the Timpanogotzis or Lagunas, offers an answer. But as a clue to the complex, mutually conflicting goals of the whole expedition, it requires the opening of another Pandora's box. The name of that mishmash of myth and native history is Teguayó.

*   *   *

INSTEAD OF SETTING OUT at once to look for the Sabuaganas, the padres sent Atanasio and Andrés Muñiz ahead to scout, while the team rested in camp beside the Gunnison River. The next day, about 10 AM, the Spaniards were surprised by five Indians who appeared on a high hill to the north and started yelling at the tops of their voices. None of them, it turned out, had been recruited by Atanasio, but D & E coaxed the boisterous strangers into camp. The padres offered them food and tobacco, then began "a long parley"—how, one wonders, with both the interpreter and the guide absent? For quite a while, according to Escalante, all the Sabuaganas wanted to talk about was the "quarrels" they had been having all summer with the Yamparica Comanches.

When I first read this passage, I did a double-take. Comanches? In northwestern Colorado? I had always thought that the vast domain ruled by those masters of raiding and warfare was the Great Plains. As far as I knew, there were no Comanches anywhere near the Gunnison River in 1776. To be sure, Puebloans and Spaniards dwelling along the Rio Grande lived in constant fear of Comanche attack, but it always came from the east.

Whoever those unpleasant antagonists of the Sabuaganas were, and however the dialogue may have been sabotaged by mistranslation, the five Yutas vehemently warned the Spaniards not to push on to the north. As Escalante irritably dismisses the Sabuaganas' advice, "We refuted the validity of these pretenses, by which they were trying to stop us from going ahead, by telling them that our God, who is everyone's, would defend us if we should happen to run into these foes."

The next day Atanasio and Andrés Muñiz returned, bringing with them five more Sabuaganas and a single specimen of that other tribe, the Lagunas. Whether these more distant peoples were Utes at all seemed in doubt, for "the Yutas told us that the Lagunas dwelt in pueblos like those in New Mexico." Once more the Spaniards "regaled" these new visitors with plentiful food and tobacco, then settled in for a discussion even longer than the one of the day before.

Something monumental was at stake for the expedition at this point, though it is hard to uncover just what. Escalante's lengthy journal entry for August 30 offers hints. The Sabuaganas now intensified their warnings about the dangers posed by Comanches ahead:

> They replied that to go to the place we were trying to reach there was no other trail than the one passing through the midst of the Comanches and that these would impede our passage and deprive us of our lives—and finally that none of them knew the country between here and the Lagunas. This they repeated many times, insisting that we had to turn back from here. We tried to convince them, first by arguing and then by cajoling, so as not to displease them.

As soon as the padres offered the Laguna man a woollen blanket, a big knife, and glass beads to serve as their guide, the Sabuaganas caved in, admitting that they knew the way to Laguna country after all. The padres rather cynically attributed the Sabuagana change of heart to jealousy, compounded by their fear of losing "the kindnesses we were doing them." Before the expedition charged on to the northwest with their Laguna guide, the Sabuaganas demanded that the Spaniards visit the main encampment of their own people, high in the forest on the southern slopes of the plateau now called Grand Mesa.

For three days, led by the Laguna guide (whom they had promptly renamed Silvestre, appropriating Escalante's Christian name), the team rode through forests and along streams, leaving behind the scrub oak thickets as they climbed into a landscape of stately blue spruces and aspens interspersed with grassy clearings, traveling 46 miles beyond the Gunnison. The padres—or more likely Miera y Pacheco—calculated that the men had now traveled 523 miles from Santa Fe during the thirty-five days they'd been on the trail. At last, at an elevation of about 8,500 feet, the twelve-man team of Spaniards was met by an impressive force of eighty Yutas on horseback. "They told us," Escalante wrote, "that they were going out to hunt, but we figured that they came together like this, either to show off their strength in numbers or to find out if any other Spanish people were coming behind us or if we came alone." After a brief exchange of courtesies, the Spaniards followed the mounted Utes another three miles until they came to the grand encampment of the Sabuaganas, "which had numerous people and must have consisted of thirty tents."

It was the most important event to occur in the five weeks since the team had left Santa Fe, and Escalante lavished on it by far the longest entry up to this point in the written record he kept. In the Sabuagana encampment, California was far from the padres' minds. But as Franciscans, they could at last carry out a duty that meant more to them than any agenda assigned to the expedition back in Santa Fe.

From Delta on September 20, Sharon and I turned east on State Highway 90, which parallels the Gunnison River. Seven miles on, we came to the forlorn little town of Austin, which bravely bills itself as the Orchard City. (All of Colorado's Western Slope is a cornucopia of fruit, and as a kid growing up in Boulder I had gorged on apples and pears and peaches grown in towns such as Fruita, Paonia, and for all I knew Austin.) Just east of today's town the Spaniards had camped on August 28, as they sent out their guide and interpreter to look for Sabuagana camps. As we continued along Route 90, following the North Fork of the Gunnison, we were driving in D & E's footsteps. Sure enough, at Leroux Creek, a wayside sign identified the spot where the Spaniards had camped on August 30. The marker was the work not of the Bicentennial Commission but of a local outfit called the North Fork Historical Society. In the next few miles, we paused at five more such signs, pinpointing the humblest incidents in the D & E campaign. It would be the only stretch on the entire 1,700-mile loop where a local group had bothered to mark the passage of the long-ago expedition.

At one of the markers I struck up a conversation with a trucker who was idling his rig in the pullout. I told him about our plan to follow Domínguez and Escalante across four states, which the man took as his cue to hold forth about the route of the Donner Party on their way to death and cannibalism on the east slope of the Sierra Nevada in 1846. I'd run into Donner aficionados before and I knew how relentless they could be. Within minutes, the hefty fellow had turned red in the face as he cursed Lansford Hastings, author of the Hastings Cutoff, the purported shortcut across the Great Basin that some historians blame for the party's demise. I'd never been very interested in the Donner saga myself, as it seemed like a classic case of sheer emigrant bungling, as well as a disaster hashed over so thoroughly that no new details were ever likely to come to light. I made a half-hearted attempt to bring Escalante back into the conversation, but the trucker was 400 miles off in Nevada, trying to fix what had gone wrong 172 years ago, if only George Donner and James Reed had listened to him. I suppose to a third passerby we might have sounded like a pair of Hyde Park zealots each on his soapbox trying to straighten out the world. I touched my forehead in a farewell salute and retreated to the refuge of our SUV.

At Paonia we turned off Route 90 to follow Forest Road 701 north, traveling close to the trail along which Atanasio led the Spaniards to the Sabuagana encampment. A couple of miles in, we stopped on an ugly gravel pullout for a picnic lunch. The temperature was dropping, and a harsh wind blew out of the west, so we put on our parkas and huddled over our cheese and crackers and oranges. But from the pullout there was a lordly view of the West Elk Mountains, 20 miles off to the east. Over there, fifty-four years before, as a gung-ho twenty-year-old fresh off my first Alaskan expedition, I had taught at the Colorado Outward Bound school in the second year of the program's transplantation from Great Britain to the United States. I managed to ignore the school's dubious rationale of character-building via the morning dip and the 200-foot rappel while I nursed my incredulity that I was getting paid, however meagerly, to hike and camp in my beloved Rockies. How unimaginably long ago that seemed now, as we stared at the dark green silhouettes of the Elk Range.

Four miles farther up Stevens Gulch Road, we entered the Grand Mesa National Forest, and a winding 13 miles beyond we came to the grassy, open basin of Hubbard Park. Bow season was upon us, and nearly every pullout was occupied by hunters wearing camo, their flatbed trucks loaded with ATVs. At our picnic spot, I had puzzled over a Colorado Wildlife Division sign that announced "Attention Hunters. Moose in Area! Be Sure of Your Target."

On the northern edge of Hubbard Park stood the Electric Mountain Lodge. A big wooden shingle at the driveway entrance proclaimed "Open Year Round" for "Horse—Snowmobile—ATV—Rentals," and small cartouches promised lodging, meals, cocktails, and wheelchair access. At the end of the driveway, a skillfully rendered bronze statue of an elk bugled at the sky. Next to it a flagpole displayed the Stars and Stripes and the Colorado state ensign. But the lodge was closed. An electrified fence and video surveillance warning signs gave the place a creepy vibe. Later I looked up the lodge on the Internet. Visitors as recently as 2014 had left reviews, but one of them hinted at problems that might have signaled the resort's demise: "OMG! This place was horrible. There were dead flies, moths, and other assorted flying things on every windowsill in the place. They were even hanging on the curtains like they were trying to get out but never made it."

Electric Mountain woes notwithstanding, Hubbard Park would have been a lovely place to camp. But the growing cold disheartened us, and all the best pullouts were taken. On a whim, I said to Sharon, "Let's stop and talk to one of these guys."

She frowned. "I don't know. Men in camo with their guns just give me a bad feeling."

"What's the worst that can happen?" I teased her. "They're not gonna shoot us."

"Okay, but—"

We drove up to a gigantic white canvas tent nestled among the aspens, in front of which a fellow with a trim white mustache and beard sat in a lawn chair catching the late afternoon sun and reading a book. I got out of our car and said hello.

Rich was from Colorado Springs, though he'd grown up in Gallup, New Mexico. He seemed happy to have company. I told him about our journey along the route of Domínguez and Escalante. Gallup, after all, lay very close to the last leg of their loop, as they rode from Hopi to Zuni.

Rich had never heard of the expedition but, unlike others we had met along the way, he was eager to learn more. He even wrote down the title of the University of Utah edition of Escalante's journal I was reading every day. I pointed out the passage that covered the team's entry into Hubbard Park.

Rich invited us inside the big tent, where he proudly showed off the folding cots that could sleep six and the pot-bellied stove that kept the men warm at night. The place was big enough to hold a town meeting. Somehow, though, it reminded me of gloomy roadhouses in Alaska.

"What game are you allowed to hunt with a bow?" I asked.

Touching each finger, he listed the prey: "Deer, elk, bear, and turkey." (Apparently moose were spared.) The other guys were out on their ATVs at the moment, scouting distant ridges. "We keep 'em within radio contact, though," he said, hefting a walkie-talkie.

"Got any game yet?"

"Nope. Seen some, but not to shoot."

"It's gotta be hard with a bow."

Rich smiled. "Not to be chauvinistic," he said, "but it's sort of manly."

Back in the car, I said to Sharon, "See, that wasn't so bad."

"He seemed like a nice guy," she admitted. "But did you see the revolver on his hip? Why does he need a gun even in camp?"

"It's sort of manly," I jibed. "Maybe I should wear one."

"If you do . . ." Her scowl, as she got behind the wheel, dissolved into a grin.

*   *   *

AT THE BIG CAMP of the Sabuaganas on September 1, Domínguez took Andrés Muñiz with him and sought out the "chieftain," then entered his tent. At once, "after embracing him and his children, [Domínguez] asked him to gather there the people who were on hand." Escalante must have been present, for the scene he narrates has the immediacy of first-person witness. It also defies credibility—at least according to my own skeptical grasp of what might have happened on that late summer day. Writes Escalante,

> When those of either sex who could attend had been assembled, he announced the Gospel to them through the interpreter. All listened with pleasure, and especially six Lagunas who were present, among whom our guide and another Laguna stood out. As soon as the padre began instructing them, the new guide mentioned interrupted them so as to predispose the Sabuaganas as well as his own fellow tribesmen "to believe whatever the padre was telling them because it was all true." In the same way, the other Laguna relayed the pleasure and eagerness with which he heard the news of his eternal salvation.

This was what the padres had come on their long, dangerous journey to do. This meant far more to them than the blazing of a trading route to Monterey. Yet from all their experience among the New Mexico pueblos—especially from Escalante's utter failure with the Hopi in 1775—surely both men knew that converting Indians of any kind to Catholicism was a difficult and even perilous business.

One of the Sabuaganas was befuddled by the exchange. According to Escalante,

> Among those listening there was one a bit deaf who, not grasp-
> ing what was being treated, asked what it was the padre was
> saying. Then this Laguna said: "The padre says that this which
> he shows us"—it was the image of Christ crucified—"is the one
> Lord of all, who dwells in the highest part of the skies, and in
> order to please Him and go to Him one has to be baptised and
> must beg His forgiveness." He emphasized this idea by beating
> his breast with his hand—a surprising gesture on his part for
> his never having seen it made before, either by the padre or by
> the interpreter. When the padre saw the evident joy with which
> they heard him, he suggested to the chieftain now in charge of
> the encampment that if, after he had conferred with his people,
> they would accept Christianity we would come to instruct them
> and set them in a new way of living that would lead to baptism.

So for the first time on the voyage, Domínguez promised to return to this high meadow and build a mission. Flush with success, not content to have won the promise of the Utes to convert, he now went on to give the Indians their first lesson in Christian ethics:

> Filled with joy by the open declaration of the Lagunas men-
> tioned, the padre asked how the latter one was called (the
> guide we had already named Silvestre), and on learning that
> they called him Red Bear he instructed them all by explaining
> to them the difference existing between men and brutes, the
> purpose for which either of them were created, and the wrong
> thing they did in naming themselves after wild beasts—thus
> placing themselves on a par with them, and even below them.
> Promptly he told the Laguna to call himself Francisco from
> then on. When the rest saw this, they began repeating this

name, although with difficulty, the Laguna joyfully pleased for being so named.

Now that Domínguez had set the natives straight about the one true God, the prospect of salvation through baptism, and the proper way to name one another, everybody settled in for a feast of jerked bison meat, for which the Spaniards offered more glass beads in exchange. D & E also wondered if the Utes would trade the Spaniards' horses with their worn-out hooves for fresh Sabuagana and Laguna mounts. The Utes said they'd think about it.

What could possibly have been going on that September 1 in the Sabuagana encampment? Except by the most devout of Franciscan apologists, Escalante's account simply cannot be taken at face value. Not only that day among the hunting camps in Hubbard Park but before and after our trip, as I reread the passage in the padre's diary, I tried to come up with a plausible explanation.

One possibility is that the entry is pure fiction, a set piece made up by the friar to please his superiors to whom the journal would be presented at the end of the expedition—not only Governor Mendinueta but, even more crucially, Fray Isidro Murillo, the head of the Franciscan custody in New Mexico, whose orders had sent the team into the field in the first place. But dissembling just wasn't Escalante's style. His very humorlessness is a badge of his honesty. When the party is in trouble, he admits it; when they think they are lost, the confusion creeps onto the page.

It's more likely that the Utes had no idea what Domínguez was talking about when he started sermonizing. As he held out his crucifix and told his magical tale, they might have thought they were listening to a shaman from some alien tribe spin out an incomprehensible but vivid parable. The 178 years of Franciscan efforts to convert the Puebloans in New Mexico prior to this meeting with the Utes were full of comparable "conversions" that the priests were only too glad to take credit for.

What was in it, after all, for the Utes to be so acquiescent? When I later raised this issue with Matt Liebmann, my Harvard anthropologist friend, he pointed out that the arrival of a team of Spaniards in Sabuagana territory held the promise of all kinds of trading possibilities, from glass beads to guns, from tobacco to cotton cloth. Why else had generation after generation of Ute entrepreneurs traveled all the way to Abiquiu with goods to barter?

To be sure, the lightly armed and woefully provisioned squadron of a dozen Spaniards led by their blue-robed medicine men hardly betokened a commercial bonanza, but perhaps these strangers were merely the vanguard. Why not strike up friendly relations and see what might come of them?

The Spaniards withdrew to their own camp. That evening the chief and several Ute elders paid a visit. Their mood was grave.

> They began trying to persuade us to turn back from here, exaggerating anew and with greater effort the hardships and perils to which we were exposing ourselves by going ahead, saying for certain that the Comanches would not let us do so—and that they did not tell us this to stop us from going as far as we wanted, but because they esteemed us highly. We acknowledged this token and told them that the one God whom we worshiped would expedite everything for us and would defend us, not only from the Comanches but also from all others who might intend to do us harm, and that we feared not a thing that they were bringing up because we were certain that His Majesty was on our side.

Plainly, the padres were determined to move on to the north and west. Yet as Domínguez tried to explain this to the Sabuagana elders, he said nothing about the need to find a route to California. Instead, all the talk was about finding the camps of that other band of Indians, the Lagunas. And D & E were counting on the Laguna whom they had named Silvestre to guide them there.

Before they could move on, however, the padres had to deal with another problem. Escalante blames it on a schism within the Spanish party and he does not hesitate to name the three men whose treachery, uncovered that very evening, he regarded as nothing short of mutiny. The malefactors were the interpreter, Andrés Muñiz, his brother Lucrecio, and Felipe, one of the *genízaros* who had stowed his way aboard the expedition by trailing the team for fifteen days before popping into sight on August 14.

This passage in Escalante's journal is one of the thorniest in the whole five-month record of the expedition. In high dudgeon, the padres apparently lectured the whole team by reminding them that they had pledged in Santa Fe "not to take along any goods for trading," because "all agreed not . . . to have any purpose other than the one they had, which was God's glory and the good of souls." This sounds like sheer hypocrisy, for that very day D & E had blithely traded glass beads for jerked bison meat and had proposed exchanging their own lame horses for the Sabuaganas' fresh ones. But now, Escalante claims, he and Domínguez discovered (how?) that the three mutineers had smuggled goods along to offer the Utes to persuade them to oppose the Spaniards' plan to push on in search of the Laguna camps.

Escalante leaves unclear just what motive the three "traitors" might have had for trying to sabotage the padres' program. The phrase "either out of fear or because they did not want to go ahead" is so vague as to be ambiguous. Yet in the same passage Escalante records that the Muñiz brothers and Felipe had tried to trade their hidden goods for weapons, because they were so afraid of the Comanches lurking ahead.

If Escalante's account of this near-mutiny is honest, there's another possible explanation for it that the padre never addresses. All three of the miscreants were *genízaros*. What if in fact they had been raised as Sabuagana Utes? That might explain Andrés Muñiz's facility as interpreter. And what more human motivation for forestalling the departure of the team could there be than wanting to linger with—perhaps even to rejoin for good—the people among whom they had been born and raised until they were sold as slaves to the New Mexico colonists? Alas, such a speculation is today beyond the reach of either proof or disproof.

One last detail in Escalante's long, indignant, and baffling September 1 journal entry only adds to the conundrum. As the Sabuaganas still tried to prevent the Spaniards from riding off into dangerous Comanche territory, they played a last trump card: "They said that if we did not turn back from here, they would not make exchanges for the hoofsore horses we had." To which Escalante replied that "we would go on even if they made no exchange, because under no circumstances would we turn back without knowing the whereabouts of the padre our brother who had been among Moquis and Cosninas and might be wandering about lost."

Good lord! Father Garcés again? Wandering, maybe lost, somewhere between here and the far end of the Grand Canyon? Perhaps the Lagunas could help them find, and thereby save, the padres' beloved Franciscan brother. No wonder the Sabuaganas were confused. What were these crazy Spaniards really trying to do?

* * *

IN THE END, the Sabuaganas gave in, even trading their good horses for the worn-out Spanish ones. On September 2, the expedition bade farewell to their temporary hosts and pushed on to the northwest, counting on Silvestre, their Laguna guide, to find the way. It took them four days to complete the traverse of Grand Mesa and reach the shores of the Colorado River.

From Hubbard Park, Sharon and I could have tried to navigate a network of old roads that looked somewhat sketchy on the map. Even if we had done so, we would have been following the D & E route only approximately. In 1975, the Bicentennial retracers had given up in the face of backcountry obstacles and ambiguities, pleading setbacks by fenced-off private land and flooded jeep roads. Instead they had plotted the course of the 1776 pioneers by their usual appeals to "likely" campsites and hill crossings divined via USGS quadrangle maps.

The weather was definitely turning for the worse, the temperature dropping, with the hint of a storm in the air. And I was starting to feel bad—a little nauseated, more fatigued than normal, with a nameless malaise hanging over my spirits. We decided to retrace our drive back to Paonia then head west to Grand Junction, where we'd spend the night in a motel. Sharon was worried about me. We had planned to get a second blood draw in Provo, the biggest city on the whole D & E loop, to see if my sodium level had dropped into the dangerous numbers. But Provo was still several days away.

As we drove back down Forest Road 701, I said, "It's hard to like these guys,"

"Who?" asked Sharon, surprised. "The hunters?"

"No. Domínguez and Escalante." Sharon didn't respond at first. I wondered if my malaise was clouding my enthusiasm for our quest. But I went on, "They show up at the Sabuagana camp. Or rather, they sort of stagger in, guided by Atanasio. The Utes greet them warmly, it sounds like. They've only been there an hour or two before Domínguez gathers them together and tries to turn them into Christians."

"Isn't that what missionaries do?" Sharon parried.

"Sure, but not usually so abruptly, or so . . . what? Condescendingly. Scolding them for calling each other by animal names. Deciding poor Red Bear should be named Francisco from here on. Give me a break."

When Sharon didn't answer, I added, "I just can't buy the instant conversion. Indians don't just drop their religion like a bunch of old clothes and say, 'Cool. We never heard about this guy Jesus before, and heaven and salvation and all that stuff. Thanks, bro!'"

At least that got a chuckle out of Sharon. I was letting off steam that had been building up for weeks, as I obsessed over Domínguez and Escalante. "What really doesn't make sense about that conversion scene is that just the year before, Escalante had had a total failure at Hopi. The men at Oraibi told him, in effect, 'We don't want your stinkin' Christianity. We're perfectly happy with our own gods. And would you please get out of here before we get really riled up? Go back to Santa Fe.'"

Sharon was resisting my disaffected tantrum. "It was Domínguez doing the sermonizing, wasn't it? Not Escalante."

"True. And in his big mission report, Domínguez was pretty intolerant of the natives when he visited the pueblos. Bitches about how lazy and dirty they are. You know, though Escalante wrote the journal, Domínguez had a hand in what he said. Maybe a heavy hand. He was the boss of the expedition, after all."

We drove slowly through the aspen trees. The bark of some had been carved by the men who had been on the crews putting in the National Forest track to Hubbard Park. Sharon slowed down so I could read one graffito from 1989: "Conrad Cisneros. Building road," it read. *No relation to Juan Pedro Cisneros, Escalante's sidekick from Zuni?* I wondered idly.

"You have to admit those guys were brave," Sharon said. "Coming all the way up here without any soldiers, or hardly any guns. Going ahead toward the Comanches even after the Utes warned them they'll all be killed."

"I guess. I suppose it's bravery. Or just blind faith. 'With God on our side, nobody can hurt us.' What's that trite old war motto, 'There are no atheists in foxholes'?"

But my spleen was ebbing. "Yeah, Escalante was brave, all right," I said. "I didn't tell you this before, but he was in constant pain all through the expedition. Somewhere he'd gotten what he called a 'urinary ailment.' One reason the expedition didn't leave Santa Fe on July 4, as they planned, was that he got a really bad attack just as they were ready to start. Domínguez ordered him to rest for a week."

"How do we know it was bothering him the whole expedition?" Sharon asked.

"He wrote a letter to Fray Murillo about his trip to Hopi in 1775. Blames his own weakness for the failure to win any converts. It's there that he talks about the pain. There's one poignant passage, as he's trying to ride his horse up to one of the hilltop Hopi villages. How does it go?" Later I found the passage. Escalante had written, "Although the ascent of the two hills is very difficult, I went up them without getting off my horse because my urinary ailment had been aggravated by the rough road, and the pain was such that I could not walk at all."

I went on, "But that was a private letter to his Franciscan superior. The journal from 1776 was more official. And there's not a word of complaint about his 'ailment' or his pain, even though Escalante records the fevers and stomachaches and illnesses of the other guys. Including Domínguez."

My mood had changed. "He was a tough bastard. You know, he never recovered from whatever it was he had. He died less than four years after the expedition, in 1780. He was on the way to Mexico City to seek a cure, but he only got as far as Parral, a little town in Chihuahua. He was only thirty years old." Sharon sucked in her breath. "John Kessell thinks the urinary ailment was prostate or bladder cancer, and that it killed him. I can relate to that."

We wound down out of the spruces and aspens, back through the scrub oak. "Also," said Sharon, "they never did any harm to the Indians, did they?"

"Nope." I was coming around. "Compare them to Oñate or Vargas."

"And they never treated their teammates badly. Even when they discovered that the three guys had smuggled along the trading goods—"

"Good point," I interrupted. "Oñate would have said, 'For that, we're going to clap you in irons.' Or when Felipe and Juan Domingo caught up with the team on August 14, these poor *genízaros* just wanting to tag along. Vargas would have said, 'Fuck you guys. Get out of here. Find your own way back to Abiquiu.'"

We reached Grand Junction after dark and chose a motel more or less at random. After dinner I had a bad case of acid reflux and almost threw up. I took Alka-Seltzer, as well as Oxycodone for my back pain, then slept poorly. In the morning I was dizzy, with the sparkly aura of a migraine making my head throb and the sky too bright to look at without squinting. Sharon would have to drive all day. During the previous two years I had suffered from so many side effects of cancer that I took these new discomforts in stride. But a glum anxiety hung over us all morning.

Grand Junction is so named because here the Gunnison River flows into the Colorado. But it's the knack of modern cities to bury the streams that gave them their reason for existing beneath grids of streets and houses and stores. Heading for the motel, very tired after the long day, we had crossed the Colorado River on South 5th Street without even noticing it.

Had we driven Highway 50 directly from Delta to Grand Junction, instead of following the Spaniards up into Hubbard Park on Grand Mesa, we would have passed only a few miles east of the Dominguez–Escalante National Conservation Area and the Dominguez Canyon Wilderness. These lands, set aside by the Bureau of Land Management in 2009, offer all kinds of backcountry enticements, from long hikes and backpacks to petroglyph panels to kayaking and canoeing on Big Dominguez Creek and Escalante Creek. In the central Dominguez Canyon Wilderness itself, neither motorized vehicles nor bicycles are allowed. It's country preserved as close to true wilderness as the government agencies in charge of preserving the American environment can designate. It's also a handsome tribute to the expedition that brought the first Europeans to this part of the great West in 1776.

I would have been tempted to spend a few days in that BLM playground, poking into places like the Potholes or Brushy Ridge or Gibbler Gulch. But the great irony is that Domínguez and Escalante never traveled within 20 miles of this outback dedicated to them. More than a week later, in southern Utah, Sharon and I would drive into the other vast domain of protected land memorializing the expedition: Grand Staircase–Escalante National Monument, which centers on the Escalante River and the venerable Mormon town of Escalante. But here, too, is a wilderness across which the Spaniards never traveled. Of the several ironies attendant upon that misnamed backcountry paradise, more below.

On the morning of September 21, the storm still held off, but the wind out of the west had increased. We drove on, glad to be tucked inside our SUV, as gusts swirled up the roadside dirt and the willows beside the river bent in submission. It was our twentieth day out of Santa Fe, and we were only a third of the way along the route of Domínguez and Escalante.

From the Sabuagana encampment on September 2, 1776, the Spaniards zigzagged through hills and ravines as they sorted out the jumbled topography of Grand Mesa. Somewhere near a butte known today as Bronco Knob they reached an elevation of 9,800 feet, the highest they would attain on the whole journey. Escalante's journal turns lifeless as the men followed Silvestre's vacillating directions, skirting scores of beaver dams and struggling with their horses and mules. They ran into no Comanches, nor even any signs of them, whoever those vaunted enemies might be. Their only human encounter was with three Ute women and a child who were out gathering berries, and who offered the Spaniards some. "The gooseberry which grows in these parts," noted Escalante, "is very sour on the bush, but when already exposed to the sun, as these Yuta woman had it, it has a very delicious sweet-sour taste."

In late morning on September 5, the team came to a big river. The Utes, they were told, called it the Red River, and said its source was a great lake far to the east. In a puzzling aside, Escalante adds that the great stream was a "river which our own call San Rafael." (Which of "our own," one wonders? Rivera never reached it.) The Spaniards noted that it ran higher than the Rio Grande near Santa Fe, but

crossing it was no problem. They were not impressed with their surroundings, "where there are no prospects of a settlement." The team
stopped to camp. Miera y Pacheco got an astrolabe reading of 41° 4' N,
still half a degree too far north. The expedition had traveled 575 miles
during their thirty-nine eventful days since departing from Santa Fe.

Without even realizing it, Domínguez and Escalante had discovered the fabled Río Tizón—known today as the Colorado. On
September 6 the men set out again, leaving the river after riding
downstream only a little over a mile, striking off northwest into a
new maze of canyons and hills.

Perhaps it was inconsequential that the men were unaware of their
river discovery. Everything they sought lay on the other side, beyond
the Tizón. Somewhere out there California beckoned, but before
it, Teguayó.

Chapter Six

TEGUAYÓ AND THE LOST SPANIARDS

Even though the Spaniards failed to recognize the Río de San Rafael as the long-sought Río Tizón, it would have made sense to follow that waterway indefinitely downstream, for it flowed west, toward far-off California, and there were no canyons in sight to box the team in, as the tortured Dolores had done. Instead, on September 6, the men struck off northwest up a side creek toward another high upland.

Even today, the Piceance Basin is little traveled, a maze of shallow draws threaded by bad dirt roads that dead-end near the headwaters of such uninspiringly named creeks as Brush, Clear, Dry, and Roan. Pronounced "Pee-ants" by locals, Piceance is a Ute word meaning "tall grass." In recent years, developers have started coveting the basin for its natural gas reserves, and the oil shale potential lights dollar signs in the eyes of fracking zealots. During four days from September 6 to 9, 1776, the Domínguez–Escalante expedition crossed the basin. In 1975, a new Bicentennial retracer named G. Clell Jacobs took over from the duo who had gamely shadowed the expedition across the Uncompahgre Plateau and down the Uncompahgre River to the Gunnison, then up onto Grand Mesa. To navigate the Piceance Basin, Jacobs stitched together transport by four-wheel-drive truck, dune buggy, and his own feet, as he guessed just where the Spaniards might have ridden and camped. At one point he interviewed a ninety-year-old rancher who'd been raised and spent his whole life on Carr Creek, one of the streams that trickles down to join the Colorado. The old-timer pointed out an ancient Ute trail that had been rendered impassable by landslides, which he guessed the Spaniards might have followed.

Those four days traversing Piceance Basin were not happy ones. It was not D & E who chose the route but Silvestre, the Laguna guide they had hired. And on the first day, the mutinous *genízaros*—the Muñiz brothers and Felipe—shared with the padres their suspicion that Silvestre had been enticed "to keep us winding about so as not to proceed further or to hand us over to a Sabuagana ambuscade that could be awaiting us." D & E scoffed at the notion of such a nefarious plot and kept the team moving northwest. That night they camped next to the teepees of a Sabuagana party, who swore that they had spent the day even farther north, in Yamparica Comanche territory, hoping to steal horses. But these raiders had found neither their enemy nor their horses, instead deducing from tracks in the sand that the Comanches must have moved out to the east, headed toward El Río de Napeste.

Once more, Escalante's diary threatened to give me a headache. The Napeste is the Arkansas River, which flows almost 1,600 miles from its headwaters near present-day Leadville, Colorado, all the way across eastern Colorado, southern Kansas, northern Oklahoma, and Arkansas before emptying its waters in the Mississippi River. The middle Arkansas was indeed Comanche territory, but its headwaters rose no nearer the Piceance Basin than 120 miles as the crow flies. Even James Fenimore Cooper would have thought it a stretch for the Sabuaganas to derive from horses' footprints in the sand a destination as remote as the Arkansas.

For several days the Spaniards had ridden on under the dire warning that they would be wiped out by Comanches. Unless the usual confusions of language skewed everything, the Sabuaganas lived in daily fear of an enemy they called the Comanches. But whoever that phantom foe really was, the Spaniards never caught a glimpse of them. And that night was the last the team spent in the company of Sabuagana Utes. The Indians whose conversion to the true God had seemed a *fait accompli* a few days earlier were left behind, entrenched in their aboriginal ways, as the Spaniards sought another tribe—the people of the lake, the Lagunas.

* * *

FROM GRAND JUNCTION, Sharon and I could have driven back up the Colorado River 25 miles to the old railroad stop of DeBeque, where D & E had crossed the great river. We could have pushed the dirt tracks up Roan and Carr Creeks, but without a dune buggy or a vigorous hike I doubted that we could have traversed the Piceance. I wasn't feeling good on the morning of September 21, and I was starting to worry that we were falling behind our own schedule. So instead we set off north on State Highway 139, where I knew we'd meet up with the D & E track, and where I wanted to revisit a prehistoric mystery along the banks of Douglas Creek.

Despite my post-migraine daze, to be on the road again was deeply satisfying. All the years when I'd bombed across country as fast as I could to link Colorado and the East Coast, or endured the gauntlet of the Alaska Highway to get to the limitless mountains of my ambition, I'd been too impetuous to enjoy each journey itself except as a means to an end. But now Sharon and I were in the middle of a true road trip, and skipping one part of the D & E itinerary gave us the leisure to stop and savor another part.

In an essay mock-heroically titled "The Rediscovery of America: 1946," Wallace Stegner celebrates the joy of setting out on an ordinary car camping trip from San Francisco to Lake Mead, Las Vegas, Death Valley, and the Sierra Nevada after four years of service during the war. In that piece Stegner tosses off a credo that I could sympathize with now: "We are a wheeled people; it seems to me sometimes that I must have been born with a steering wheel in my hand, and I realize now that to lose the use of a car is practically equivalent to losing the use of my legs."

About 30 miles up Route 139, we crested a low pass that separates the watersheds of Salt Creek and Douglas Creek. And 20 miles farther north, as low cliffs on either side began to shelter the winding valley from the mesas surrounding it, we suddenly came upon the first painting. On the sandstone wall on our left, someone had drawn a pair of uplifted hands in white, their edges gilded in red. Other panels followed, the figures painted in red, white, and brownish purple. Some depicted humanoids with horned heads or headdresses; others plainly represented dogs and bighorn sheep as well as long stalks of plants, probably corn.

On September 9, after completing the traverse of Piceance Basin, the Spaniards discovered the same paintings. Writes Escalante, "Halfway in this canyon toward the south there is a quite lofty rock cliff on which we saw, crudely painted, three shields, or 'Apache shields,' of hide, and a spearhead." The "Apache shields" panel, which is held together today by a rusted metal cable to prevent the collapse of the sandstone slab the prehistoric artist used for canvas, looked to me like a red figure carrying shields (or other blobs) as well as a spear or staff, while also playing a flute held sideways before his face. This stretch of Douglas Creek is still called Cañon Pintado, or Painted Canyon, the name Escalante gave it. The sites are maintained by the BLM, with signboards giving their modern names: "Waving Hands Site," "Carrot Man Site," "White Birds Site," and the like.

It's odd that Escalante shows no curiosity about who might have created these tableaux. At the ruin beside the Dolores he had at least pointed out the kinship that village seemed to have with the mud-and-stone structures of the New Mexico pueblos. He may have assumed the art in Douglas Canyon was the work of Utes, but if so, he would have been wrong.

Sharon had never been to Cañon Pintado before, but I had spent a day here in 2005 as I researched an article for *National Geographic* about a canyon in east-central Utah that a single rancher named Waldo Wilcox had kept in pristine condition for fifty years by fencing it off and scaring off curio hunters and archaeologists alike with stern "no trespassing" signs and (rumor had it) the shotgun he toted around his spread. Nearly all the ruins and rock art in Range Creek were the work of Fremont people, prehistoric farmers and hunter-gatherers whose culture bore some resemblance to that of the Anasazi, but also crucial differences.

Much less is known about the Fremont than about their neighbors to the south, but both peoples were afflicted by a combination of environmental degradation (drought, deforestation, the depletion of big game, "arroyo-cutting") and perhaps a spiritual mandate to move elsewhere that led to the wholesale abandonment of the Colorado Plateau by 1300 AD. A profound difference between the cultures, however, lies in the fate of the peoples after the abandonment. We know that the Anasazi moved south and east and assimilated with the Puebloans in New Mexico and with the Hopi in Arizona. But the experts have no clear handle on what happened to the Fremont. They may have assimilated so thoroughly with Utes and Shoshone as to be invisible today. One scholar believes they migrated all the way to western Kansas and "became" the Kiowa. But they may also have died out completely, spiraling into cultural extinction.

Douglas Creek is named for the last Ute chief to call this valley home, before the government forced his people to move to the reservation in Utah. What's so interesting about Cañon Pintado is that that shallow canyon, almost treeless today, its muddy stream fringed with intrusive growths of tamarisk and cheat grass, way out on the eastern edge of the Fremont domain, seems to have been the very last refuge of the Fremont. Archaeologists have detected them flourishing there as late as 1500 AD. What survival tricks might they have learned that the proud builders of Mesa Verde and Keet Seel and Lowry and Yellow Jacket never mastered? As Sharon and

I studied the paintings—yes, they're crude compared to the brilliant
Fremont panels at McConkie Ranch or in Nine Mile Canyon—I
was beguiled again by the thought that the last bands of Fremont
might have hung on almost into the decade when the Spaniards first
entered the Southwest.

At the town of Rangely, Douglas Creek pours its meager flow into
the White River. We had intended to stop there for a picnic lunch,
but a nasty 30 mph wind out of the west was blowing dirt and trash
through the streets. No one was about in the sleepy burg. We found
a concrete picnic table in a city park, but because of the wind ended
up dining in the front seat of our SUV. Brie cheese and Ritz crackers
again, rice pudding, a handful of nuts, a Reese's peanut butter cup, a
bottle of Starbuck's Frappuccino, but also a gloriously ripe peach: one
more of my patented meals for survivors of radiation therapy to the
mouth and throat. There's something regressive about eating lunch in
a car. Perhaps it conjures up childhood snacks on the road when Mom
and Dad were too irritable to stop and lay out a proper picnic spread.
I felt a glum mood creep over me. The high school next door proclaimed itself "Home of the Panthers." Ever since Tierra Amarilla,
where the Escalante Mid–High School was "Home of the Lobos,"
we had been driving past schools whose students embraced as their
totems wildcats, eagles, bulldogs, bobcats. I thought of Domínguez
lecturing Red Bear about the difference between brutes and humans
and rechristening him Francisco.

The Spaniards reached the White River late on September 9 and
named it El Río de San Clemente, camping on its north shore. They
noted that the stream, like the San Rafael (Colorado), flowed west,
but dismissed its banks as "offer[ing] no prospect for a settlement." It
would have made good sense to follow the White River downstream
to where it joins the Green. But now Silvestre, the Laguna guide, was
calling the shots, and he led the team off to the northwest, through
a parched badlands of "rockless hills and brief plains with neither
pasturage nor trees," as Escalante dispiritedly observed. The team

camped that night without water, keeping guard until dawn over the horses and mules. On September 11, more of the same.

The route D & E followed between the White and Green rivers roughly parallels State Highway 64 and U.S. Highway 40. E. Clell Jacobs, the Bicentennial retracer, made a brave effort to rediscover the precise path the Spaniards followed across what is today a bleak plain of oil fields. He consulted old maps that indicated "Indian trails" and chatted with old-timers, but as was so often the case with the Commission's effort to pin down the Spanish itinerary, Jacobs ended up reverting to likely guesses and hints of corroboration. For instance, Escalante describes the campsite of September 11 only as an arroyo with running water near a poplar (cottonwood) grove. Writes Jacobs, "After making many trips to this region and driving and walking the route, this researcher has concluded that the party was east of Snake John Reef and that the campsite was near the present K Ranch." Perhaps.

That day, for the first time, Escalante admits that his team is beginning to run low on food: "By now we had few provisions, in view of the long traveling we still had to do, because of what we had spent among the Sabuaganas and other Yutas." That the men thought they could possibly carry enough food for the whole journey, no matter how many pack animals they allocated for the purpose, signals a disastrous miscalculation. Yet before the trip, Domínguez had blithely claimed as much. In a letter to Fray Isidro Murillo, the head of the Franciscan order in New Mexico, written on the day of the team's departure from Santa Fe, he expressed his gratitude to Governor Mendinueta, who "not only applauded our plan but also opened up his heart and his hands, giving us supplies and everything we might need for the journey." So on September 11, in the midst of the wasteland near today's Colorado–Utah border, when the team discovered bison tracks, D & E sent "two companions" off to track the great animals. They returned after noon saying they had spotted a buffalo. The hunt was on. "We dispatched others on the fleetest horses and, after chasing it for about three leagues, they killed it; then at seven-thirty at night they brought back a grand supply of meat." This was also the first time on the whole journey that Escalante recorded shooting any game, or even trying to live off the land more aggressively than pausing to sample handfuls of the local berries.

On September 13 the team came to the Green River. It was a moment of high importance, for several reasons. Escalante noted that "the river is the most copious one we have come by"—larger, in fact, than the Colorado, which the team had forded eight days earlier. No doubt Silvestre told him that the new river was joined somewhere far to the west by the San Clemente (the White), "but we do not know if it does [come together] with the preceding ones." In other words, even the Laguna guide was ignorant of the cardinal fact that the Colorado River ultimately joins the Green to form the mighty current that flows through Cataract Canyon, Glen Canyon, and the colossal gorge of the Grand Canyon—the most powerful river in the American Southwest. Several weeks hence, that ignorance would plunge the Spaniards into a life-threatening predicament.

Unfazed for the moment, the padres named the big river the San Buenaventura—literally, the Saint of Good Fortune. Silvestre told them there was only one place to ford the river, "on the west side of the hogback on the north, very near to a chain of small bluffs of loose dirt." Today's Highway 50 crosses the Green on a sturdy bridge at the derelict farming town of Jensen, Utah. A ramshackle visitor center was staffed by a small, ancient lady. I asked her, "Do you know where the Ute crossing of the Green River was?" "What?" she cried, her mouth agape. I explained our mission retracing the route of Domínguez and Escalante. Those names meant nothing to her. (What kind of information, I wondered cruelly, was this old crone capable of dishing out?) She urged me to head north to another visitor center at the gateway of Dinosaur National Monument. I thanked her and fled.

Fortunately, the Bicentennial Commission had done the research I craved. In 1975 two new retracers, Jerome Stoffel and George Stewart, fused local lore with Escalante's careful description to pinpoint the place of the ford. They were aided by the memory of a Jensen old-timer named Demar Dudley, who recalled that in 1917 a big flood had altered the course of the Green. With Stoffel and Stewart's coordinates in hand, Sharon and I took a back road three miles north along the west bank of the Green to the spot where Brush Creek trickles into the main current. Staring across the surging water, we could imagine the ford just as Silvestre had described it. Not for the first time, I realized that in 1975 the Commission men had been able to call upon the long memories of local residents to enhance their rediscovery of the Spaniards' route. By 2017, that link of oral lore seemed to have gone extinct—as exemplified by the stare of incomprehension of the old lady in the visitor center. (I would have wagered that Demar Dudley, may he rest in peace, knew who Domínguez and Escalante were.)

In the same journal entry on September 13, Escalante notes that the big river is "the same one which Fray Alonso de Posada . . . relates in his report as separating the Yuta Nation from the Comanche." The mention of Posada is the key to just what goals the padres were pursuing in mid-September 1776, besides the desire to find a route to Monterey, which by that point in the journey seems to have been pushed to a back burner.

Writing in 1686, in the midst of the shock that the Pueblo Revolt had dealt the Spaniards six years earlier, Posada attempts a grandly ambitious survey of the geography of all of North America, despite the fact that half the continent remained unknown to Europeans. But more particularly—and more vitally for Escalante—Posada tries to fix the geographical location of a mysterious place known alternately as Teguayó and Copala. The history of the idea embodied in those names intermingles native origin myths and the Spanish passion to discover a fabulously rich land somewhere beyond the frontiers of Old Mexico. When Coronado entered the Southwest in 1540, he was in the grip of a zeal to discover Quivira, loosely synonymous with the

Seven Cities of Cíbola, or the Seven Cities of Gold. As related in chapter 1, Puebloans invented Quivira and located it far to the east of the Rio Grande, out on the plains of today's Kansas, to lure the genocidal conquistador into a wild goose chase and thereby spare their own settlements. After Oñate's conquest of New Mexico in 1598, Spaniards became dimly aware of the belief of the Tewa Indians, who occupied six pueblos ranging from Ohkay Owingeh to Tesuque, that long ago their people had migrated from an origin place many leagues to the northwest of their present villages—the semi-mythical Teguayó. And in 1604, on a foray in search of the great South Sea, or the Pacific Ocean, Oñate was told by natives near the lower Colorado River about a place equally far off to the north called Copala.

Copala became conflated with Quivira. Oñate listened hungrily to a story of men and women wearing bracelets and earrings made of gold but who somehow spoke Spanish, living in utopian splendor in distant Copala. Writing six years after the Pueblo Revolt, Posada was well aware that, during an unsuccessful attempt to win back the colony in 1681, an elderly Puebloan who was captured and executed provided the first testimony about Popé, the shaman who had directed the great uprising. According to that informant, as Popé meditated in a kiva at Taos, three supernatural beings appeared who gave him the vision of a homeland rid of the oppressor, and those spirits "said they were going underground to the Lake of Copala." To make matters even more complicated (and more baffling to the Spaniards), Cortés and his men had learned that the Aztecs believed they had migrated from a mythical homeland far off in the little-known north. Moctezuma himself was supposed to have come from Teguayó/Copala.

Posada notes that for almost a century, geographers have confused the "provinces" of Quivira and Teguayó. The main thrust of his scholarly report is to disentangle these two lands. What galvanized Escalante (and no doubt Domínguez) was Posada's fairly precise claim that Teguayó lay 180 leagues (or 475 miles) northwest of Santa Fe. Moreover, "the land which the Indians of the North call *Teguayó*" is one and the same as the territory that "the Mexican Indians by an old tradition call *Copala*." According to Popé's vision, unearthed in 1681 by the tortured informant, Copala was a lake.

One of the major goals, then, of the Domínguez–Escalante expedition was to find Teguayó and to discover whether or not it was the rumored land of incalculable wealth and luxury. Thanks to Posada, Escalante knew that Teguayó/Copala was centered on a big lake. Not by accident did the padres call the Ute tribe supposed to inhabit that land the Lagunas (*laguna* is Spanish for "lake"). Whether Silvestre promised the Spaniards a lake is uncertain, but likely, for when D & E eventually reached the vast inland body of water known today as Utah Lake, they professed not an iota of surprise.

Oddly enough, Posada doesn't say a word about Comanches, despite Escalante's assertion that the 1686 report fixes the boundary between the territory of the Yutas and that of the Comanches. What Posada does define is the well-known border between the "Apacha" and the Yutas. Apacha was a standard appellation for "Apaches de Navajo," which ethnographers identify today as the Navajo of New Mexico and Arizona. This only deepens the mystery of the Yamparica Comanches. Did Escalante willfully equate Posada's "Apacha" with the Comanches the Utes kept warning him against? Or did he simply forget? The point is that by September 1776 D & E were far more motivated to find the mythic stronghold of Teguayó than they were by their mandate to blaze a trail to Monterey.

All this is murky and complicated enough. But we know that the padres were equally entranced by another thread of legend and rumor. Much of it sprang from the electrifying report received by Escalante's colleague at Zuni, Fray Damián Martínez, sometime in the early 1770s. According to Martínez, a Navajo whom the Spaniards trusted reported as follows:

On one of the forays he made with them [his people] they traveled between north and west as far as the river called El Tizón, on the shore of which he found a white man on horseback with clothing and armament of the type we use. He spoke to him in Castilian and in his Navajo language, and he says that the man did not reply but only smiled to himself when he used our language. This Indian and his companions observed among the groves on the opposite bank of the river a number of smokes, as if from chimneys and some plantings. . . . They waited a while to observe the ford and the route which the white man was taking, but the said man remained motionless on this side until, tired of waiting, they turned back.

This startling encounter reinforced an old idea in the New Mexico colony that there might be a band of "lost Spaniards" hanging on somewhere beyond the Río Tizón. Other reports specified that these men grew full beards, which seemed to prove that they could not be Indians. Ever since Coronado's *entrada* in 1540–42, the idea had taken hold that some band of allies sent to support the conquistador's massive army had been waylaid or captured or had simply gotten lost somewhere in the uncharted wilderness to the north. The rumors of bearded men beyond the Tizón, perhaps still wearing armor and speaking Castilian, provided yet another dramatic spur to the quest of 1776: not only to discover Teguayó, but to find and save the countrymen lost more than a century before. Escalante himself alluded to this goal in a letter he wrote from Zuni to a Franciscan brother in August 1775, as he first contemplated the great expedition he would co-lead the next year. Wrote Escalante: "Here it is believed the Spaniards or white people whom the Yutas say they have seen many times may be descendants from those 300 soldiers whom Captain Alvarado left when he entered by the Río Colorado at the beginning of the conquest."

Whew. Hernando de Alvarado was the commander of Coronado's advance guard, leading 75 to 100 soldiers (not 300) first to Zuni, then out onto the Kansas plains in the fruitless search for the riches of

Quivira. He returned to Mexico after the expedition and died peacefully in Mexico City in 1550. But by the 1770s, Spaniards in New Mexico had invented, or evolved, the legend that Alvarado himself, or at least a substantial portion of his troops, had gotten separated from the expedition and never returned. It was this legend, reinforced by the Navajo's account of the man in armor speaking Castilian on the other side of the river, together with the stories of bearded strangers in the far northwest, that Escalante wholeheartedly bought into. And what cause could be more noble than the rescue of fellow countrymen enslaved or lost three generations before? The lost Spaniards were the original POW/MIAs.

* * *

ESCALANTE DOES NOT say whether the team thought the San Buenaventura was the fabled Tizón. But it was the biggest river they had crossed on the whole journey, bigger even than the Rio Grande, by which yardstick they measured all the waterways they discovered. The men spent two days on the banks of the Green, resting their horses. They managed to kill another bison, a small one, from which "we enjoyed little meat." Yet there was a sense within the party that something monumental had been accomplished. On the very edge of the river there were "six big black poplars [cottonwoods] which had grown in pairs," as well as another standing alone. On that solitary tree Joaquín Lain used his adze to cut a rectangular "window" in the bark, then wielded a chisel to carve "Year of 1776," his last name, and two Christian crosses. It was a conscious imitation of the inscription Rivera had carved in the big cottonwood on the banks of the Gunnison in 1765, which D & E had searched for in vain.

Herbert E. Bolton, retracing the expedition route in 1950, believed he had found the same grove. "The six giant cottonwoods still stand at the site described by Escalante," he wrote in *Pageant in the Wilderness*, "but the inscription, perhaps covered by the growth of a century and three-quarters, is not visible." The historian's claim was one more example of partisans of D & E needing to be more certain than they had any right to be that they had found traces of the long-ago journey. Later a team of botanists from the University of Utah cored the cottonwoods and found that none of them was more than seventy-five years old.

Celebratory those days on the banks of the Green may have been. Escalante envisioned a future settlement here, complete with irrigation ditches to water the fields. But as soon as the team moved on, a mood of paranoia and mistrust took hold. On the far side of a dry arroyo, the Spaniards discovered the tracks of "about twelve horses and some people on foot." They could of course have been left by any party venturing near the crossing of the Green, for all kinds of purposes, but D & E studied the markings closely and concluded that "they"—the authors of the prints—"had been lying in wait or spying for some time on the ridge's highest part, without letting go of the horses. We suspected that they might be some Sabuaganas who could have followed us to deprive us of the animal herd at this place, where we would likely attribute the deed to the Comanches instead of the Yutas, since we were no longer in the latter's country but the former's."

Where was the padres' serene faith in God to protect them from all enemies? In its absence, the miasma of suspicion wrapped itself around Silvestre. The Spaniards recalled that the night before, the guide had "casually and without being noticed" slipped out of camp to sleep alone. Back on the Gunnison, the team had given Silvestre a blanket to wear, but the man had never put it on. Now, on September 16, he wore the blanket all day. "We suspected," wrote Escalante, "that, for his having had an understanding with the Sabuaganas, he wore it so as to be recognized in case they attacked us. He increased our suspicion all the more when he lagged behind for a while, pensive and confused, before reaching the ridge where we found the tracks." Rather than confront Silvestre, the padres "dissembled," pretending nothing was wrong. And indeed, nothing happened.

By now I thought it was high time to settle this pesky Comanche business for good, but of course in our baggage on the road we lacked the research materials to dig into this ethnographic puzzle. It was only months later, back home in Massachusetts, that I could make a stab. In Pekka Hämäläinen's definitive culture history, *Comanche Empire* (2008), a well-drawn map of the tribe's homeland in the 1770s and 1780s covers a vast territory stretching from eastern New Mexico into what are now Kansas, Oklahoma, and northern Texas. Small zones of Comanche raiding focus on Santa Fe and the pueblos along the Rio Grande, but extend no farther west than Jemez pueblo or north than a few miles beyond Abiquiu. Yet on that map, a small blob of separate land is glossed as "Comanche raiding zone." And that blob stretches from Grand Mesa to the Green River, where the Sabuaganas warned D & E about Comanches to the northwest.

That analysis sounds authoritative. But as I read more closely, I realized that Hämäläinen's only source for the presence of Comanches way up in northeastern Utah was Escalante's journal, reinforced by Miera y Pacheco's map, which affixes the legend "Comanches Yamparicas" across the blank space just north of where the team forded the "Rio de S Buena Ventura" (the Green). If the D & E expedition is Hämäläinen's sole source for this anomalous Comanche presence, perhaps he is simply passing on undigested the padres' misconception that the indomitable warriors of the plains had established a stronghold in far-off Ute country. Hämäläinen seems to admit his own surprise at such an intrusion, observing that that stronghold would have been "separated from Comancheria proper by four hundred miles of rugged mountains, deep canyons, and thick forests."

I think the most likely explanation of the phantom enemy whom the Sabuaganas lived in dread of, and who rattled the nerves of the Spaniards as they pushed beyond the Green, is that they were another tribe of Utes, or perhaps Shoshone, who threatened the existence not only of the Sabuaganas but also of Silvestre's Laguna people. "Yampirica" seems to echo the Yampa River, a tributary of the Green, which flows about 60 miles north of Grand Mesa. "Yampa" is a Snake Indian word for an edible plant that grows along the river—and the Snakes include the Eastern Shoshone. A band called the Yamparica, or Yampa Utes, eventually emerges in the historical record, but not until 1850, or three-quarters of a century after the Spaniards rode through Utah. That tribe, of course, could have been there all along. None of this explains, however, why D & E insisted that the Yutas with whom they made peace consistently swore that the bad guys against whom they sporadically warred were Comanches.

*   *   *

ON SEPTEMBER 21, Sharon and I hoped to camp out. But the weather, which had turned for the worse as we drove up into Hubbard Park the day before, was further deteriorating, as the thermometer steadily dropped and the clouds smudged with hints of rain. After Jensen, we drove north into Vernal, the biggest town for miles around, and found a motel. That evening, in a gloomy cafeteria-like restaurant, we watched as a large family of Utes came in and occupied the long table next to ours. They ranged in age from a pair of toddlers to a grandma robed in a fine dress, spangled with necklaces and bracelets. Every member, sad to say, was obese. On the Navajo reservation I'd often witnessed the equivalent. In historic photos of both Navajos and Utes from the end of the nineteenth century, all the men and women look lean and fit. But the traditional diet of corn and mutton and berries has relentlessly morphed into platters of fry bread and tacos and burgers, supplemented with jumbo-sized Cokes and Twinkies and Hostess cupcakes, not to mention booze. The family next to us, though, looked stone-cold sober, and they were having a good time, laughing and teasing one another.

Simply to make an observation such as this one is to tiptoe on the edge of ethnic stereotyping, not to mention cultural condescension. But in 2017 it was hard for me not to see the legacy of Silvestre and the Sabuaganas as marginalization, anomie, and the reservation blues.

On September 17, 1776, the day after the expedition found the prints that warned them of what they feared was an impending "ambuscade," Silvestre led the team up a high ridge, from the summit of which he pointed southwest to show the men where the Green and White Rivers meet. That junction today is the site of the little town of Ouray, Utah, named after the vacillating chief who in the early 1880s bowed to manifest destiny and traded his people's Colorado domain for the Uintah and Ouray Reservation, whose four million acres cover, after the Navajo reservation, the second-largest Indian reserve in the United States. From Vernal on September 22, we drove along U.S. Highway 40 and at Fort Duchesne turned south on dirt roads to creep onto the reservation. At the junction, a scattering of shops gave us our choice among Ute Gas, the Ute Coffee House, and the Ute Crossing Grill.

The houses on either side were small and poor. Yards were decorated with defunct trucks and cars, their tires removed, rust invading the chassis. The ditches along the roadside collected the trash. For some reason, the beer of choice for both reservation Navajos and Utes is Bud Lite, either in cans or brown bottles. We crossed the Duchesne River and turned west. On either side barbed wire fences paralleled the roadway. We stopped to read several signs hung from the upper strands. The wording was uniform:

NOTICE!
TO ALL NON-MEMBERS OF THE UTE INDIAN TRIBE
THIS IS INDIAN LAND
NO TRESPASSING
NO HUNTING

The hostility baked into that printed message seemed hard-earned. A century and a half ago, Ouray's people had given away their homeland to politicians who coveted canyons and mountains rich with gold and silver. Whatever the four million acres the tribe had received in exchange might be good for, it was not to fuel such nineteenth-century bonanzas as the Camp Bird and Tomboy mines, nor such twentieth-century temples to Sybaris as Aspen and Telluride.

About ten years earlier, I had tried to get permission to hike on the Uintah and Ouray Reservation, which I knew must be swarming with prehistoric ruins and rock art left by the Fremont people, just as I'd found in Range Creek, which borders the rez on the west. Many times I'd paid for a permit to hike on the Navajo Reservation, and some of my most rewarding Anasazi discoveries had come in canyons seldom visited by Anglos. Even in the most culturally sensitive areas, such as Canyon de Chelly and Monument Valley, I'd been able to explore in the company of a Navajo guide I hired.

Several phone calls and emails to the Ute headquarters in Fort Duchesne went unanswered. Finally I got an agent from the tribe's Fish and Wildlife Department on the line. He was perplexed. For decades, Ute guides had charged decent fees to guide Anglo hunters on the reservation, where they stalked trophy elk and black bear. But no one, the man claimed, had ever asked about hiring a hiking guide. For want of a pigeonhole in which to insert my request, it floated in bureaucratic limbo. Nothing came of my inquiry.

On the evening of September 17, the Spaniards camped near here, where Sharon and I trundled along the dirt road beside the Duchesne River. From their camp, staring at a distant mountain range (probably the eastern edge of the Uintas) they caught sight of wisps of smoke rising from distant campfires. "When we asked the guide who in his opinion had sent them up," wrote Escalante, "he said that they could be Comanches or some of the Lagunas who usually came hunting thereabouts."

During the next five days, the Spaniards moved steadily westward, driven by the paramount desire to reach the main encampment of the Lagunas. The way ought to have been straightforward, following first the Duchesne and then the Strawberry rivers upstream. But Silvestre seemed to guide the team into arbitrary byways and incomprehensible tangles of vegetation. Escalante's diary is rife with complaint—and suspicion. On the 18th, "Because the guide wanted to cross over to the river's other side and follow it, he stuck us through an almost impenetrable willow bosque, or thicket, and into marshy estuaries which made us backtrack and cross the river thrice while making many useless detours." The next day, Silvestre chose a route that required "making several turns over almost impassable terrain" that "caused one of our horses to be injured and made us backtrack another mile." A different horse died on September 20. So the litany proceeds: "a stretch of sagebrush, flat but bothersome, and with a lot of prickly pear cactus"; "narrow valleys of very soft dirt and many small holes in which, because they lay hidden in the undergrowth, the mounts kept sinking and stumbling at every instant"; "breaking through almost impenetrable swaths of chokecherry and scruboak and passing through another poplar forest so thick that we doubted if the packs could get through unless they were first taken off." On the 21st, Silvestre managed to infuriate the padres and ratchet up their suspicion. "The guide, anxious to get there sooner than we ourselves could make it, was hurrying so fast that he vanished in the forest at every step, and we knew not where to follow him. . . . He was ordered to go slow and always within our sight."

In our SUV, we watched the temperature on the dashboard sink to 43°, and a light rain began to fall. Along the same stretch of the Duchesne River, the Spaniards endured a comparable weather change. "Tonight it was so cold," Escalante reported on September 20, "that even the water which stood close to the fire all night was frozen by morning."

The moment we crossed the invisible boundary between Uinta and Duchesne counties, the highway improved, potholes replaced by smooth tarmac. The road stopped curving and instead abruptly changed direction by jolts of ninety degrees aligned with the points of the compass. In place of peevish "no trespassing" placards proclaiming Indian sovereignty, we found neat green signposts announcing

8850 South, 3500 East, and the like. We had left the Ute reservation and entered greater Myton, a venerable Mormon town (2010 population 569). But when at last we entered the village center, we found trailers and cottages that looked every bit as poor as the rez shacks. One lane, however, bore the proud signature Escalante Way.

We traveled on west of Myton on U.S. 40 toward Duchesne, the biggest town we would visit between Vernal and Provo. The origin of the name of that high plains outpost, like the Scottish romance informing Montrose, piqued my fancy. Rose Philippine Duchesne was born in Grenoble, France, in 1769, seven years before D & E hit the trail. (I'd climbed and hiked a lot in the Vercors and Chartreuse, using Grenoble as my home base. The region is one of my favorite parts of France.) At the age of eighteen, Rose Philippine became a nun, but when the French Revolution forced her underground, she longed to light out for America.

Her wish was answered only in 1818, when she traveled to Louisiana to serve in the Catholic missionary effort on the frontier that Jefferson had purchased from Napoleon. She ended up in St. Charles, Missouri, where she ran a school that struggled to stay afloat. Her grand passion, like that of D & E, was to bring the Gospel to American Indians. She got her one chance at age seventy-two, as part of a Jesuit campaign to educate Potawatomi girls. Too ill to do much in the way of teaching, she gained the sobriquet "the woman who always prays." After a single year among the Indians, she was recalled to St. Charles.

What Sister Rose Philippine, who never got closer to Utah than Sugar Creek, Kansas, had to do with naming the thoroughly Mormon town of Duchesne, I never got straight. She was beatified in 1940, but six years before that, the Daughters of Utah Pioneers installed a plaque in the center of Duchesne, which we stopped to ponder. The inscription vaguely hailed the nun as "having links" with the explorer William Clark and the mountain man William Ashley. I think the town was named after the river, and it's likely that French trappers bestowed the tribute, but when and exactly why, who knows?

Domínguez and Escalante camped just west of today's town of Duchesne on the night of September 21–22. But any effort to find the site of their bivouac today is thwarted by one more man-made lake that obliterates the Spaniards' trail—the Starvation Reservoir, smack in the middle of Starvation State Park. Alas, that designation alludes not to the lean rations the Spaniards were consuming by the end of September 1776 but to some desperate wintering-over by homesteaders around 1900.

About 30 miles beyond Duchesne on Route 40, we came to an even larger dammed lake, the crown jewel of the Strawberry Reservation Recreation Area. From here, the easiest way to cross the Wasatch Range to get to Provo is to continue on Highway 40 northwest to Heber City, then jog southwest on Route 189. But the Spaniards, guided by Silvestre, took a more circuitous route over several high passes, through a maze of forests and crooked creeks. By the time we got to the Strawberry Visitor Center the rain was coming down steadily, and it was cold enough that we thought it could be snowing up higher. But the ranger on duty gave us a map, circled the national forest roads (mostly dirt) that we should follow, and judged that our SUV would have no problem negotiating the outback.

The barren surroundings of the reservoir, mostly treeless, coated with heather turning brown, reminded me of a Scottish moor. I was pleased to see that the displays outside the visitor center once more hailed Domínguez and Escalante. The Bicentennial Commission had persevered here, for the plinths of white stone holding the black-and-gold panels were in the same style as the ones we had seen at the ramada on the outskirts of Montrose.

Ever since our drive had begun on September 2, I had been anticipating a calendrical quirk that I thought would bind us closer to Domínguez and Escalante. I thought of it as a kind of syzygy, like the moment every twenty-six months when Mars and Earth come closest in their orbits, aligned in a perfect vector away from the sun. Somewhere that afternoon, on the dirt roads of the Uinta National

Forest, it happened. The date was September 22, 2017, and the relevant passage in Escalante's journal covered the events of September 22, 1776. Our conjunction, of course, would occur only once, because the Spaniards traveled so much more slowly even than Sharon's and my balky pace.

For the expedition, it was a day of keen anticipation, though the team found it rough going. Escalante reports "many dangerous defiles and slides," "the sierra's corrugated ruggedness," and "lofty shoulders, some of them craggy with rock." But from a high ridge the Spaniards saw "a large number of big smoke signals being sent up, not too far away."

> Silvestre the guide said they belonged to some of his people possibly out hunting. We returned the message with others to avoid being mistaken, should they have seen us, for hostile people and so have them run away or welcome us with arrows. Again they began sending up bigger smoke clouds at the pass through which we had to go toward the lake—and this made us believe that they had already seen us, for this is the handiest and the regular signal used for anything worth knowing about by all the peoples in this part of America.

D & E beseeched the guide "to be on the lookout tonight in case one of his own, who knew of our arrival, approached the king's camp to find out what people were coming." At 2 AM, Silvestre suddenly "spoke for a long while in their language"—apparently broadcasting his message into the empty night. But, wrote Escalante, "We did not learn if anyone heard him."

We had driven only a few miles south on Forest Road 131 when we abruptly saw three hunters trudging back to their pickup from the slope below the road. They looked hypothermic, but the man in front had a grimace of pride on his face, for on his shoulders he was hauling the severed head and antlers of a big stag. The other two men were apparently lugging nothing but their rifles. We could only hope that the trio had not abandoned the rest of the carcass to scavenging animals, although it was so miserable out that we could imagine the faint-hearted violating this cardinal rule of the big game hunter's credo.

For the next two hours, as we followed forest roads 131, 042, and 051, we crept slowly through an enchanted landscape. As we climbed, patches of forest, dark green Engelmann spruces mixed with aspens just entering their autumnal gold, sprang up on either side. But from a ridgeline near 8,500 feet, we stared down on the charred wreckage of some gigantic recent forest fire. The only other vehicles we passed on the roads were hunters' pickups and RVs, and half the pullouts were occupied by their white canvas tents. The rain did not quite turn to snow, but on the higher benches we passed patches of new drift.

Once more, the Bicentennial retracers had to guess just where the Spaniards had passed 199 years before. Their commentary resorts to the usual phrases: "we propose that," "we surmise," "it must have been," "it would have been necessary." After much driving back and forth, Jerome Stoffel and George Stewart convinced themselves that "there seems little doubt that the campsite the night of September 22 is at the junction of Wanrhodes Canyon and Diamond Creek." Escalante specifies only "a brief plain which lies between two rivulets that join each other," but I had to admire the retracers' gumption. As we crested Unicorn Ridge, we were four or five miles away from that junction, but even in good weather I doubted that we would have hiked cross-country to behold the empty meadow of the Commission's conjecture.

On September 23, the Spaniards found their way out of the convoluted upland as they emerged in the broad valley of the Spanish Fork River. It is just possible that that place name, which first appears on a John C. Frémont map published in 1845, echoes the Domínguez–Escalante expedition, but it more likely derives from trappers in the 1820s who gradually sketched out what would come to be called the

Spanish Trail. Once the team started down that generous corridor, bisected today by U.S. Highway 6, they could barely contain their excitement. Yet eagerness was tempered by wariness, for despite Silvestre's reassurances, the men did not know how they would be received at the main Laguna encampment. Rather than ride boldly ahead, they stopped to make an early camp, roughly where today's Route 6 meets Interstate 15, the main Utah thoroughfare linking Salt Lake City in the north with St. George in the southwest corner and on to Las Vegas. From that site, which the padres named the Vega del Dulcísimo Nombre de Jesús (The Plain of the Most Sweet Name of Jesus), Domínguez, Andrés Muñiz, and Silvestre rode ahead, "racing their horses as much as they could, even to the point of exhaustion, so as to get there this afternoon."

The next two days, from the afternoon of September 23 to midday on the 25th, would furnish in several respects the true climax of the whole expedition. On these events Escalante lavished two of the longest entries in his journal, and later he appended to its pages a "Description of the Valley" that serves as a kind of gazetteer to the bounteous basin and its inhabitants, outlining its promise as the site of a future Spanish settlement. Yet those entries must be read with more than a healthy dose of skepticism. It is almost impossible to believe that the encounter with the Laguna Utes occurred the way Escalante insists that it did. His narrative reads rather like a script from some Franciscan passion play.

The Spaniards' caution was well-advised, for Domínguez's advance party was met by "some men [who] came out to meet them with weapons in hand to defend their homes and families." It is at this point that the reader must suspend his disbelief—or else try to probe just what ends the apparent fiction of the journal narrative serve. According to Escalante,

> As soon as Silvestre spoke to them the show of war was changed into the finest and fondest expressions of peace and affec-

tion. They very joyfully conducted them to their little humble abodes, and after he had embraced each single one and let them know that we came in peace, and that we loved them as our greatest friends, the padre allowed them time to talk at length with our guide Silvestre, who gave them an account so much in our favor of what he had observed and witnessed ever since he had become one of us, and about our purpose in coming, that we could not have wished for anything better.

Escalante, of course, was not present to witness this joyful embrace between two alien cultures; he would have listened to Domínguez's account of it later that evening, back at camp on the Spanish Fork. Perhaps Silvestre was indeed as smitten by the padres' kindness as the journal makes him out to be. "With greatest awe," the guide cited as proof of the miraculous power of the Spaniards the way the team had blithely passed through Comanche country. Gone from the narrative now is any of the paranoia and suspicion that attended the team's hesitant movements after crossing the Green River. Once more, serene faith trumps peril. According to Escalante, Silvestre told his fellow Lagunas "how, after the Sabuaganas had said that the Comanches would surely kill us or deprive us of our herds of horses . . . they had not attacked us nor had we seen them—what the padres had said thus coming true, that is to say, that God would deliver us from all our enemies and . . . that even if we passed through their very own country they would not detect us nor we ourselves see them." This seems to hint at supernatural intervention, as if to escape harm the Spaniards had made themselves invisible. Sounding like a brainwashed yes-man, Silvestre doubled down on his praise: "He ended by saying that only the padres spoke the truth, that in their company one could travel all over the earth without risk, and that they were nothing but good people."

Now, once the ice was broken, Domínguez offered tobacco to his hosts, then launched into a speech about the padres' purpose in coming. It was the preamble to a mass conversion effort such as the one he had attempted among the Sabuaganas. Through Silvestre and Andrés Muñiz as interpreters, Domínguez explained that the team's principal motivation

> was to seek the salvation of their souls and to show them the only means whereby they could attain it—the chief, primary, and necessary one being to believe in a single true God, to love Him and obey Him wholly by doing what is contained in His holy and spotless Law—and that all this would be taught them with greater clarity and at greater length, and the water of holy baptism poured on them, should they wish to become Christians and for the padres to come to instruct them and Spaniards to live among them, and that in this event they would be taught how to farm and raise livestock. . . . For, by submitting themselves to live in the manner ordered by God and as the padres would teach them, our Great Chief whom we call King would send them everything that was needed, because, on seeing how they wished to be Christianized, He would already be guarding them as His children and would be caring about them as though they were already His people.

Who knows what the Lagunas made of this extraordinary tirade? The passion play was launched. "They listened gladly," Escalante reported second-hand, "and replied that they were ready to do all this, revealing from the start their great docility." After what must have been an exhausting day, Domínguez returned to the camp on the Spanish Fork and shared his glad tidings with his team.

Yet even as he left the Laguna encampment, Domínguez could not resist warning his new hosts that the team's stay in their homeland would of necessity be brief. Not because they had to get on to California, but because "we had to continue our traveling in order to learn about the other padre, our brother." When I first read this passage, I was incredulous. Were D & E still obsessed with finding out the fate of Fray Francisco Garcés? Did they really think they could locate him in the vast wilderness through which they sojourned? So far Escalante's journal says nothing about the lost Spaniards or the white strangers with beards, but in view of later events, I would come to think that this throwaway allusion to Brother Garcés was a kind of coded tag for that larger quest into the topography of myth and rumor.

*   *   *

As WE DROVE into Provo, the rain became torrential and the temperature dropped to 36°. Through gaps in the smothering clouds we glimpsed new snow coating the slopes of Mount Timpanogos north of town. It felt like a day in late November, with winter just around the corner. We found a motel not far from the campus of Brigham Young University, lugged our gear up to the room, and turned the thermostat high. We had called ahead to a hospital to get another blood draw, my first since Durango two weeks earlier. Because I seemed so susceptible to the cold, and because it took so little exercise to exhaust me, Sharon was worried about my sodium level.

The next day, we drove to the edge of town to look at Utah Lake, the body of water that D & E had so keenly anticipated, for which they had named Silvestre's Utes the Lagunas. The gray-green lake, choppy with whitecaps, disappeared into the fog. We were the only visitors in a city park that on a nice day would have teemed with picnickers. Staring out into the gloom, I felt as though I had ventured to the edge of some subarctic ocean. It looked like the kind of day even seasoned mariners might fear.

The night before, worn out by the long drive from Vernal, addled by the cold and rain, I'd had my first meltdown on the trip. Having settled into our motel only at dusk, we tried to find a nearby restaurant for a quick meal. A steakhouse called Ruby River stood just across the street. Sharon looked up the reviews on TripAdvisor, which rated the place "#7 out of 229 restaurants in Provo." One patron summarized his dining experience as "good but slow"—a warning I should have heeded. It was a Friday night, but Ruby River didn't take reservations. Instead, over a bedlam of noise on the phone, the hostess took our name and guaranteed us "priority seating."

We should have turned around at the door upon discovering large families patiently hovering in the lobby and even out the door in the rain. We should have opted for McDonald's. Instead, we succumbed. Since it was Mormon Provo, there was no bar. To get a beer or a glass of wine, we had to snag the attention of one of the waitresses, all of whom were dressed as cowgirls. Despite the Western theme, Frank Sinatra's gooeyest hits blared from the sound system. Still standing in the vague space between waiting line and tables where the 5:30 crowd was just tucking into their dinners, we were handed our drinks after only forty-five minutes. Half an hour after that we were seated on skimpy stools. Sometime thereafter we were allowed to order.

When two hours went by without the appearance of any food, I lost it. As soon as I could rein in the eighteen-year-old in her Stetson and chaps, I started screaming, "Where the hell is our dinner?" Other patrons looked on in horror—this sort of thing wasn't done in have-a-nice-day Provo. The waitress started crying. Sharon put her hand on my sleeve and begged me to stop making a scene. In the end, the only consolation was that Ruby River decided not to charge me for the soggy mashed potatoes drenched in white chicken gravy that I couldn't eat.

On September 24, 1776, Domínguez and Escalante had a much more fruitful meeting on the shores of Utah Lake than Sharon and I did as part of the hungry mob inside Ruby River. The day before, Domínguez had been told that not all of the Laguna "chiefs" had gathered to hear his electrifying message. But on the 24th, he could flatter himself that the entire Laguna nation hung on his words.

The padres had learned that the Lagunas called themselves the Timpanogotzis. The name can be translated as "people of the rock water-mouth" or "rock canyon." Their neighbors the Sabuaganas, however, somewhat less poetically referred to the tribe as the "fish-eaters," in allusion to their dependence on the catch from the great lake. Now Domínguez repeated his promise that the padres would come back soon to live among the Indians, would baptize them and thus save their souls, and would teach them how to farm and raise livestock. According to Escalante, the Timpanogotzis "all unanimously replied that the padres should come, that they would live as the tatas (thus the Yutas call the friars) taught them, and that they offered all their land to the Spaniards for them to build their homes wherever they pleased."

As I pondered these passages in the journal, I vacillated between thinking that Escalante wrote only what he wanted to hear and wondering why the Timpanogotzis might have been so welcoming and servile. When I posed the riddle to Matt Liebmann, my Harvard anthropology professor friend, he instantly replied, "From the Ute point of view, the coming of the Spaniards might have meant access to trading resources. And they might have seen the Spaniards as allies against their enemies—the so-called 'Comanches,' whoever they were."

Sure enough, on the 24th Domínguez offered the head chief ("who had a genteel appearance") some special gifts: "a big all-purpose knife and white glass beads, and Don Bernardo Miera gave him a hatchet." The padres also parceled out those time-honored European baubles for appeasing natives, the glass beads, to other Timpanogotzis in attendance, "a few to each one since they were so many." In return, Domínguez demanded from the chief a "token sign" of their pledge to become good Christians—some object to take back to Santa Fe to prove the efficacy of the conversion the padres had wrought so far away in the wilderness. The next day, the Timpanogotzis presented the Spaniards with a remarkable thing: a painting on deerskin of their main warriors, each adorned with splotches of red ocher to signify the blood spurting from "wounds in battles with the Comanches."

Thus, for the first and only time on the expedition, the padres explicitly pledged to return and build a mission and settlement among the Indians. Why the Lagunas and not the Sabuaganas? Although Escalante never mentions Teguayó or the lake of Copala, it's clear that the fertile basin of the great lake met Spanish expectations of a wealthy land beyond the Río Tizón. If the Timpanogotzis were not actually wearing bracelets and earrings made of gold, they nonetheless embodied an affluence beyond any the padres had yet encountered among the Utes. The "Description of the Valley" that Escalante inserted in his journal gushes with visions of the prosperity of the basin. "As many Indian pueblos can fit inside the valley as there are those in New Mexico," he marvels. The place had the "finest of advantages." Not only "flat meadows with good land for farming" and "good soil that can be irrigated," but "plenty of firewood and timber in the adjacent sierra." As for game, the valley "abounds in several species of good fish, geese, beavers, and other amphibious creatures which we did not have the opportunity to see"—not to mention rabbits and "fowl," as well as bison herds off to the northwest. On the strength of a day and a half spent in the region, Escalante could swear that "the climate here is a good one, for having experienced cold aplenty since we left El Río de San Buenaventura, we felt warm throughout the entire valley by day and by night."

Even as the Spaniards admired the big lake that gave the Timpanogotzis a way of living, their hosts told them about an even larger one off to the north. "Its waters are harmful and extremely salty, for the Tipanois assured us that anyone who wet some part of the body with them immediately felt a lot of itching in the part moistened," Escalante recorded. You would think the Spaniards would have been keen to explore that topographical wonder, but they seem to have been in too much of a hurry to contemplate the 40-mile detour northward to explore the strange salty lake. Yet Miera y Pacheco drew it on the map he compiled after the expedition. Instead of a 40-mile gap between the lakes, he shows them connected by a short, narrow inlet, and gives them both a common name, Laguna de los Timpanogos.

On no authority mentioned in Escalante's journal, Miera also drew a major river flowing straight west out of today's Great Salt Lake. The wish-fulfilling fantasy of a river leading from the Rocky Mountains across the West to the Pacific would tantalize and frustrate explorers for another three-quarters of a century.

It must have been a shock to the padres to discover that many of the Timpanogotzis men grew beards. Escalante reports the fact almost offhandedly, not in the journal itself but in the set piece of "Description of the Valley." Only a week later, when the team came across Indians with even fuller beards, Escalante would muse on the connection between those bearded men and the old story about lost Spaniards beyond the Tizón.

By noon on September 25, the Spaniards were ready to make their getaway. They persuaded two young Lagunas, whom they had named Joaquín and José María, to accompany them as guides to the unknown lands ahead. And now the padres explained the main reason for their haste in moving on, besides the search for Father Garcés. Once the two guides had been secured, Escalante wrote on the 24th, "we decided to resume our journey next day toward the establishments and port of Monterey." Although orders given to the padres before the expedition posited the main goal of the venture as linking Santa Fe to California, this is the first time in the journal that Escalante explicitly mentions the need to find a route to Monterey.

Having made such powerful promises to the Timpanogotzis about the salvation of their souls and the mission and town they would return to build, the padres must have felt chagrined as they begged for food. Writes the chronicler, "At the very last, we let them know that we now had but few provisions and that we would be grateful if they sold us some dried fish. They brought it and we bought a good portion." Bought with what? More glass beads?

Escalante paints the actual departure as an emotional rupture. Should any of the natives fall ill, D & E counseled, "they were to call upon God by saying, 'God, the True One, help us, protect us.'" Those words in Spanish were too much of a mouthful for the Timpano-gotzis, so the padres gave them instead the mantra "Jesús–María." "This they began repeating with ease . . . and during all the time we were making preparations to leave they did not cease repeating these holy names."

At the hour of leave-taking, "all bade us farewell most tenderly, especially Silvestre, who hugged us tightly, practically in tears." The Timpanogotzis had taken the padres' promises to heart. As the men mounted their horses, the Utes "began charging us once more not to delay our return too long, saying that they expected us back within a year."

Those parting words would haunt Escalante through the rest of the expedition—and beyond.

Chapter Seven

DECISION

As we drove out of Provo on the morning of September 24, the storm showed no signs of letting up. On Interstate 15, the going felt a little treacherous, with the windshield wipers swiping in a frenzy, semis barreling along behind and beside us. On Summit Ridge, a barely perceptible rise that separates Provo Valley from Juab Valley, the rain turned to snow. We had good news, though, in the form of a blood draw that recorded my sodium level at 130—still below normal, but high enough to portend another week or so of smooth sailing.

The route the expedition followed south of Utah Lake pretty much follows I–15 for about 60 miles. But this was the first time on the whole journey that we'd driven on an interstate, and between the foul weather and the 70 mph traffic, we felt divorced from the Spaniards as never before. A couple of days later, as we drove another section of I–15, I realized with a thud that we had covered three days of D & E's adventures in twenty-five minutes.

During the first several days after the monumental meeting with the Timpanogotzis, Escalante's journal reverts to spiritless accounts of the terrain: streams, woods, sagebrush flats. The team advanced only five miles on each of the first two days, though the chronicler gives no hint as to what retarded their progress. On September 27, the two guides, José María and Joaquín, rounded up five Indians and brought them into camp. Apparently the Spaniards had already left the Laguna domain, for these newcomers had heard nothing about the promise of salvation the padres had brought to the people of the lake. D & E fed the five Indians, gave them tobacco, and "found them as docile and agreeable as the rest." When the friars repeated their promises about transforming the natives' lives, those five "display[ed] great joy on hearing that more padres were to come and the Spaniards live among them."

The next day, September 28, the expedition made contact with Utes apparently living in an even more primitive state. As the team took a break from the "great heat" in a grove of cottonwoods, "scarcely had we sat down when from among certain thick clumps of willows eight Indians approached us with great fear, most of them naked with only a piece of buckskin over the private parts." Unfortunately the guides were off on some errand, so communication with these timorous newcomers was sketchy at best. Escalante insists that "we made them understand by signs that we were people friendly to them and came in peace." On the 29th, somewhere near today's town of Nephi, "we came upon a very old Indian of venerable countenance. He was alone in a tiny hut, and he had a beard so full and long that he looked like one of the ancient hermits of Europe."

Ever since leaving Abiquiu on August 1, the expedition had proceeded relentlessly north and west, with major detours eastward to cross the Uncompahgre Plateau and Grand Mesa. But after the meeting with the Timpanogotzis, for the first time the team headed south. Escalante never explains why. At each Indian encounter, the Spaniards grilled the natives about the geography ahead, with particular attention to how the rivers ran and where there might be reliable springs. Could the abrupt southward turn signify a general change of plans, or at least a weakening of the resolve to plug on to California? Did the men feel the tug of far-off Santa Fe?

It's clear that by now the expedition was, if not lost, at least thor-

oughly befuddled by the lay of the land. Miera y Pacheco kept taking latitudes with the astrolabe, and every reading continued to err
toward the north by about half a degree. On September 29, the team
camped on the banks of a good-sized river, which, "according to the
name these Indians had for it, appears to be the San Buenaventura."
In other words, the team believed that after making a long semicircle
to the west, they had come back to the banks of the Green—perhaps
the Tizón—many leagues downstream from where they had forded
it on September 16. In fact, the new river was the Sevier. At that
moment, the Green flowed a full 120 miles to the east as the crow
flies, where it plunges through the spectacular gorge of Desolation
Canyon—so named by John Wesley Powell almost a century later.

Early the next morning a delegation of Indians, twenty strong,
showed up in camp. These men wore "blankets of cottontail and
jackrabbit furs," had their nostrils pierced with animal bones, and
were "more fully bearded than the Lagunas." At last Escalante makes
explicit the connection with the old legend. These Indians with the
luxurious beards—the first of many the Spaniards would run into
as they moved on southward—nonetheless "employed the same language as the Timpanogotzis." They must be, therefore, the natives
"who perhaps gave rise to the report about Spaniards who were said
to exist on the other side of El Río de Tizón." Miera would draw
a vignette that he plunked in the middle of his map showing two
bearded Indians accompanied by two bare-breasted native women
(see image in insert). Oddly enough, the men are wearing leather
capes and caps and carrying quivers full of arrows, and one is carrying a dead jackrabbit. They also help the women unfurl a fishing net.
Miera's caption is "Barbones Tuavichis"—*barbones* meaning "bearded
ones," "Tuavichis" being the name of a tribe of Utes.

If D & E were crestfallen to have the myth of the lost Spaniards—
white men with beards, wearing armor, adrift in the heart of Yuta
country—exploded, Escalante's journal gives no hint of that reaction.
A letter the padre wrote before the expedition had voiced a certain

skepticism about the myth. In any event, some modern commentators identify the fully bearded Indians as Paiutes, whom ethnographers long after 1776 found sporting beards a conquistador might envy, though the Pahvant Utes, who occupy the region today, are also known to grow beards. (As Matt Liebmann told me, "Moctezuma himself had a beard.")

Sometimes modern highways incorporate the age-old wisdom of native trails. I–15 south of Provo links a string of Mormon towns—Santaquin, Mona, Nephi, Levan, Scipio—as it takes the best route through former wilderness, first following the Sevier River, then skirting the subranges of the Wasatch on the west. For five days since parting with the Timpanogotzis, the Spaniards had adhered to this sensible route. Yet suddenly on October 1, the team backtracked a mile and a half to the north, then set off westward. Their new bearing required the crossing of the small massif known today as the Canyon Mountains. There was no trail. Once beyond the peaks, the men rode onward looking for water. Speeding their horses to reach a lake they saw in the distance, they discovered instead a mirage, as the "lake" turned into a salt-and-alkali flat. All day the men searched for water in vain. After a remarkable day's jaunt of 36 miles, one of the longest on the expedition, the team reconciled themselves to a waterless camp.

What was going on? Escalante offers no explanation for this grim westward veering. There is no mention of the Laguna guides urging such a change in direction. Had the tug of Santa Fe been preempted by the tug of Monterey? For once the padres named their campsite not after a saint but with the laconic tag Llano Salado, or Salt Plain. Two of the men who had scouted ahead to look for water came back to camp swearing they had seen another lake two or three miles farther off. In the night, once the moon had risen, five men took the whole horse herd ahead to drink. The plan was for those five to return with water for the whole team.

What ensued turned into full-blown fiasco. Back in camp, October

2 dawned without any news from the missing five. Shortly thereafter, one of the scouts stumbled back into camp, unable to account for
the other four, or for the horses. It turned out that the second lake
had likewise been a mirage. Under moonlight, three of the five had
pushed ahead to search for water. The two left to guard camp had
fallen asleep. When they woke, they found all the horses missing.
Frantically they set off in two different directions to look for the runaway steeds.

Escalante does not bother to castigate the sleeping sentries for their
dereliction, but it is clear that a kind of panic had set in among the
fractured team. At once, Juan Pedro Cisneros "rode off bareback"
(evidently at least one horse had remained at Llano Salado) as he
tried to track the missing herd. Desperately thirsty horses will usually
backtrack to find the last water they encountered, and sure enough,
Cisneros found the whole herd halfway back to the previous night's
camp. He managed to return with the missing horses by noon. It was
a spunky performance, riding bareback without water 36 miles and
rounding up the spooked horses in a mere six hours.

Shortly after Cisneros's return, the three who had gone ahead
to look for water came back to camp, accompanied by six bearded,
nose-pierced Indians, but without water. The second sentry was still
missing. The "chief" of the Indians promptly sent four of his men to
search for the vagabond, each on a different vector. "It was a gesture
deserving the greatest gratitude," wrote Escalante, in an uncharacteristic tip of the hat to native savvy, "and worthy of admiration in so
wild a folk who had never before seen people like us." Before too long,
one of the searchers produced the hapless refugee.

Even in the wave of relief that must have attended the roundup of
the horses and the reuniting of the party, Domínguez and Escalante
sprang into missionary mode. Having noted that the Indians called
themselves Tirapangui, and having admired their facial hair ("the
five . . . were so fully bearded that they looked like Cachupín padres or
Bethlehemites"—monks forbidden to shave—) D & E commenced to

preach. "We announced the Gospel to them as well as the interpreter could manage it, explaining to them God's oneness, the punishment He reserves for the wicked, the reward He gives to the righteous, and the necessity of holy baptism and of the knowledge and observance of the divine law."

Other Indians straggled in. The friars redoubled their efforts, promising the natives that "we would come back with more padres so that all could be instructed," with the added benefit that in the future "they were not to live scattered about as now but gathered together in towns."

The joyous and instantaneous acceptance of a new Catholic doctrine that Escalante reports among the Utes and Paiutes defies credibility. One might be tempted to attribute it to willful blindness on the part of the padres, as they mistook the politeness of strangers for spontaneous conversion. Or worse: that Escalante deliberately falsified the success of the padres' sermonizing to claim glorious triumphs among the savages in the report he would submit to his superiors after the expedition. But Escalante was too certain of the holy truth of his faith, and in a certain sense too naive, to be capable of such Machiavellian cunning. The clear-eyed recounting of his missionary failures among the Hopi, both in 1775 and a month and a half after his encounters with Utes and Paiutes, stands as a corrective to any suggestion that he fictionalized the responses of the bearded men at Llano Salado.

The scene Escalante paints on October 2 is a literal tearjerker. After listening to the padres' promises, the Indians "all replied very joyfully that we must come back with the other padres, that they would do whatsoever we taught them and ordered them to do." They even agreed to go live with the Lagunas on Utah Lake to await the return of their benefactors. The farewell was wrenching.

Scarcely did they see us depart when all—following their chief, who started first—burst out crying copious tears, so that even when we were quite a distance away we kept hearing the tender laments of these unfortunate little sheep of Christ, lost along the way simply for not having the Light. They touched our hearts so much that some of our companions could not hold back the tears.

The chaos of the waterless camp and the separation of the team that seized the expedition on the night of October 1–2 is the first strong hint in Escalante's journal of a wholesale collapse of morale, a psychological unraveling, that set in after two months on the trail. Soon the Spaniards would be involved in a fight for their very survival. The fragmenting of the team, the indications of bitter disagreement among its members, even the inklings of mutinous strife, all prefigure the desperate predicament that lay only weeks ahead.

A few miles south of Scipio, Sharon and I left Interstate 15 with a sense of relief as we followed U.S. Highway 50 northwest, then west. We stopped for lunch in the town of Delta, once the alfalfa capital of the whole West. The Ranger Café was filled with weatherbeaten Mormon veterans and with younger Utes. A pair of teenage Anglo lovebirds shared their French fries in the booth next to ours, the guy showing off his biceps in a T-shirt despite the 40° weather. After we ate, I asked the woman at the cash register if the locals knew about Domínguez and Escalante. "Yes," she allowed without much enthusiasm, "but they were mostly farther east. Around Bryce Canyon. That's where Escalante made his highest survey station." Like the school supposedly plunked on top of Escalante's mission in Tierra Amarilla, this was news to me. "They say," the cashier went on, "they found stuff from the expedition all around the state."

One wonders just how such folklore comes into being. Not a scrap of certifiable artifact from the 1776 expedition has ever been identified. Yet the same was true until a couple of decades ago about the Coronado *entrada,* and by now all kinds of relics, ranging from crossbow parts to horseshoe nails to brass bells jettisoned by the conquistador's party between 1540 and 1542, have been discovered. On the other hand, D & E left a much smaller footprint than did Coronado.

About 12 miles west of Delta, off a short side road, stands the Gunnison Massacre Monument. Ever since I wrote a book about Kit Carson and John C. Frémont called *A Newer World,* I had been intrigued by Captain John W. Gunnison. Frémont's fourth expedition, the first he tried to conduct without the skillful guiding of Carson, turned into one of the great debacles of Western history. The only reason it's not better known today is that Frémont, who would soon make a bid for the U.S. presidency, did all he could to cover it up.

Pursuing a cockamamie scheme to survey a railroad route along the 38th parallel, Frémont led a team of thirty-three men into Colorado's La Garita Mountains in the dead of the heavy winter in 1848–49. The party got stranded in blizzards at timberline, and the retreat turned into every-man-for-himself chaos. Ten of the thirty-three men died, and survivors cannibalized the corpses. Instead of leading rescuers back into the mountains to save the stragglers, Frémont took off for California, leaving the dirty work to more humane men out of Abiquiu.

In 1853, on an army expedition, Gunnison trumped Frémont's failure by completing the survey route in admirable fashion. As he did so, he made the Anglo discovery of the Black Canyon, one of the most dramatic gorges in the United States. The Gunnison River is named after the captain. Seventy-seven years before Gunnison, in their camp on the San Xavier River on August 27, Domínguez and Escalante were only 10 miles north of the mouth of the Black Canyon, but the Sabuaganas gave the Spanish team no inkling of the great abyss nearby.

In late October 1853, Gunnison was wrapping up his survey when his camp on a nondescript bend of the Sevier River was attacked in the night by Pahvant Utes. Eight men were murdered, including the captain, and, according to the survivors, their bodies were horribly mutilated. Among the dead was Richard H. Kern, the gifted artist who had survived Frémont's catastrophe in the La Garitas five years earlier.

The Pahvant attack was presumed to be revenge for the murder of a Ute chief by an emigrant wagon train passing through Utah shortly before. But to this day a strong vein of rumor has it that Brigham Young "ordered" the Pahvants—or worse, men dressed up as Indians—to attack the government expedition. The motivation would have been the fear that a railroad would threaten the autonomous kingdom Young thought he had founded in Zion. The whole scenario sounds far-fetched—except that we now know that very much the same treachery was played out in the Mountain Meadows Massacre in 1857, which for more than a century afterward was blamed on the Paiutes. The case against Young in the Mountain Meadows tragedy has been brilliantly laid out by historian Will Bagley in *The Blood of the Prophets*. Until a Bagley puts his hand to the Gunnison Massacre, the true story may never be unearthed.

On this gray, gloomy day, we drove up to the lonely monument. Tamarisk thickets lined the nearby bank of a sluggish bend of the upper Sevier River. A stern iron rod standing vertical proclaimed the deed on the fateful date of October 26, 1853. Beside it, a lump of black stone had been cemented upright, like some Maya stela, to a concrete base festooned with white river cobbles. The plaque that explained the massacre had been pried loose from the plinth. The cashier at the Ranger Café had told us that the plaque had been stolen a few years earlier—by whom, no one knew. All in all, the grave marker seemed a desolate and inadequate memorial to one of the most gifted nineteenth-century explorers of the West. Yet the loneliness of the site seemed also to evoke the mood that had apparently overtaken the Spaniards near here in early October 1776.

As we headed back east on Route 50, just before the town of Hinckley, we came across another sort of memorial. A dead cottonwood tree standing alone beside the highway, all naked branches, served as the skeletal framework from which hung literally hundreds of pairs of tennis shoes, dangling by tied-together shoelaces. Since my teenage years in Colorado, I had seen sneakers tossed high into trees or across telephone wires. I'd always assumed that the practice reflected some high school hazing ritual. But after our trip, I found a fascinating site online that analyzed "shoe tossing" or "shoe dangling" with all the cultural rigor of a sociological treatise. Yes, the site granted, shoes could be thrown up into trees or wires by teenage bullies intimidating their victims, or by passersby to taunt drunkards, but as the practice was prevalent not only in this country but in Europe and Latin America, it could apparently also celebrate school graduations or marriages. I thought of stopping back at the Ranger Café to get the cashier's exegesis of the Hinckley cottonwood, but I doubted that even her best insider knowledge would elucidate the tribulations of the Domínguez–Escalante expedition.

After the debacle at Llano Salado, with the horses and men at last rounded up and watered and a new batch of Indians enlightened about the Gospel, the team headed south on October 3. Troublesome marshes got in the way, yet drinking water was hard to find. The interpreter, Andrés Muñiz, was thrown from his horse and pitched into a marsh, where he received "a hard blow on one cheek." After a 15-mile jaunt, the team settled for a bad camp on the treeless flats by a small gulch. "All over the arroyo," wrote Escalante, "there was a kind of white scum, dry and thin, which looked from afar like linen spread out, for which reason we named it Arroyo de Tejedor"—the Arroyo of the Weaver.

To follow the Spaniards' route, Sharon and I took State Highway 257 out of Hinckley. Escalante does not explain why the team, after making their 36-mile thrust dead west on October 1, chose now to head south once again. The second day's march, on October 4, gained only 13 miles, since the horses "were very much exhausted because the brackish waters had done them much harm."

On October 5, the team trudged another 13 miles before calling a halt. The whole day hung under the cloud of a bizarre and disturbing chain of events. In the morning, before the horses were saddled, the guide José María simply walked out of camp without a word to any of the Spaniards, heading alone back to the encampment of his people on Utah Lake. D & E saw him go but decided not to chase after him and beg him to stay on, even though, as Escalante lamented, the guide's desertion meant that "we were left without anyone who knew about the country ahead, even if from hearsay." (What was Joaquín, the other Timpanogotzis recruit, good for, if he was useless as a guide?)

At first D & E were baffled by José María's desertion, but Andrés Muñiz furnished an explanation. The night before, Juan Pedro Cisneros had summoned Simón Lucero, who was his servant, to pray the Virgin's rosary with him, but Lucero had refused. Cisneros's fury escalated from verbal abuse to blows, or at least to "grappling with him arm to arm."

This event had evidently terrified José María, especially when D & E went on with their own morning prayers without interceding in the fracas. Perceiving the guide's upset, the padres attempted to reassure him: "We tried to convince him that those involved were not angry at each other, and that even when a parent corrected his youngster as it now had happened, they never reached the point of killing each other as he was thinking, and therefore that he should not be scared." This explanation failed to placate José María, who must have thought he had fallen in with a team of strangers whose solidarity was coming apart at the seams, and who were capable of serious violence when they got angry. Even as he records his annoyance at watching José María desert, Escalante professes sorrow for the man's soul: "We felt very bad about this incident because we had wanted to hasten his salvation, which now he will not be able to attain that soon."

From this unhappy camp, the padres sent two scouts ahead "to find out if the sierra's western side . . . could be negotiated and furnished any hope of finding water sources." The men returned after dark with bad news: "They had not found any pass for traversing the sierra, that it was very high and rugged from this direction, and that ahead of it lay a wide plain without any pasturage or water source whatsoever."

As Sharon drove slowly south on Route 257, I stared out the passenger-side window, trying to make Escalante's account fit the landscape. It simply made no sense—except perhaps for the comment about the scarcity of water and pasturage. The "high and rugged sierra" that Escalante cites as a serious barrier simply doesn't exist. A pair of short chains of rocky hills stretching north to south, called the San Francisco Mountains and the Wah Wah Mountains, rise some 2,000 feet above the plain, but both are easily skirted on the north. The Spaniards' camp on October 5 was very close to the old Black Rock railroad siding. From there today a dirt road stretches, mostly in straight lines, some 60 miles to the Nevada border. Nothing but the lack of water and pasturage could have blocked the expedition. Yet Escalante claimed that the scouts' brief reconnaissance proved that "we could no longer take this direction—which was the best for getting to Monterey, where our goal lay."

Was the whole team simply psychologically played out? The weather could not have helped. "On the two previous days," wrote the chronicler, "a very cold wind from the south had blown fiercely without ceasing. This brought on a snowfall so heavy that not only the sierra's heights but even all the plains were covered with snow tonight."

For the next two days, the Spaniards never budged from camp. Snow fell all day on October 6. Exasperated, at nightfall the padres prayed, "implor[ing] the intercession of Our Mother and Patroness by praying aloud in common the three parts of her rosary and by chanting the Litany, the one of All-Saints. And God was pleased that by nine at night it should cease to snow, hail, and rain." Still the team could not pull itself together to move on the 7th. "We were in great distress, without firewood and extremely cold, for there was so much snow and water the ground, which was soft here, was unfit for travel."

Domínguez and Escalante had still not abandoned their plan to forge a route to Monterey. On October 8 they finally set out, heading south once more. The going could hardly have been worse. The ground was "so soft and miry everywhere that many pack animals and mounts, and even those that were loose, either fell down or became stuck altogether." In addition, "We suffered greatly from the cold because the north wind did not cease blowing all day, and most acutely." After a march of only nine miles, the team called a halt and set up camp. That night Miera y Pacheco used the astrolabe to get a latitude reading from the North Star. He came up with 38° 3' 30' N—about half a degree too far *south*. (Curiously, throughout the expedition, the several readings the team took by Polaris erred by half a degree to the south, while the readings by the sun were half a degree or more too far north.)

The grim conclusion that had been dawning on the padres for most of the previous week—and perhaps for even longer—now thrust itself to the forefront of their thinking. The team was too depleted. The country was too rough. Monterey was still too far away.

The primary goal of the expedition would have to be abandoned. The trip was, in its most fundamental sense, a failure.

Escalante's long journal entry on October 8 intermixes a sober reckoning of the facts with a certain amount of rationalizing. During the seventy-two days the team had been in the field since leaving Santa Fe, they had gained, by their own calculation, only about 355 miles of westward progress. In a day before longitude could accurately be measured, no one could say how much farther west Monterey stood. (In actuality, as the eagle flies, 550 miles stretched between the glum camp of October 8 and the mission Father Serra had founded in 1770.) But there were potent hints that the gulf yet to be traversed was a massive one—most saliently, "not having found among all these latter peoples [i.e., the Timpanogotzis and the bearded Indians south of Utah Lake] any reports about the Spaniards and padres of the said Monterey."

Moreover, it seemed that "winter had already set in most severely."

All the mountains the men could see in the distance were covered with snow. Passes blocked with snow could force the team to hole up for "two or three months in some sierra where there might not be any people or the wherewithal for our necessary sustenance." Despite the dried fish the Spaniards had bought from the Timpanogotzis, "the provisions we had were very low by now, and so we could expose ourselves to perishing from hunger if not from the cold."

Where the rationalizing came in was when Escalante argued that even if the team made it to California, there would be no hope of getting back to Santa Fe until June 1777. This "could be very preju-dicial to the souls which . . . yearn for their eternal salvation through holy baptism." D & E had promised the Timpanogotzis they'd be back within a year to build a mission and a town. Failing to keep that promise could lead the jilted Utes to suspect the padres had lied to them. And that in turn might jinx all efforts to "[extend] his majesty's dominions . . . in the future."

Thus D & E decided to give up the quest for Monterey and instead return directly to Santa Fe via Hopi and Zuni—with the long-cherished visit to the Cosninas (the Havasupai) as an added bonus. The padres further rationalized that by heading south and east toward home they might discover a faster and better route from Santa Fe to the land of the Timpanogotzis. Teguayó might yet be enfolded in the New Mexico colony.

In the long view of history, it was unquestionably the right decision. The only problem was that several of the padres' teammates were vehemently opposed to it. In particular, Bernardo Miera y Pacheco, Joaquín Lain, and Andrés Muñiz wanted to push on toward Monte-rey. For two days those dissidents bit their tongues as the team moved on southward, covering 16 miles each on October 9 and 10. But on the 11th, the conflict came to a head.

As the team moved sluggishly on, D & E let the three malcon-tents ride ahead, as they discussed "the means we ought to take . . . to remove from our companions . . . the extreme dissatisfaction with which they were abandoning the trip to Monterey." In the zealotry of their faith, the padres were convinced that God, "for Whom we solely wanted to travel and were ready to suffer and, if need be, to die," had ordained the decision to head toward home. But the dissenters were not about to bend to the Franciscans' resolve. "And so, from this place onward," recorded Escalante, "they came along very peevishly; everything was very onerous, and all unbearably irksome."

As they rode on, the Spaniards bickered among themselves. In vain D & E argued that the expedition had already achieved the noble goals of "having discovered such a great deal of country and people so well disposed to be easily gathered into the Lord's vineyard." The three who wanted to push on toward Monterey were adamant. Miera y Pacheco was the chief troublemaker. According to Escalante, the veteran of so many Indian campaigns "conceived without any reason whatsoever . . . grandiose dreams of honor and profits from solely reaching Monterey." Even worse, he rallied Joaquín Lain and Andrés Muñiz to his cause "by building castles in the air of the loftiest." In his scorn, Miera y Pacheco swore that if the men pushed on to the west, they would reach Monterey within a week.

The October 11 entry in Escalante's journal, covering the team's bitter internal strife, reveals the twenty-seven-year-old priest at his most sanctimonious. He berates the three objectors for everything from trying to trade with the natives to failing to keep in mind "the sole aim of this undertaking, which has been and is God's greater glory and the spreading of His faith." In Escalante's view, the dissidents were placing their worldly desires before "the business of heaven." They were "clos[ing] their eyes to the Light."

On the afternoon of September 24, Sharon and I drove south on Route 257 past Black Rock siding toward the crossroads town of Milford. There were hardly any other cars on the highway. I tried to float empathically between the clashing visions of Miera and the friars. The storm that had smothered Provo for two days was dispersing only slowly, and the scrub-and-sagebrush flats on either side of

the road announced a desolate landscape that made the padres' decision seem a logical one. The cold, the snow, the lack of firewood, the
dwindling food supply—all the conditions under which the team had
struggled in early October made the call of Santa Fe all too easy to
embrace. Miera y Pacheco's vow that Monterey lay only a week's ride
away was wildly mistaken, of course. In hindsight, had the Spaniards
heeded his dare and plunged on toward the west, they might well
have perished, all twelve of them.

But it was hard not to admire the grizzled veteran's resolve and
nerve. In a Western movie version of the Domínguez–Escalante saga,
Miera y Pacheco would be played by Gary Cooper. As he sits easily
in his saddle, hands crossed over the pommel, I can hear him taunt,
"You men of God, you're somethin' else. You can finger them beads
till the cows come home, but that ain't gonna get us to Monterey.
Head on home if you like. I'm movin' out." A twitch of the reins, a
bugle arpeggio . . .

In our agnostic twenty-first century, it's all too easy to dismiss the
faith of the padres as blind fanaticism. Escalante's insistence that God
Himself had pointed the way toward Santa Fe smacks of the righteous piety by which true believers always justify their whims and
impulses. As leaders of the expedition, Domínguez and Escalante
could have simply ordered Miera and his two henchmen to obey their
commands. Instead, on October 11, the padres did an extraordinary
thing. In Escalante's words, they chose "to search anew God's will by
casting lots—putting *Monterey* on one and *Cosnina* on the other—
and to follow the route which came out."

Back on August 19, on the banks of the Dolores River, D & E had
likewise chosen to leave the decision of the team's itinerary up to the
apparently random process of the casting of lots. But then, the matter
at hand was far less consequential, a choice merely among trails leading in three different directions. This time, the fate of the whole team
hung in the balance.

Before submitting the party's route to the crucial test, Domínguez harangued his teammates. He "set before them the obstacles and difficulties which continuing the trip to Monterey entailed," as he "held them responsible for all the evil which could now result by going on to Monterey." And he warned darkly that if the westward course prevailed, "there was to be no other leader or guide than Don Bernardo Miera."

In a footnote to the 1995 Chavez translation of Escalante's journal, editor Ted J. Warner speculates about this dramatic crux in the voyage:

> The question of just how they "cast lots" has caused considerable discussion. They probably put the two names in a hat and drew one out. Some believe they wrote the names on a flat stick and tossed it in the air and followed the route which came out on top. Some cynics have suggested that the two padres, leaving nothing to chance, put two slips in the hat each with the name *Cosnina* on it.

Whatever the actual process may have been, Escalante insists that all the men, including Miera y Pacheco, submitted to the casting of lots "in a Christian spirit," before praying fervently and "reciting the Penitential Psalms with the Litany and other orations which follow it." Then the men put their destiny in the hands of God, or chance. In what is perhaps the most anticlimactic passage in the whole journal, Escalante writes, "This concluded, we cast lots, and the one of *Cosnina* came out."

One can imagine Miera's bitterness and disappointment. But the chronicler has the last and only word: "This we all heartily accepted now, thanks be to God, mollified and pleased." In his biography of Miera y Pacheco, John Kessell demurs: "Mollified and pleased? . . . The return would test every man, regardless of what he thought of the decision."

In 1975 another pair of Bicentennial retracers, Thomas Alexander and Ted Warner (who two decades later would edit Escalante's journal), tried to fix the location of the momentous event on October 11, 1776, where the casting of lots dictated the party's homeward course toward Santa Fe. They concluded that the pivotal turn had taken place very near a point marked as "Hill 5343" on the USGS map, about five miles south of Brown Knoll. They went so far as to propose renaming the hill "Dominguez Dome" in honor of the "stern lecture" the padre had delivered to his teammates thereabouts. Sharon pulled off Highway 257 and we parked beside the nondescript bump of Point 5343. Needless to say, the hill remains officially unnamed today. Scrutinizing the journal, I decided that once more the urge to be more precise than even the most careful historiography might justify had led Warner and Alexander to pinpoint the place. Seized by a kindred temptation, I shot a meaningless photo of Point 5343 before we drove on.

Escalante could barely contain his enthusiasm for the homeward trek. As the team rode on southward from the casting of lots, the landscape, no longer stark and cold and snow-struck, turned into "good terrain," with "some hills fully clad with pastures," debouching at last into a "beautiful valley" where the team pitched their tent after dark, naming the place the Valle y Río del Señor San José, after the Virgin's husband, Joseph. Today the dry streambed of the "Río" bears the humdrum name Coal Creek.

Homeward bound the Spaniards may have been, but they were still effectively lost. Confusing the Sevier River with the Green had addled their instinctive geography. Their sole remaining Laguna guide, Joaquín, was evidently out of his depth in this southern outback, so far from the lake of his people. Escalante credits the Ute with no advice as to where to direct the team's wandering. The next day the Spaniards stumbled upon another group of Indians, in perhaps the strangest encounter with natives the explorers had experienced during their two and a half months out of Santa Fe. Riding ahead of the padres, several "companions" surprised a group of twenty men and women who were out gathering wild seeds. The whole band fled, but not before two women were "detained by force."

Escalante's account of this meeting reads as a travesty of cultural exchange. "It pained us to see them frightened so much," he writes, "that they could not even speak." Well, what would you expect, I was tempted to annotate when I first read this passage, of women "detained by force"? "We tried to take away their fear and misgivings through the interpreter and Joaquín the Laguna." Modern commentators identify these Indians as Paiutes, whose language, though cognate to the Ute that Joaquín and Andrés Muñiz spoke, may have been almost unintelligible to the Spaniards' interpreters. Throw in the women's terror at being held captive and you have a recipe for confusion. To make matters worse, both Domínguez and Escalante were deeply shocked by the appearance of the women, who "were so poorly dressed that they wore only some pieces of deerskin hanging from the waist, barely covering what one cannot gaze upon without peril." At last the team released the captive women, beseeching them "to notify their people that we came in peace, that we harmed no one, that we loved everybody."

The only reliable scrap of information the two Paiute women conveyed was that a great river lay "not very far from here." Escalante calls it El Río Grande, not to be confused with the Rio Grande in New Mexico that flows just west of Santa Fe. In a stab of geographical reorientation, the padres suspected for the first time that the river the women talked about might be the Colorado—even though when the team had crossed the same river on the outward track, back on September 5, they had called it the San Rafael and had failed to recognize it as either the Colorado or the Tizón. How the San Buenaventura, or Green River, fit into all this muddled topography seems at this point to have been beyond the friars' ken.

Eight miles farther on, the Spaniards scared up another small band of Paiutes, who also fled. Desperate for a guide who could lead them to the Cosninas, Joaquín the Laguna apparently being useless for that task, the padres sent Joaquín Lain off to capture another runaway. Lain brought the prisoner back seated behind him on his saddle. This poor man was even more traumatized than the women who had been "detained by force." He was "overly vivacious, and so intimidated that he appeared to be out of his mind. He stared in every direction, watched everyone closely, and any gesture or motion on our part startled him beyond measure."

The Spaniards tried to calm the freaked-out Paiute by giving him food and a ribbon to pin to his scanty clothes. Then they questioned him about the Cosninas, "but he gave us no clue concerning them, either because these ones called them by another name, or perhaps because he figured that if he admitted knowing them, we would forcibly take him along to lead us to them, or finally because he didn't know them." I added my own gloss to this sorry cross-examination. The captive Paiute no doubt feared for his life, and he probably could barely understand what the strange-looking white men were asking him. If he knew about the existence of the Havasupai across the Colorado River near the end of the Grand Canyon, he surely didn't call those Indians the Cosninas. But above all he wanted to survive. Tell them what you think they want to hear? An impossible task, given the linguistic gulf and the man's catatonic state.

Still the padres questioned on. Had the captive seen or heard anything about other Spaniards, especially any padres, in this region? (The wills-of-the-wisp of Father Garcés and the lost Spaniards from Coronado's time were still flitting through the brains of D & E.) The wretched prisoner had to say no: there were folks all over hereabouts, but they were all Indians like himself.

When D & E asked the man to guide them to another camp of Indians farther south, the Paiute "willingly" agreed. The next day, October 13, after a ride of only six miles, they came to the camp, where the Spaniards were disappointed to find only "a very old man, a young man, several children, and three women," though "all of them [were] handsome." The ancient Paiute agreed to join the frightened captive in guiding the Spaniards farther south. Even at the time, the "great eagerness" of the two Paiutes to accept the role of guide struck the Spaniards as fishy. Toward midday, the guides led the whole party into "a ridge-cut entirely of black lava rock which lies between two high sierras by way of a gap." In "the roughest part of this cut," the two Paiutes simply "vanished from our sight." Uncharacteristically tongue-in-cheek, Escalante writes, "We applauded their cleverness in having brought us through a place so well suited for their ruse." In retrospect, the padres realized that the very old Paiute had agreed to guide the team just so that his family could make their escape from these terrifying intruders. On a very small scale, the two Paiute "guides" had performed the same trick as the Turk who led Coronado out onto the plains of Kansas in his vain quest for Quivira. And unlike the Turk, strangled for his treachery, they managed to slip away as the Spaniards struggled with the obstacles of the black lava canyon.

* * *

WITH THE WEATHER still cold and unsettled, Sharon and I chose a motel in Cedar City over a campsite along the trail of the homeward-bound explorers. The next morning, September 25, we resigned ourselves to Interstate 15 once more, for the route the Spaniards followed for three days, from October 12 to 14, follows Kanarra and Ash Creeks down an increasingly tight canyon that the modern divided highway irons out in 33 miles of stress-free motoring. It was here that the canny Paiutes guided the expedition into the maze of black lava corridors so that they could slip away unnoticed. At 70 mph, we had to squint hard to glimpse the complexities of the terrain. Only an exit called Black Ridge rang the faintest echo of the landscape that so vexed the half-lost pioneers. As we glided along, I thought of a passage from W. H. Auden's sly poem "Et in Arcadia Ego":

> I well might think myself
> A humanist,
> Could I manage not to see
> How the autobahn
> Thwarts the landscape
> In godless Roman arrogance . . .

At Toquerville, we exited. Here the expedition camped on the evening of October 14, after negotiating sandstone cliffs and a *malpais* (badlands) that Escalante likened to volcanic slag. The travelers were exhilarated by the "very temperate country" in which they had arrived, after the brutal cold and bleakness of the plain where they cast lots and gave up on California. "The river poplars [cottonwoods] were so green and lush, the flowers and blooms which the land produces so flamboyant," marveled the chronicler. Sharon and I likewise stepped out of our SUV into a radiant sun and the warmest morning we had enjoyed in almost two weeks. I realized with mild surprise that for the first time on our whole journey, we had dipped below an altitude of 4,000 feet.

According to Warner and Alexander, the Bicentennial retracers, the Spaniards' camp was located "inside the boundaries of the town of Toquerville about two blocks due west of the old LDS chapel." On this genial Monday morning ("Comic Book Day," according to an online calendar), we paid a dutiful visit to the residential neighborhood where Escalante had admired the flowers and foliage, then stopped at the city office for further enlightenment. The two women behind the counter were fuzzy about Domínguez and Escalante but eager to be of help. One of them named a local old-timer who she said "was given a mass of documents" by an even older-timer. "I could call him up for you." By now I had learned to evade such passings of the buck. I thanked the woman, then, on the way back to the car, perused the civic plaque on the lawn. I learned that Toquerville had been settled by Mormon pioneers in 1857 and incorporated in 1882. The town was named after the local Paiute chief, one Toquer, whom the plaque praised as a "friendly" Indian with unusually "clean habits." *Toquer*, I was further informed, was the Paiute word for "black."

I wondered idly whether Toquer, had I been around in 1857, might have told me some stories his grandfather had bequeathed him about the strange white men who had passed through his homeland eight decades earlier. In my fantasy, Granddad was one of the guides who had slipped away from the expedition in 1776. The WPA guide to Utah, published in 1941, revealed that Toquerville had once been a polygamist enclave. The anonymous authors interviewed a longtime resident named Lorine Isabelle Lamb Higbee, who vividly recalled the raid of her home in the dead of night by U.S. marshals on a "polygamy hunt": "They . . . started around the house. One going one way and one the other. I had some wooden tubs filled with clear water . . . at the back. They stumbled over these and fell into my yellow rosebush. You could hear them swear a mile." Despite their ineptitude, according to Higbee, the marshals ferreted out a father of two families with numerous children and killed him. "He was a big active young man and a fighter. . . . They shot him in the back as he was crossing the field."

Between Cedar City and Toquerville, I–15 passes just west of Zion National Park. If your gaze isn't glued to the passing lanes, you can catch glimpses of the soaring red cliffs of that geologic wonder as you speed southward. Escalante makes no mention of Zion's sandstone towers and walls, but by now I'd grown accustomed to the expedition's indifference to nature on a monumental scale. And no wonder: for travelers in 1776, a generation before the Romantic poets discovered wilderness, landscape was a gauntlet of nuisances that blocked your path, not scenery to be admired.

On many previous trips, I had driven State Highway 9 through Hurricane, La Verkin, and Springdale to traverse Zion on the way to Grand Staircase–Escalante National Monument. Now, following the D & E trail, we arrowed south of Apple Valley on dirt roads that paralleled Rock Canyon and Clayhole and Hurricane washes. After the fertile oasis of Toquerville, we plunged back into desolation. Mile after mile rolled by with nary a tree in sight. Despite the three-day rainstorm just past, the creeks were bone dry. In two hours of 25 mph driving, we passed only one other vehicle. Spotting us, its driver slammed to a stop to pose an urgent question. She worked for some outfit called the Three Points Center, apparently a residential facility for troubled adolescents based in Hurricane. A bit frantically, she told us that three boys had "taken off" that morning. She was out looking for them. She enjoined us to give a call "if you see anything going on." It was only after she had receded in our rearview mirror that I realized that the woman had failed to specify whether the runaways were on foot or had stolen a car. (If the former, I thought, they wouldn't get far without water.) Nor had she indicated whom we were supposed to call if we saw anything going on. Resisting the woman's fussy anxiety, I found myself silently rooting for the delinquents' flight to freedom.

Crossing this sterile badlands on October 15, desperate to reach the Colorado River, the Spanish expedition was in trouble. That day Escalante closed his journal entry with the complaint, "Tonight our provisions ran out completely, with nothing left but two little slabs of chocolate for tomorrow." The next day, pushing on south, the team abruptly heard shouts behind them. Eight Indians were hailing the party from atop a low ridge. Returning in hopes of a parley, the padres told Andrés Muñiz to "advise them to come down without fear because we came in peace and were friends." Coaxed into approaching, the wary natives laid out strings of turquoise and seashells in hope of some kind of trade. "But they speak Yuta so differently from all the rest," Escalante mused, "that neither the interpreter nor Joaquín the Laguna could make them understand." For three hours the conversation continued in sign language. Somehow the Spaniards gleaned the information that the Colorado lay only two days' march away, "but that we could not go by the route we intended because there were no water sources, nor could we cross the river by this route for its being very much boxed in and very deep, and having extremely tall rocks and cliffs along both sides." Sign language or not, the advice the Indians gave was sound. At the place of the three-hour consultation, the team stood about 50 miles due north of the Colorado, but in a stretch where the great river plunges through some of the deepest gorges of the Grand Canyon.

Disappointing the Indians by signing that they had no goods to trade, the Spaniards begged the men to guide them, promising to pay them for their trouble. (With what? I wondered.) Somehow the natives signed back that they would lead the team partway, but that "from there we could make it alone, since they were barefoot and could not walk far." So needy were the hungry explorers that they offered to cut up hides from their saddlebags as makeshift moccasins, and at last a pair of natives—they may have been Paiutes or perhaps Mojaves, whose Yuman tongue is unrelated to Ute—agreed to guide the team a short distance.

In a long day of grim toil, the Spaniards covered less than four miles. Escalante's account is a narrative of despair. Entering the canyon the Indians led them to (today's Rock Canyon), the team stumbled and flailed, "because of the presence of so much rubble, flint, and recurring difficult and dangerous stretches. We came to a narrow defile so bad that it took us more than half an hour to get only three saddle mounts through."

In the midst of this ordeal, the two guides deserted, "prompted no doubt by their mean timidity," Escalante griped. When the men led their horses to a stagnant pool of water, the animals refused to drink. Camp that night was waterless for both men and beasts. Escalante records the hopelessness the team felt: "Tonight we were in direst need, with nothing by way of food, and so we decided to deprive a horse of its life so as not to forfeit our own; but because there was no water we postponed carrying it out until the place where there would be some."

At this point in Sharon's and my journey, and in my rereading of Escalante's journal, I began to doubt a conclusion I had come to before we left Santa Fe. All the commentators on the 1776 expedition assume that the team traveled with both horses and mules; MacGregor and Halus throw in twenty head of cattle to boot (an addition I had discounted from the start). I too had been picturing a pack train of horses and mules. But Escalante never mentions mules (in Spanish, *mulos*). Although mules were the beast of choice for carrying loads on colonial expeditions, it's possible that the four-legged caravan with which D & E traveled was made up only of horses. Escalante sometimes refers to "the animals," and he repeatedly employs the curious phrase "horse herds" (implying two different species?). But when starvation forced the men to sacrifice a pack animal for food, they might well have pondered the choice between horse or mule—and if so, the chronicler might have commented on that decision. So I began to think that perhaps there had never been mules at all—only horses.

Does it matter? Probably not. Yet for all the richness of detail in the journal, it's maddening what sorts of basic things Escalante never explains: what the men ate day after day, what weapons they carried, how they camped and cooked, even what they wore. (Surely by mid-November, their boots were wearing out!)

On September 25, driving the obscure dirt roads south of State Highway 9, even with plenty of food and water and a full tank of gas in our RAV4, Sharon and I could feel the hostility of this barren outback. In early afternoon, we stopped for a windy picnic on a stretch of road that crested a low pass in the hogback called the Hurricane Cliffs. In 1975, pausing here themselves, Bud Rusho and Gregory Crampton, two of the most accomplished retracers in the whole Bicentennial Commission platoon, proposed a signpost to celebrate the passage of the expedition. "In this area," they wrote, "the BLM has erected an elaborate historical marker commemorating the Mormon road. This would also be a good place to mark the trail of the Spaniards who opened the route a century before the Mormons."

One more Bicentennial pipe dream. Not only did Sharon and I

find no plaque or monument to hail the Domínguez–Escalante expedition, but the "elaborate" BLM marker of 1975 had vanished. In the words of Shelley, from that bleak pass across the Hurricane Cliffs, "the lone and level sands stretch far away."

The twelve men of the expedition had reached their lowest ebb in two and a half months on the trail. In the three weeks to come, things would only get worse. Much worse.

Chapter Eight

THE CROSSING OF THE FATHERS

ON SEPTEMBER 26, SHARON AND I DECIDED TO TAKE A short detour off the Spaniards' trail. Except that it wasn't really a detour so much as a shortcut into the realm of historical irony, of which the West owns more than its fair share. If the name Escalante rings any bell in the brain of the casual traveler today, it is the one that peals in Grand Staircase–Escalante National Monument, the vast federal reserve of canyons, mesas, and streams decreed by President Bill Clinton in 1996—2,937 square miles of backcountry that ought to gladden the heart of the most jaded outdoor aficionado. Three months after Sharon's and my journey, President Trump ordered that the monument be reduced in size by 47 percent, though as of this writing lawsuits brought by environmental groups have pushed the ultimate fate of that wilderness into judicial limbo.

Escalante's name on the monument derives from the Escalante River, the last major tributary of the Colorado to be discovered by Anglos, which shares its appellation with the Mormon town first settled in 1875 (population 797 in 2010). The irony is that the Domínguez–Escalante expedition never came closer to the town or river named after the junior friar than 55 miles as the raven files its flight plan. Even the farthest-sprawling corners of Clinton's generous monument keep a 15-mile distance from any of the Spaniards' 1776 footprints.

During the past quarter century I'd spent many of my best hiking and camping days within the monument. In the early 1990s, before Clinton acted, Sharon and I joined our friend Matt Hale to pack with llamas for eight days along the Escalante River and tributaries such as the Gulch, Wolverine Creek, and Little Death Hollow without running into a single other soul. In September 1996, just a week after Clinton's fiat, I'd hiked the canyons for a magazine assignment and interviewed the townsfolk of Escalante, most of whom were in favor of tarring and feathering the president who (they said) hadn't had the guts to visit the town but instead had delivered his proclamation from the rim of the Grand Canyon.

Since then, I've hiked the slot canyons, set out on four-day solo circuits, and made forays up onto remote Kaiparowits Plateau, all in homage to one of my favorite wildernesses in the Southwest. Escalante was the last town the vagabond poet Everett Ruess passed through in 1934 before he vanished. For a pair of magazine articles, and then for a book, I'd quizzed the old-timers in town who still remembered the youth sauntering through with his two burros in 1934, and I'd prowled through every corner of Davis Gulch, where Ruess's last camp was found the next spring.

Even in 2017, before Sharon and I set out on the D & E trail, friends I mentioned my "project" to assumed I'd start my researches in Grand Staircase–Escalante National Monument. By way of demurral, I recounted my favorite irony about the name and the place.

In 1875, Almon H. Thompson, a government geographer who was John Wesley Powell's brother-in-law, undertook a vast pioneering survey of some of the ruggedest country in southern Utah, including the Henry Mountains, the Aquarius Plateau, and the Kaiparowits Plateau. Coming down from Fifty-Mile Mountain (as the locals called Kaiparowits) in early August, he ran into a group of Mormons from Panguitch who were starting to lay out a town on the banks of the river that bisects this desert-like outback. Those settlers were hoping that a town at a lower elevation than Panguitch would provide a longer growing season. They had tentatively named the new settlement Potato Valley.

Thompson struck up a conversation with these hardy pilgrims. In his diary entry for August 5, he wrote, "Saw four Mormons from Panguitch who were talking about making a settlement here. Advised them to call the place Escalante." No doubt Thompson filled in the men about the glorious failure the expedition led by two Franciscan priests out of Santa Fe had prosecuted a century earlier. The locals liked the idea, and slapped the name of Escalante on the fledgling settlement.

Thompson was already referring to the river as the Escalante, even though its discoverer had called it Birch Creek. Thompson's team thus honored the padre because the river's mouth "was not a great distance up from where Escalante had crossed the Colorado." In any event, it's clear that the architects of Potato Valley knew nothing about the Domínguez–Escalante expedition until they consulted with Thompson.

Jump ahead forty-eight years. In 1923, a sociologist named Lowry Nelson came to Escalante, intent on including the town in his study of Mormon villages. He found that the locals uniformly pronounced the name "Es-ca-LANT," rhyming it with "slant" and rendering the Spanish final "e" silent. Just so the citizens pronounce the name today. When Nelson asked his informants about the origin of the name, they said that it was an old Indian word whose meaning had been lost.

Sharon and I were eager to camp out again, and it seemed appropriate to do so on some corner of the monument named after Escalante, whether or not the padre had ever set foot on the precise patch of land where we would pitch our tent. From Kanab we drove nine miles east on U.S. Highway 89, then headed north on a numberless side road. A few miles along, we stopped to behold a tableau that had outraged me ever since I discovered it five or six years earlier.

Near the turnoff for Johnson Canyon, a fenced nook of ranch land, furnished with an old corral and a sagging shed, a carpet of cow dung, a live calf or two, and forbidding entry with the usual dire "no trespassing" signs, backed against the nearly vertical sandstone cliff. More than 700 years ago, and perhaps as long as several thousand, artists had used that wall to carve a dizzying panoply of spirals, humanoids, animaloids, and abstract designs. Taken as a whole, the wall was a frenzied masterpiece.

Some of the crudest desecrations of ancient art in the West are the work of the first Anglo settlers. We found names and inscriptions dating back to 1871, and bullet holes everywhere, all of it deliberately splashed on top of the petroglyphs. John English, a painter from Omaha, had stitched his calling card here in 1895, as had John Allen, an attorney who had just hung his shingle in Kanab. Another section of the wall read like a billboard from the 1920s, inscribed in neat white painted letters:

Jensen & Brooksey
STORE & GARAGE
FREDONIA ARIZONA
GASOLINE OIL & SUPPLIES
ICE CREAM

And on the edge, like a last-minute addendum:

EASTMAN
KODAKS
AND
FILMS

Those Kilroys could have painted and carved their messages across any part of the adjoining cliff that was barren of Anasazi art. What impulse, I wondered for the nth time, made it gratifying for them to obliterate the ancients? What lost visions did they feel the need to neutralize? What spasm of nihilism did each well-placed bullet scar unleash?

We drove on, turning east on the dirt road that leads to the old Deer Springs Ranch. Here we were tiptoeing by SUV on the border between private land on the left and national monument on the right. Yet even on the Grand Staircase–Escalante side of the road, barbed wire and "no trespassing" signs flipped the finger at Clinton's 1996 decree.

I was still in a bad mood from the Johnson Canyon obscenities, but now I gave full vent to an anger that had smoldered in me for decades. What is it about the American psyche that turns private property into a sacred fetish? Which aliens is the barbed wire strung to keep out? In France, England, and Scotland I'd often hiked across private land—fenced but without barbed wire—to admire a dolmen or a set of standing stones erected more than four millennia before, in homage to gods or worship of ancestors whose identities we will never know. In Mexico, Guatemala, and Belize I'd found decorated sacrificial vessels in situ deep inside caves on private land. In these countries—indeed, in almost all the nations of the world except the United States—if you find antiquities in your front yard or back pasture, those relics belong not to you but to the state. But in the U.S., you can do whatever you want with a prehistoric clay olla or yucca basket you dig up as you plow a new field or excavate a cellar. You can display the artifact on your mantel, or sell it on eBay, or—like the cronies of the father of the woman I'd talked to in Dove Creek—set it up on a rock and blast it for target practice. At the Edge of the Cedars Museum in Blanding, Utah, there's a room stacked from floor to ceiling with stunning pots and effigy vessels, some of them unearthed on private property, but most illegally dug out of public land by "owners" who then lied about the artifacts' proveniences.

I could go on about what dark traits in the American character this peculiar conception of ownership, not only of land but of the immemorial past, seems to validate, but pontificating is not my favorite pose. Let me mention, though, a certain basin in New Mexico, all of it owned by ranchers whose deeds date back to the colonial land grants with which Spain enriched its favorite citizens in the seventeenth and eighteenth centuries, and whose descendants have put up some of the most threatening "no trespassing" signs (warning of "full prosecution under the law") for the most timid encroachments on their sacred acres. That basin also happens to be one of the richest repositories of dazzling Anasazi rock art, much of it blazoning forth nascent images of the kachina religion that still glues together the spiritual life of the pueblos—as well as the locus of the slumbering ruins of at least seven major villages. I'm proud to say that I've made more than a dozen "illegal" visits to this wonderland, ducking under the barbed wire, slinking from arroyo to outcrop, without pocketing a single potsherd or touching a single petroglyph. Each time I return, it's with a dark song in my head, the refrain of which goes something like, *No one has the right to "own" these prodigies of the human soul.*

By 4 PM, Sharon and I had found a perfect pullout on the monument side of the road, unblemished by barbed wire, to serve as our campsite. We pitched our tent, gathered downed wood for a fire, and then sat in our camp chairs drinking (without intentional irony) Mexican beer. The wind that had gusted all day died to a whisper. We were perched on the edge of a drop-off that opened on a panoramic view northeast. As the sun lowered behind us, we gazed down on the distant hamlets of Cannonville and Tropic (where Everett Ruess had picked apples with the local kids and "almost" fallen in love with a Mormon girl). Beyond that valley, softening in the last sunlight, stretched the long massif of the Escalante Mountains, and way beyond that, reduced to blue silhouettes, the Henry Mountains.

My mood had shifted by 180 degrees. I felt a weary contentment. In two hours, only a pair of cars passed by, their occupants tossing us waves of the hand. "You know," I said to Sharon, "now that they're in serious trouble, I feel more sympathetic with those guys."

"Domínguez and Escalante, you mean."

"Yeah. They all get really pissed off at each other, but they never split up."

After a moment or two, Sharon said, "I was surprised by the casting of lots."

"Because?"

"The padres could just have decided for the whole team. Ordered the others to turn back. Instead, they were willing to put it up to— what would you call it?"

"A cosmic test?"

"Something like that."

I took a sip of beer. "If they didn't rig it, the casting of lots shows how much they believed God would decide for them."

"They could have held a vote."

"Yep. And I'll bet it would have come out nine to three in favor of Cosnina. Of turning back. If you can trust the journal, only the three guys led by Miera really wanted to go on to Monterey."

Sharon rummaged through our food bags. "What do you want for dinner?"

"I don't know," I sighed. "I'm never hungry." I knew I needed to eat, but I said, "Let's wait an hour or so."

After a longer silence, I went on, "You know, when we started out, I wasn't sure I could finish this whole trip." Sharon nodded. "I half expected some collapse like at Mammoth or Hanover. Or a really bad sodium reading in Durango or Provo."

"We're lucky. Or we're doing it right."

"And now," I said, "I'm sorry it's almost over."

"Me, too."

We looked at each other. There was a flicker of nervousness in Sharon's smile. It wasn't just the trip, I realized, that we didn't want to end. That's what cancer had come to mean.

"I could eat a salad," I said. "Are the vegetables in the cooler?"

Later, with a few pieces of lettuce soaked in blue cheese dressing wilting on my paper plate, I threw out a thought. "One thing you can't get around is that D & E were pretty brave. They're in such bad shape they're about to eat one of their horses, but the whole point of the journey is still in their heads."

"It helps to believe in God," said Sharon.

"Blind faith. Why do we say that true belief is blind?"

"But you admire them, don't you? They're like Joan of Arc."

"Or John Brown at Harpers Ferry. It helps if you yourself believe in their cause. Otherwise they're just fanatics."

Sharon chuckled. "I can't even remember what Joan of Arc's cause was."

"Something to do with saving France from the Brits. You could look it up." I moved my camp chair to catch the last rays of sun angling through the junipers. "You know," I went on, "I don't believe at all in the padres' cause. Converting the savages. Cramming Jesus and the Gospel down the throats of polytheistic Indians. But in 1776, cultural relativism hadn't yet been invented." I took a slow breath. In my voice I heard the long-dormant tone of the professor I'd once been, but I had to finish the thought. "I don't for a minute respect what they were trying to do with the Utes. But I admire them anyway."

Now Sharon's smile was unconflicted. "This would be a hard trip to do if we didn't. Admire them, I mean. Yes, they were like Joan of Arc. What they were after was all worth dying for."

"You mean Monterey?"

"No," said Sharon. "Something more abstract. Something to do with God."

"God's hand in the wilderness?"

As if the team's plight was not already desperate enough, on October 17 Miera y Pacheco fell seriously ill. He "became so weakened that he could barely talk," wrote Escalante. Even so, the team covered 12 miles by midday. In an arroyo they discovered some weeds they thought might be edible, "but we could gather only a very few, and these tiny." Later they searched the saddlebags in which they had carried their food for months, hoping to find "leftovers," but all they dug up was some pieces of squash that the "servants"—presumably men such as Simón Lucero, whom Juan Pedro Cisneros had beaten on October 5, triggering the desertion of José María, the Laguna guide—had traded with the Paiutes to obtain the day before "and had hidden to avoid having to share them with the rest." The team added these scraps to "a bit of brown sugarloaf" the men had found in a saddlebag, and "made a concoction for everybody and took some nourishment."

As Escalante's entry about the "servants" hiding food indicates, the fragile solidarity of the team was crumbling. That afternoon, D & E disagreed with "the companions" about which way to proceed. An unauthorized scout to the east led its adherents to predict "flat country with many arroyos where there had to be good water." The padres were in favor of a beeline south toward the Colorado River, but they decided to humor their "companions." By evening, Escalante—addict of the second guess—recorded the error of the scouts' prognostication. Without water after a day's ride of 23 miles, the padres declared a camp. At once two of the "scouts" set off again, swearing they had seen water from a distance and promising to bring some back for the whole team. They were gone all night and failed to return by morning. Escalante peevishly concluded that the men had ridden ahead to find Indian camps, had bartered there for food, and had in effect deserted. On the morning of October 18, the rest of the team saddled up and headed onward without bothering to search for their missing teammates.

Despite the loyalty to one another the Spaniards had nurtured on the long trail out from Santa Fe, now their sense of a common purpose was disintegrating. Even if some of the men weren't hiding pieces of squash so they wouldn't have to share them, the fact that Escalante would accuse them of such a fundamental breach of comradeship betrays the collapse of the team's unity. And though one or two (or five) men had gotten separated from the others at various points on the expedition, now for the first time the padres refused to search for their missing comrades.

During the next three days, Miera's serious illness failed to heal. Somehow the veteran kept up with his marginally healthier teammates, as they pushed on south and east toward their fateful confrontation with the Colorado River. On October 18, frantically searching for water, the men discovered five Indians peering down on them from a high mesa. When D & E redirected their course in hopes of a meeting, four of the natives hid while the fifth ignored the padres' entreaties to approach. "We could not persuade him to come down," noted Escalante. "At each step we took, as we came closer to him, he wanted to take off. We let him know that he did not have to be afraid, that we loved him like a son and wanted to talk with him."

At last the Spaniards achieved a tête-à-tête with the skittish Paiutes. With Andrés Muñiz and Joaquín the Laguna doing their best to interpret, after an exchange lasting an hour the Indians revealed that a good water source lay near at hand. "We begged them to come along and show it to us, promising them a swatch of woollen cloth, and after much urging three of them consented to go with us." The Paiutes led the men, "very much exhausted from thirst and hunger," about five miles across "a bad and very rocky route," to two good water holes. When the horses were brought up, they drained the pools dry. Even so, the team was too played out to move on. Escalante indicates that the Indians were shocked to learn that the Spaniards were out of food. Enticed by the promise of more goods in trade, one of the Paiutes offered to set off for their "humble abodes, which were somewhat distant," and come back with food. After midnight the man returned with "a small quantity of wild sheep meat, dried cactus prickly pear done into cakes, and seeds from wild plants."

The next day twenty Paiutes arrived at the Spaniards' camp with more food. "We paid them for everything they brought, and we charged them to bring meat, piñon nuts, and more cactus pear if they had any, that we would buy it all, especially the meat." Escalante does not record what goods the team "paid" for the food with—more swatches of cloth, perhaps, or more glass beads? If the Spaniards were humiliated to be begging food from Indians whose own supplies of cactus pear and wild seeds were probably limited, the chronicler does not confess to any such chagrin. Foremost in the minds of the Spaniards was anxiety about the impending crossing of the Colorado, so that when the Paiutes not only conveyed the distance to the great river but "a few vague directions with regard to the ford," the men were heartened.

In camp on October 19, one way or another the padres orchestrated a far-ranging discussion with their visitors. None of the Paiutes would admit to knowing anything about the Cosninas, though the usual linguistic confusion must have hindered the exchange of information. Even though the men had given up the quest for California eight days before, they were still hoping to learn how far away the original goal of the expedition might be. But when they were asked about "the Spaniards at Monterey," the Paiutes showed "not the least indication of their having been spoken of." Improbably, one of the Indians reported that "he had heard about the journey of the Reverend Padre Garcés."

Puzzling over this entry in Escalante's journal, I wished for the umpteenth time that we could know what really took place in the October 19 camp, that we could somehow retrieve the Paiute perspective on the parley. It seems likely that the natives still harbored a deep distrust of the white-skinned strangers who had staggered into their homeland, for when D & E pleaded with the men to guide them on to the Colorado, they refused.

* * *

FRESH FROM OUR CAMP in the national monument, Sharon and I caught up with the Spaniards on U.S. Highway 89A east of Fredonia, Arizona. Here the road, and the route the Spaniards took, climbs from the desert up onto the ponderosa-thronged Kaibab Plateau. In 30 miles of easy driving we gained almost 2,400 feet of elevation, from 5,500 feet above sea level at Fredonia to 7,925 at Jacob Lake. The Spaniards had hoped to avoid the plateau, but it seemed as though there was no bypassing the arduous climb if they hoped to reach the Colorado River at a place where it could be forded. In that stretch of highway the temperature gauge on the dashboard of our SUV dropped from 66° to 52°.

Writing for the Bicentennial Commission in 1975, Gregory Crampton insists that the precise path the Spaniards followed here was not today's Highway 89A but "the Winter Road, an alternate route across the Kaibab used in the 1930s when U.S. Highway 89 was closed." My maps gave no hint of this old thoroughfare, so as we pulled into Jacob Lake—an outpost on national forest land and the main gateway to the North Rim of the Grand Canyon—I was hopeful that local knowledge would fill in the blank.

It was only September 27, but already the touristy village felt as though it was shutting down for winter. At 1:30 PM on a Wednesday, the visitor center was closed. The only alternative was the motel-cum-gift shop. Judging from the kitschy Indian knicknacks on sale, we had made the transition from Ute to Navajo, even though the Spaniards had encountered only Paiutes hereabouts. I asked the woman behind the counter about the old winter road favored by travelers in the 1930s. "You should talk to Tommy in the dining area," she replied. "He's lived here his whole life."

It took me a few minutes to locate Tommy. At once he said, "I don't know about that. You should ask my uncle Johnny. He's in the gift shop." I trudged back to the racks of fake silver bracelets and dreamcatchers. Johnny indeed worked there, but at the moment he was "not available."

I sighed. The old winter road would have to go undiscovered, at least by me on our present journey. I wished I'd gotten to know Crampton before he died in 1995, for no one was master of more half-forgotten Southwest lore than he. As a teenager I had pondered the marvels of his classic celebration of the canyonlands, *Standing Up Country*, long before I'd ever seen Shiprock, let alone the Totem Pole or Spider Rock.

By nightfall on October 22 the Spaniards had crossed the Kaibab Plateau, despite "plenty of difficulty and fatigue experienced by the horse herds, because it was very rocky, besides having many gulches." Darkness fell as the men were still descending from the divide, so they headed for a pair of fires they saw glowing in the distance. D & E had sent the two interpreters ahead to search for water, so the team assumed it was they who had built the fires. But when they arrived, they found Andrés Muñiz and Joaquín the Laguna attempting to converse with Indians around their own fires. As the whole team came up in the darkness, the Paiutes panicked and all but three men and two women fled. One of the women pleaded with Joaquín, "Little brother, you belong to our very own kind; do not let these people with whom you come kill us."

The padres tried to convey their usual reassurances, emphasizing that the team came in peace and harbored only fond, loving feelings for the natives. "They calmed down a bit," noted Escalante, "and in an effort to please us presented us with two roasted jackrabbits and some piñon nuts." They also led the Spaniards to a nearby spring, where the horses greedily drank.

Gregory Crampton located this camp with great certainty at Coyote Spring, in the cleft that connects House Rock Valley with Coyote Wash, since "there is no other springwater north or south for several miles." In 1975 a rancher from Kanab told Crampton how the source got its name. At some point after the Spaniards passed through, drifting sands completely covered the spring. It was only when coyotes dug through the sand to get to the water that local ranchers rediscovered and developed the font. D & E named their campsite San Juan Capistrano, after the fifteenth-century Italian saint and fellow Franciscan, Giovanni da Capistrano, whose accomplishments included burning fifty Jews to death in the Polish city of Wroclaw in 1453. The cliff swallows of Capistrano, made famous in a 1940 hit song, allude to the California town named after the saint, where a Catholic mission was founded during the months the Domínguez–Escalante expedition was in the field.

At the Capistrano campsite, the team rested only 25 miles in a straight line from the Colorado River, but it would take them four more days to reach its banks. One of the reasons for the delay was something that happened in the wee hours of October 22–23, an event that so disturbed the padres that it provoked by far the angriest outburst against any of their teammates in the whole of Escalante's journal.

That evening, Miera y Pacheco was still as sick as he had been since October 17; if anything, his ailment had grown worse. After the friars had gone to bed, Miera, with several of his teammates, conveyed his distress to the Paiutes. On hearing the Spaniard's complaint, one elderly Indian "set about to cure him with chants and ceremonials." In the journal Escalante professes not to know whether the veteran soldier asked for such treatment or was spontaneously offered it by the old shaman. From the Franciscan point of view, Indian cures, "if not overt idolatries (which they had to be), were wholly superstitious."

Domínguez and Escalante were wakened by the medicine man's chanting. Soon they learned that not only Miera himself but the unspecified teammates had "gladly permitted" the cure. Most leaders of Spanish expeditions would simply have shrugged at Miera's turning to the Paiutes for a remedy, but Domínguez and Escalante were horrified. In their view, Miera and his accomplices "hailed [the curing ceremony] as indifferent kindly gestures when they should have prevented them for being contrary to the evangelical and divine law which they profess, or at least they should have withdrawn."

It's hard not to see this whole fiasco from Miera y Pacheco's point of view. For six days straight he had been seriously ill, with stomach pains so severe that he had trouble riding his horse. Over the years he'd spent so much time among Indians that he'd surely witnessed curing ceremonies performed by the medicine men of various tribes. Perhaps he'd even seen victims miraculously recover. Whatever treatment the padres were offering him for his ailment—treatment never specified in Escalante's journal—it wasn't working. Why not give the Paiute shaman a whirl?

Intriguingly, though Escalante never says that Miera felt better after October 22, there are no more entries recording the victim's illness. Maybe Paiute medicine—or the placebo effect—had done the trick.

What begins in Escalante's journal as a rebuke of Miera and the teammates for trafficking in Indian superstition quickly turns into a tirade. It's as if, in the padres' minds, everything that had gone wrong on the expedition could be blamed on the "companions" who interacted with the savages either for the wrong reasons or in ways that betrayed their dangerous ignorance. Escalante verges on blaming all that's rotten in the state of New Mexico on Spaniards who failed to distinguish between truth and idolatry. Even at a distance of 241 years, Escalante's shock at Miera's transgression is itself shocking.

On the morning of October 23, having learned of the shenanigans that Miera and crew had participated in, D & E were "extremely grieved by such harmful carelessness and we reprimanded them, instructing them in doctine so that they would never again lend their approval to such errors." This lecture by the young, unworldly priests must really have stuck in Miera's craw. But of course we don't have the veteran's own journal (if he kept one) to give the other side of the story.

Escalante's tantrum had only begun. Behavior like the midnight séance with the shaman, he insisted, was "one of the main reasons why infidels who have most dealings with the Spaniards and Christians in these parts show more resistance to the truth of the Gospel, and their conversion becomes more difficult each day." As an example of his teammates' malfeasance, Escalante digs up the little speech Andrés Muñiz had made to the first group of Sabuaganas the team had met near the Gunnison River. Trying to convey Catholic doctrine to the Utes, poor Muñiz had explained, "The padre says that the Apaches, Navajos, and Comanches who are not baptized cannot enter heaven, and that they go to hell where God punishes them, and they will burn forever like wood in the fire." That sounded to me like a fair (if slightly crude) exposition of the Church's position on heaven and hell, but according to Escalante, the Sabuaganas "became overjoyed on hearing themselves excluded, and their foes included, in the unavoidable destiny of either being baptized or of being lost forever." The padres attributed Muñiz's oversight to the venal motive of trying to get in the Sabuaganas' good graces so that at some future date he could return to engage in "the despicable fur trade." Back on September 22, on hearing what Muñiz had told the Sabuaganas, the padres had "reprimanded" the interpreter, so that "he changed his conduct on seeing his stupid puny faith exposed."

D & E had apparently heard tales from their teammates of other occasions when Spaniards, including themselves, had participated in Indian "idolatries." Thus, Escalante sorrowfully imagines, "what will they not do while wandering three or four months among the infidel Yutas and Navajos with no one to correct them or restrain them?"

The despicable fur trade was not the only temptation for weak-willed Spaniards in Indian country. The padres knew that "when some go to the Yutas and remain among them in their greed for pelts, others go after the flesh which they find here for their bestial satisfaction." Sex with savages was a kind of ultimate horror for the padres, who had found the sight of Paiute women in skimpy loin-cloths intolerable. Escalante closes his diatribe of October 22—unique in the journal—with a chilling prayer: "Oh, with how much severity should similar events be attended to? May God in His infinite goodness inspire the most suitable and practical means."

Throughout Sharon's and my long journey, and for months before and after, I had found my greatest challenge to be trying to see the world through the Franciscan eyes of Domínguez and Escalante. About that matter, I had consulted both my professor mentors, Steve Lekson and Matt Liebmann. Steve had jauntily replied by email, "If you want to get inside D & E's heads, take Franciscan orders. Or you could do like Sir Richard Burton getting into Mecca, wear the cowl and infiltrate a Franciscan monastery." Matt gave me a more practical answer. "I always tell my students that in the eighteenth century the worldview of the friars in New Mexico was closer to that of the Puebloans than it is to ours today. Both believed that forces for good and evil were abroad in the world. They might have been invisible, but they were real, active, powerful. For the Franciscans, the devil was there in the room when they dealt with natives."

This exegesis helped me understand why from D & E's point of view, Miera's seeking a cure from a Paiute shaman was so much worse than merely accepting "indifferent kindly gestures." It was entering into a compact with evil beings.

I realized that to understand Domínguez and Escalante, I needed to go back to Francis of Assisi himself, of whom I had little more that the Disneyfied image of the patron saint of animals with adoring birds flitting about his head. What struck me on further probing into the life of the founder of the Franciscan order (1182–1226) was the man's hunger for martyrdom as the fulfillment of God's design. As a young missionary he sailed to Jerusalem, only to have shipwreck turn him back to Italy; on the way to Morocco he fell ill and never got beyond Spain. On the Fifth Crusade, he was captured by Muslims and brought before the Sultan of Egypt, who somehow took a liking to the earnest priest and sent him back to the Crusader camp unharmed.

Francis died peacefully at age forty-four in Italy while singing Psalm 142. But one of the dicta for which his followers most admired him was the statement that "a servant of God ought always to desire to die and to end by the death of a martyr." That genuine death wish, so anathematic to our modern sensibility, helped explain, I thought, Domínguez and Escalante's repeated answers, whenever Indians warned them that the tribe the next valley over would surely kill them, that they had nothing to fear because God was on their side.

Father Garcés himself managed to achieve true Franciscan martyrdom. Having survived his bold eleven-month ramble with no European partners across California and Arizona, he was trapped by a violent upheaval among the Yuma Indians to whom he was ministering in 1781. As he took refuge with soldiers and settlers in the church, he listened to them quarreling bitterly about who was to blame for the predicament. "Let's forget now whose fault it is," said Garcés, "and simply consider it God's punishment for our sins." Those were his last words before the Yumas clubbed him to death.

It was by no means inevitable that it would be Franciscans, rather than Dominicans or Jesuits, who would be in charge of the formidable job of making Christians out of the natives of New Spain. Shortly after conquering the Aztecs, Cortés asked Emperor Charles V of Spain to send Franciscan friars to minister to the natives (secular priests, Cortés believed, would fall into corruption). In 1524, only three years after the end of the conquest, twelve Franciscans arrived, "animated," writes Fernando Cervantes in *The Devil in the New World*, "by a fervent millenarian hope in the rebirth of the Church in the New World."

The early success of the Franciscans in New Spain, as thousands of Indians thronged the plazas to listen to the word of God and to undergo baptism, not only convinced the friars that the Puebloans were eager to have their superstitious veils torn from their eyes but that the millennium was at hand. Priests gathered up pagan idols and systematically destroyed them with little apparent native resistance. It took some time to realize that Puebloan religion, far from being obliterated, had simply gone underground, to be practiced in secret.

When the Franciscans learned that the old pagan religion was still being observed in clandestine rites performed in hidden sanctums, fury replaced benevolence. Seizing and smashing the stone and wood and feather idols did little to suppress the religion. As Cervantes writes, "Idolatry was deemed so widespread that in the early 1530s the Franciscan Archbishop of Mexico . . . saw fit to implement the first inquisitorial practices against idolatrous and superstitious Indians."

The padres believed not merely that native shamans had lapsed into their old ways but that the devil himself was alive and subverting the common good in New Spain.

The war against heresy and false gods came to a climax in 1562, under the aegis of Diego de Landa, archbishop of the diocese of Yucatán in Mexico. On learning of rampant idolatries being practiced in the small town of Mani, he ordered all the codices—the folding-screen "books" on which the only thoroughly written language to evolve in North America carried on the tradition of the hieroglyphic literacy of Classic Maya civilization (250–900 AD)—burned in a great public bonfire. For the epigraphers at the end of the twentieth century, Landa was the arch-villain; yet, ironically, the *Relación de las Casas de Yucatán* that he was later compelled to write contained a half-digested explanation of the alphabet of the codices that served for the epigraphers as something like a Maya Rosetta Stone that finally cracked the code.

Landa was not content to burn books. According to Cervantes, his inquisition ended up executing 158 natives, mostly priests, and mostly by burning at the stake. "At least thirteen committed suicide rather than face the inquisitors," writes Cervantes. "Eighteen disappeared; and many were crippled for life."

As recounted in chapter 1, the Franciscan predilection for cruel and violent treatment of heretics or even underlings deemed insufficiently servile persisted into the seventeenth century, as exemplified by Father Guerra's beating of the Hopi man, then smearing turpentine in his wounds until he died. Against that legacy of tyranny and physical punishment, the treatment of the Indians by Domínguez and Escalante stands as a strong counterexample, for no matter how forcibly the two padres harangued the Utes and Paiutes about the true Way, they never once (if the journal can be trusted) laid a hand or a whip on a native in anger.

In New Mexico, the Dominicans and Jesuits never really got a foothold. The history of the colony would have been quite different if they had. The Dominicans, in particular, were critical of how facilely the Franciscans baptized the natives; for, once baptized, an Indian could not be abandoned. Bartolomé de las Casas, the priest whose early treatise *A Short Account of the Destruction of the Indies* stands today as an astonishingly prescient condemnation of slavery and the mistreatment of Indians in the colonies, was a Dominican. As for the Jesuits, they went out of their way to learn the native languages, as the Franciscans almost never did. How differently Escalante's journal would read—indeed, how differently would the journey have proceeded—if Domínguez or Escalante had been even semi-fluent in Ute, Paiute, or Hopi.

Because Escalante never mentions the Pueblo Revolt of 1680, I found myself wondering how large that cataclysm, which took place some seventy years before he was born, had loomed in his thoughts as he set out in 1776 to convert the heathens. His hopefulness of success at Hopi, both in 1775 and 1776, seems almost naive when weighed against the torture and killing of the priest and burning of the church to the ground in 1680.

An excellent scholarly book written by a Franciscan, Jim Norris's *After "The Year Eighty,"* gave me a vivid answer. The high point of Franciscan power in the colony came in the 1650s, when about seventy Franciscan priests served in forty-three different missions. By 1680 their number was down to thirty-three, of whom twenty-two died in the Revolt. So scarifying had that insurrection been for the Franciscan order that ever after it was referred to as *el año ochenta,* "the year eighty." Throughout the eighteenth century, the church struggled to regain its power and importance in the colony. But by 1776, when D & E set out, the whole Franciscan establishment was in tawdry decline. Domínguez's assignment to survey all the missions, which resulted in the important book *The Missions of New Mexico, 1776,* was an ambitious effort to take stock of the state of Franciscan affairs in the colony. For Domínguez, it was a deeply dismaying year's work. Norris quotes not from the finished compendium so much as from Domínguez's letters to his superior, Fray Isidro Murillo. There he condemns friars in El Paso for being too lazy to teach the neophytes anything, as well as priests who were having affairs with married women. Padres at Sandia and Isleta were getting rich and fat by robbing their charges. Others were too ill or feeble-minded to carry out their duties; two were "notorious drunkards"; some were embezzlers; others had let the missions' holdings fall into rickety disrepair. Of seven particular friars among different pueblos, Domínguez observed, "They are depraved, disobedient, bold characters and brothers who carry knives and blunderbusses as if they were highwaymen." Summing up the sorry state of affairs, Domínguez concluded that fully half the Franciscans serving in New Mexico should be fired.

Against this sordid backdrop, the expedition Domínguez and Escalante undertook in 1776 to find a route to Monterey ought to be seen as an attempt to build a valedictory monument for 250 years of Franciscan stewardship in New Spain. Viewed in that light, D & E were unquestionably heroes, even if their great journey ended in failure.

* * *

ON OCTOBER 23 the Spaniards slaughtered a horse, then cut it up into pieces suitable for carrying. Yet that day they never left camp at San Juan Capistrano, because now Domínguez himself fell ill with "a severe anal pain, so that he could not even move about." The next morning twenty-six Indians arrived in camp. Despite their fearfulness, the Paiutes were evidently intrigued by the advent of the strangers. And despite the Spaniards' weakened and demoralized condition, D & E seized the missionary opportunity: "We preached the Gospel to them, decrying and explaining to them the wickedness and futility of their evil customs, most especially with regard to the superstitious curing of their sick. We made them understand that they should seek help in their troubles only from the one and true God, because His Majesty alone has power over health and sickness, over life and death, and is able to help everyone." According to Escalante, rather than resist this spiritual dressing-down, the Paiutes "listen[ed] with pleasure," and when the friars asked them if they would like to become Christians, they readily assented. As they had with the Timpanogotzis, the padres promised to come back with settlers and more priests.

At last the team got moving, but it was not until October 26 that they reached the banks of the Colorado, about where the Paria River flows into the great current, just downstream from today's boat launching point of Lees Ferry and the Navajo Bridge, across which Route 89A effortlessly whisks vehicles ranging from convertibles to Winnebagos. Perhaps this is the spot where the Paiutes had indicated the river could be crossed, for that very afternoon the Spaniards made their first attempt. Escalante's account of the effort sounds almost comical, until one considers just how dire the failure threatened to become.

Ever since August 14, when they had sneaked up on and then reluctantly been allowed to join the expedition, the two "hitchhikers," Felipe and Juan Domingo, had gone virtually unmentioned in Escalante's journal. Now, however, the chronicler identifies them as the two best swimmers on the team. So the trial crossing was up to them. The pair "entered the river naked with their clothes upon their heads."

It was so deep and wide that the swimmers, in spite of their prowess, were barely able to reach the other side, leaving in midstream their clothing, which they never saw again. And since they became so exhausted getting there, nude and barefoot, they were unable to walk far enough to do the said exploring, coming back across after having paused a while to catch their breath.

Presumably the hypothermic *genízaros* were given clothes by their teammates to replace the ones lost in the bold swim.

But it was a grim omen. For the next eleven days, the Spaniards poked and prodded through the cliffs and creases of the tortured landscape on the northern bank of the Colorado, searching for a viable ford. By October 29, every scrap of the slaughtered horse had been consumed, so the padres "ordered another horse killed."

The campsite at the mouth of the Paria River served as an unwelcome base. With uncharacteristic humor, the friars named the camp not after a beloved saint but rather San Benito de Salsipuedes. "Salsipuedes" means "Get out if you can." And editor Ted J. Warner points out that "a 'San Benito' to the New Mexican Franciscan of the eighteenth century referred to a garish white cassock with colored markings worn by errant brothers as a mark of punishment."

On October 28 the team made a second attempt to cross the raging current, this time with a driftwood raft. Escalante himself and the "servants" set out on the fragile craft. The poles the men had cut from driftwood to use instead of oars were 15 feet long, but only a short way off shore they failed to touch bottom. Three times the raft drifted back to the near bank.

After this setback, the padres sent Andrés Muñiz and his brother Lucrecio off to scout a route upstream and look for a better ford. This was no matter of simply hiking along the bank, for a high cliff and mesa blocked all progress only a few miles upstream from Salsipuedes. The brothers would have to scramble inland to summit the mesa, then find their way back to the river through other cliffs and draws. For three days the rest of the team simply waited, starving and scared.

Sharon and I got to Lees Ferry by early afternoon on September 27. Curiously, we had found a trailside marker on Highway 89A at the site of the Spaniards' camp on October 24 on a low mound called Emmett Hill, just east of House Rock Valley, but no memorial of the expedition at Lees Ferry, where the fate of the team hung in limbo. Instead all the signage commemorated John D. Lee, the renegade Mormon, exiled from Brigham Young's Zion, who established the crossing of the Colorado by homemade ferry here. In 1887 Lee was executed for his role as a ringleader in the Mountain Meadows Massacre, the sole conspirator among a cadre of prominent Mormons that may have had the approval of the Prophet himself ever to be brought to justice.

I'd been to Lees Ferry several times before, including on the launch of a two-week rafting trip down the Grand Canyon in the mid-1990s. But Sharon had never visited the Grand Canyon, and even though its gateway at Lees Ferry gives only the faintest hint of the glories to come downstream, she was transported by the grandeur of the place. "Right away, I couldn't believe how fast the river was running," she said later. "I wanted to get in a boat and just go down into that mystery. And all around us the cliffs were magnificent. Everything was beautiful except for the parking lot." Indeed, the massive boat-launching platform, dirt shelving into metal ramps, scattered with empty vans that had dropped commercial rafts here, was the usual put-in eyesore times three.

On the afternoon of November 1, the Muñiz brothers returned from their three-day scout with great news: they had found a way up and over the mesa to the northeast, then a way back to the river where a ford was possible. Meanwhile the temperature had dropped, and the men waiting in camp had added an "exceedingly cold" night to their privations.

Full of hope, the whole team set out on the Muñiz bypass on November 2. It took them two days to cover 17 miles. Escalante's journal is a laundry list of complaints about the terrain: "extremely difficult stretches and most dangerous ledges," "cliff-lined gorges," "a stretch of red sand which was quite troublesome for the horse herds," "such terrible rock embankments that two pack animals which descended the first one could not make it back, even without the equipment." And then, when at last the team got to the promised ford, the padres judged it impossible. Escalante, so quick to criticize the "guides" and "experts" within his party, was unsparing in his contempt for the brothers Muñiz: "Here we learned that they had not found the ford either, nor in so many days made the necessary exploration of so small a space of terrain, for their having wasted the time looking for those Indians who live hereabouts, and accomplished nothing."

On three separate outings in 1973 and 1974, Bud Rusho, Gregory Crampton, and another Bicentennial researcher, Don Cecala, pieced together what they thought was the tortuous route reconnoitered by the Muñiz brothers and followed by the expedition with the horse herd. Their research demanded approaches by foot from the west and by jeep from the east. Even so, at least one of their forays was terminated when "exhaustion set in." All in all, this clever traverse of the ridges and mesa that caused the starving Spaniards so much trouble represents the Commission's finest effort on the whole route to rediscover the pathway of the pioneers where it was most enigmatic. Rusho named the high saddle at about 4,800 feet where the descent begins Dominguez Pass, "in honor of the often-neglected head of the 1776 expedition."

On my USGS maps, I could follow the precise route the retracers took. Dominguez Pass even appears on the map, apparently an official name. Before cancer, I would have set out at once to hike the beguiling route as it twists between fins and slots. The maps indicate a "pack trail" along that outback, but I doubted that nowadays more than a tiny handful of hardcore desert rats bothered to explore it. Even in 1975, Rusho reported that "cattlemen in the area are unaware of the long unused pass." Today all the "recreation" in this part of Arizona focuses on raft trips down the Grand Canyon and on houseboats on Lake Powell. If you simply want to cover the eight airline miles between Lees Ferry and the town of Page (which is what the Spaniards had to do), U.S. Highways 89 and 89A offer an effortless alternative. That was the route Sharon and I took that afternoon, saving the rugged trail through the slickrock domes and pockets for another life.

Thoroughly disgusted by the false expectations the Muñiz brothers had raised, D & E balked at descending all the way to the river, for fear that if the ford didn't "go," the horses might not be able to backtrack up the steep and rocky slope. They could see that the river was slower and broader here than at Salsipuedes, but the glitch was a narrow canyon on the far side that offered the only way onward. If that canyon boxed out, the expedition could be caught in a trap. Still, several "companions" were ravenously urging the team to give the ford a try. Instead, the padres delegated their ace swimmer, Juan Domingo, to make the crossing and explore the narrow canyon beyond. (No mention in the journal if this time the *genízaro* swam naked with his clothes on his head!) The man was beseeched to return by late afternoon so the party could move on if the ford proved untenable. Shortly thereafter, humiliated perhaps by his scolding from the padres, Lucrecio Muñiz volunteered to ride a horse bareback across the river and support Juan Domingo's reconnaissance. He "[took] along the things needed to make a fire" and promised to "[send] up smoke signals in case he found an exit." Lucrecio, too, was enjoined to return before nightfall.

At this point, virtually without food, wasting precious effort to find water holes in the slickrock, effectively lost in a sandstone *malpais*, the team was at its lowest ebb in the three months since leaving Santa Fe. And now the expedition flirted with a fatal collapse.

The team waited until dark, then all through the night. Neither Lucrecio nor Juan Domingo returned. No smoke signals came from the far bank. Camp was on a rim overlooking the Colorado where the two brave scouts had forded it, but maddeningly it was waterless. D & E were unwilling to take the horses down to the river to drink for fear they could not get the weary animals back up the treacherous slope.

By morning the men had eaten every last scrap of meat from the second horse they had slain. Their only food that day was "toasted pads of low prickly pear cactus" and some kind of berries crushed and boiled in water, whose taste was "insipid." By late afternoon, with no sign of the missing scouts, the exasperated padres decided to risk the descent to the river. Several horses lost their footing and rolled through the rocks, injuring themselves.

Finally, just before dark, Juan Domingo arrived. He reported that the canyon opposite had no viable exit, but that Lucrecio had stayed on, following Indian tracks in the sand. (If there were footprints in the far canyon, there had to be a way out—but not necessarily one that horses could negotiate.) The *genízaro*'s testimony settled the question for D & E. They resolved to push on toward the northeast in the morning, leaving Andrés Muñiz with the dolorous assignment of waiting for his absent brother, then catching up to the expedition.

The team's march, or stumble, on November 5 was a disheartening one. Their route lay across a gauntlet of "many ridges and gullies," "a dry arroyo," and a "very high-walled canyon." At a paltry water hole they stopped for the night, still well inland from the river, after a journey of only eight miles. As the men pitched camp a heavy rain fell, then turned briefly to snow. It was still raining in the morning. All day the exhausted men had had nothing to eat.

At 6 AM on November 6, Andrés Muñiz arrived in camp. He told his comrades that he had waited through the previous day with no sign of his brother. These dismal tidings stirred a germ of pity and apprehension in the hearts of the padres. As Escalante wrote, "This news caused us plenty of worry, because [Lucrecio] had been three days without provisions and no covering other than his shirt, since he had not even taken trousers along—for, even though he crossed the river on horseback, the horse swam for a long stretch and the water reached almost to the shoulders wherever it faltered." At this point Juan Domingo volunteered to go back to the camp of November 5, swim the Colorado again, and search for Lucrecio where the two men had parted two days earlier.

The padres readily accepted this heroic offer, and piled new orders on top of the *genízaro*'s mission. Juan Domingo was told to find the footprints where he had last seen his fellow scout, follow them wherever they led, and after catching up to Lucrecio, leave the latter's horse behind and somehow strike out along the southern bank of the great river as the two men tried to keep up with the main team on its parallel path on the other side of the Colorado. Or, if the rendezvous could be accomplished soon enough, both Juan Domingo and Lucrecio were to recross the river (Juan Domingo for the fourth time) and "try to overtake us as quickly as possible." The men must have slaughtered another horse, for D & E gave Juan Domingo some meat to fortify his desperate backtrack and search.

Throughout the long expedition, Domínguez and Escalante had shown a remarkable sense of responsibility toward their ten companions, even as they castigated them for their stupid mistakes as guides. Other Spanish expedition leaders, especially those of martial mien like Coronado and Oñate, never hesitated to dole out corporal punishment for even the slightest of derelictions. But except for the squalid incident on October 5, when Juan Pedro Cisneros had beaten his "servant" (or at least "grappled with him arm to arm") because the man refused to pray the Virgin's litany with his master, Escalante's journal records not a single case of physical violence among the team members, much less as punishment meted out by the padres themselves. When teammates went missing overnight, the expedition usually halted in its tracks until the errant members could be found.

Yet in the dire predicament of November 6, trapped in the maze of canyons on the wrong side of the Colorado River, famished and demoralized, the padres seemed to countenance the option of effectively abandoning Lucrecio and Juan Domingo to give the rest of the team a chance to survive. The other eleven men (including the Laguna guide, Joaquín) set out in mid-morning on November 6, only to be "stopped for a long time by a strong blizzard and tempest consisting of rain and thick hailstones amid horrendous thunder claps and lightning flashes. We recited the Virgin's Litany, for her to implore some relief for us, and God willed for the tempest to end." Another grueling day's ride produced a gain of only nine miles, before the team stopped to camp where "some rock cliffs blocked our way." They were only about a mile north of the river but could not see it from camp. Juan Pedro Cisneros set out in the waning light to find a way to the bank of the Colorado and judge whether here, at last, a successful crossing could be made by the whole team.

A single dry sentence at the end of the journal entry for November 6 condenses and conceals an extraordinary exploratory deed: "Before night came the genízaro arrived with the said Lucrecio." (No mention of Lucrecio's horse.) For three days, without trousers, Andrés Muñiz's brother—scarcely mentioned in the journal during the three months out of Santa Fe—had crossed the Colorado twice, pushed the far canyon along the track of Indian footprints to an unspecified distance, and together with Juan Domingo followed the onward track of the main expedition through 17 miles of convoluted slickrock canyons and domes. For three nights the ill-clad Lucrecio had bivouacked through rainstorms that had drenched and chilled his comrades even in their tents and around their campfires. The reconnaissance of these two scouts stands as one of the gutsiest accomplishments of the whole expedition, yet Escalante deigned it an episode not even worth enlivening with the barest details, since in the end, as a way to cross the Colorado River, the scouts' attempted route failed to find an answer.

That afternoon of November 6, however, Juan Pedro Cisneros, off to check out the mile of trackless country between camp and the river, came back with the most promising report yet, though D & E, with their habitual caution, gave it only provisional credence. Cisneros said that where he reached the Colorado it was very wide and apparently not very deep. The glitch was that the only approach lay through a troublesome canyon. For want of a better alternative, the padres sent out two more teammates to corroborate Cisneros's intelligence. They came back with the vague admonition that "everything was difficult to negotiate." Still, it was the best hope for a ford the team had found during the last eleven days.

Very early on November 7, the padres set out to investigate the route themselves, bringing along their two crack swimmers, Felipe and Juan Domingo, to test the ford. At one point in the canyon of approach, D & E saw that the horses they were riding might be unable to descend a slickrock ramp, so they wielded axes to chisel out broad horizontal steps across a crux section about 10 feet long. With the aid of those steps, all four men reached the bank of the Colorado without mishap. From there they pushed downstream "for about as far as two musket shots," where the river appeared to be widest. One of the *genízaros* "waded in and found it all right, not having to swim at any place." D & E followed on horseback. About halfway across, the horses "missed bottom and swam through a short channel." But by then, either Felipe or Juan Domingo had completed the crossing and found the best route through the ford. He led the friars to the south bank, across a line consistently shallow enough that neither horse had to swim again. On the far side, the way looked open ahead. Escalante reports no sudden burst of joy, no sense that the team had escaped its potentially lethal trap. Instead, at once, the padres sent word to the nine men lingering at camp to come ahead.

The ford of the Colorado River that was destined to become famous had been solved. Thanks to their scouts, so often maligned, Domínguez and Escalante had discovered the Crossing of the Fathers.

* * *

FROM OUR MOTEL in Page, Sharon and I would have loved to follow the itinerary of the Spaniards during those eleven desperate days as they searched for a way to cross the impossible Colorado. Alas, nearly all the complex topography through which the team forced its painful way in early November 1776 is drowned under that Mother of All Reservoirs, Lake Powell. I had thought that other impounded lakes like the Abiquiu and Strawberry reservoirs thwarted our determination to go where D & E had gone. But here, during the dramatic crux of the whole expedition, our desire to relive it through the sympathy of travel was defeated by silt and stagnant water. Even in 1975, the Bicentennial retracers found Glen Canyon already partly obliterated by Lake Powell. That didn't keep Bud Rusho and David Miller from racking their brains to pinpoint campsites and trails on the Spaniards' route, as they identified such landmarks as Castle Rock, Warm Creek, Ramona Mesa, and Gunsight Butte. Miller, the distinguished historian who headed the Commission and edited its report, had had the good fortune to walk in the footsteps of the expedition with Gregory Crampton back in 1950, before Lake Powell was even a gleam in the eye of the Bureau of Reclamation. By then the ledge where the expedition had gouged steps for the horses had become a legendary stop for backcountry sleuths. The two men also visited a bronze plaque installed nearby to salute the key to the Crossing of the Fathers. Old photos capture the haunting power of the staircase that eased the Spanish horses' descent to the great river (see photograph in insert).

As soon as the padres and Felipe and Juan Domingo had made the ford, they sent back word to the last camp to bring the whole team down to the river. Saddles, saddlebags, and other gear were lowered with ropes down short sections of cliff. Only at 5 PM on November 7, with the team and all the horses safely across, did the whole expedition stop to celebrate, by "praising God our Lord and firing off some muskets in demonstration of the great joy we all felt in having overcome so great a problem."

There is no doubt that the Crossing of the Fathers had been a ford well known to the Indians for centuries, maybe even millennia, before 1776. Domínguez and Escalante knew as much. In the same paragraph in which he announces the team's joy and gratitude to God, the chronicler bitterly complains about "our having no one to guide us through such difficult terrain. For through the lack of expert help we made many detours, wasted time from so many days spent in a very small area, and suffered from hunger and thirst."

There had to be a reason for the Paiutes' unwillingness to show the Spaniards the way. The padres had no trouble discovering it, for "God doubtless disposed that we obtain no guide, either as merciful chastisement for our faults or so that we could acquire some knowledge of the peoples living hereabouts."

That night, in the camp on the south bank the padres named

La Purísima Concepción de la Virgen Santísima (the Immaculate Conception of the Most Holy Virgin), the men slept well. The way onward was not quite a yellow brick road, but Escalante could sense across the canyons and plains the relative proximity of Moqui, the great multi-village pueblo of the Hopi, which he had visited the year before in his futile attempt to convert the most recalcitrant of all the Puebloan peoples.

In 2006, quite by accident, a ghostly talisman of the long-ago expedition appeared out of nowhere. A group of volunteers attached to the Glen Canyon National Recreation Area were out in a motorboat on Lake Powell, as part of a project to remove graffiti from the sandstone walls. In an area called Padre Bay, several hundred feet of water directly above the Crossing of the Fathers, they discovered, underneath the crudely gouged boasts of "AJ" and "Rob" and "Kathi" from 1994, a faint, cursive *"paso por aquí 1776"*—"passed by here [in] 1776." According to Siegfried Halus and Greg MacGregor, in their picture book *In Search of Domínguez and Escalante*, "Extensive testing using laser scanning, lichen-growth comparisons, handwriting style, lead analysis, and rock-varnish comparisons have [sic] led to the conclusion that the inscription dates prior to the twentieth century and is likely to be two or three hundred years old."

To my mind the stone message is unmistably the work of the D & E expedition (see photograph in insert). It's curious that the padres carved it not on the bank of the Colorado where they found their life-saving ford, nor beside the steps they chiseled in the bedrock to ease the horses' passage, but on a nondescript wall several hundred feet above the river, on the trail of their approach to the ford. The obscurity of that location explains why the record of the team's passing was not discovered before 2006. In its simplicity—three words and a date, bereft of names—it remains unique, and haunting: the only inscription ever found from the Spanish discovery of the American Southwest.

Pictograph in Cañon Pintado (Douglas Creek). *Photograph by David Roberts.*

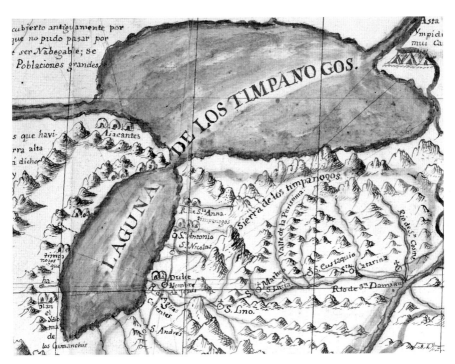

Detail from Miera y Pacheco's map of the Valley of the Timpanogotzis, where D & E promised to return to minister to the Utes. Note the mythical river flowing west out of Great Salt Lake, which is shown as connected to Utah Lake. *By permission of the British Library; Cartographic Items Add. MS. 17,661.d.*

Detail from the Miera y Pacheco map—bearded Indians, not lost Spaniards. *By permission of the British Library; Cartographic Items Add. MS. 17,661.d.*

Sharon driving, in the middle of nowhere. *Photograph by David Roberts.*

The barren plain where the expedition gave up the quest for Monterey and turned toward home. *Photograph by David Roberts.*

Lunch break in the desolate country where the expedition first sought the Colorado River. *Photograph by David Roberts.*

The author at camp in the Grand Staircase–Escalante National Monument. *Photograph by Sharon Roberts.*

Our tent lit by lantern. *Photograph by David Roberts.*

A beat-up memorial to the expedition at the San Bartolomé camp, near the Colorado River. *Photograph by David Roberts.*

The Vermilion Cliffs, approaching the Colorado River. *Photograph by David Roberts.*

Historic photo of steps carved in the bedrock by the team near the Crossing of the Fathers, now hundreds of feet beneath Lake Powell. *Used by permission, Utah State Historical Society.*

"Paso por aqui 1776"—the only known inscription from the Domínguez–Escalante expedition. *Photograph by Siegfried Halus.*

Plot of corn, Hopi Cultural Center, Second Mesa. *Photograph by David Roberts.*

The mission church at Zuni, founded in 1629, to which Escalante was posted in 1775. *Photograph by David Roberts.*

High butte near Zuni Pueblo. *Photograph by David Roberts.*

Last camp on the edge of El Malpais, between Zuni and Santa Fe. *Photograph by Sharon Roberts.*

Chapter Nine

HOPI AND BEYOND

HAVING FINALLY CROSSED THE GREAT RIVER, ESCALANTE paused to sum up the experience the team had undergone with all the various bands with which they had interacted after leaving the Timpanogotzis on Utah Lake. (It's entirely possible that he inserted this set piece later, as he may have done with the more extensive "Description of the Valley" that paints such a rosy picture of the Laguna homeland as a venue for future settlement and missionizing.) There's a kind of anthropological urge for order going on in this mini-essay, as if sorting out the tribes might clarify the confusion in which the team had traveled for the last month and a half. Escalante names no fewer than ten distinct peoples, supposedly according to the names they learned through Andrés Muñiz's interpreting efforts, but most of those tags—Ytimpabichis, Pagampachis, Payatammunis, and the like—are meaningless today.

Escalante further declares that these six southern tribes could all be lumped together as Yutas Cobardes, a term the padres made up. (*Cobardes* is Spanish for "cowards"! Presumably the label refers to the tribes' unwillingness to guide the Spaniards to the best ford across the Colorado, as well as to the timidity of Indians who were as likely to flee from the strangers as to engage with them.) Modern ethnographers would classify these southern natives as Paiutes, with their own various bands, none of which can be convincingly matched with Escalante's tribes.

In his effort to offer a neat package of Indian experience to the superiors for whom he was compiling his account, Escalante belies the ambiguity of all the encounters from Utah Lake to the Colorado River. He insists that "all whom we met speak the Yuta language," forgetting the several times the team's interpreter could barely comprehend the natives' speech, and the one time the men had to resort to sign language. What's more, Ute and Paiute are cognate languages but far from the same tongue, and the kind of dialogue that might have taken place between a hunter-gatherer near the Colorado and a fish-eater on Utah Lake might have been at least as muddled as, say, a confab between a Kansas farmer and a crofter from the Orkney Islands.

Escalante also commits the eternal mistake of Europeans dealing with Native Americans, as, despite the team's experience—with the Indians, for instance, only a few dozen miles south of the Laguna homeland who had no awareness of the great encounter by the lake—he states, "All the Yutas known heretofore composed a single nation, or let us call it a kingdom, divided into five provinces." Habituated by the notions of monarchy that obtained in Spain or Great Britain or France, European explorers could scarcely grasp the autonomy of native peoples in the Americas. Well into the nineteenth century, the fallacy of a tribal "kingdom" would plague efforts to make peace with Indians in the American West. Time and again a U.S. Army general would conclude a treaty with a "chief" who the Americans assumed spoke for all Apaches or Sioux or Comanches, only to have other bands "violate" an agreement they had never made.

From the camp of the Immaculate Conception on the south bank of the Colorado, the reunited team set out southward on November 8. "Today we found many footprints of Indians but did not see any of them," recorded Escalante. The men were still on the verge of starvation, so they slaughtered another horse—the fourth they had sacrificed for food. The coming winter was in the air. "Tonight we were very cold," complained Escalante, "more so than on the other side [of the Colorado]."

The Spaniards were still so confused about the terrain that they were desperate to find Indians who could guide them or at least direct their course. On November 9 they came upon a Paiute camp but could not persuade the fearful Indians lurking at a distance to come near, "because they suspected that we were friends of the Moqui [Hopi]," Escalante guessed, "with whom they share great enmity." Early that day the team "lost the trail" and were forced by encroaching cliffs to backtrack five miles to the northeast.

Finally, on November 10, only after Andrés Muñiz "had cajoled them for two hours" from a distance, five Paiutes consented to a parley, not with the whole Spanish team but only with Muñiz and Joaquín, the Laguna guide who was still with the expedition even though by now he was far beyond the country he knew. The Paiutes not only explained to the two interpreters how to find the trail they had lost, but passed on the exciting news that "a short distance from here we would find two trails, one toward the Cosninas and another to El Pueblo de Oraibi in Moqui."

The terrain the Spaniards crossed after fording the Colorado is today by far the most remote from roads of any sector of their 1,700-mile route. In addition, all of it lies on today's Navajo Reservation. In the Bicentennial Commission report, Bud Rusho writes, "From the camp at La Concepcion at Crossing of the Fathers the trail enters a region seen only by occasional Navajos. All previous investigations of the trail have avoided this section as being too remote and difficult to penetrate."

With his usual perspicacity, in 1975 Rusho recruited his comrade Don Cecala to try to find the long-lost route of the Spaniards on the ground. They were ferried across Lake Powell in a Bureau of Reclamation boat, past a lone plug of rock sticking out of the water officially named Padres Butte. Deposited on the south shore, they had no trouble finding an apparently ancient trail they were confident the Spaniards had followed. Several miles along, they came to a Navajo hogan occupied by two sheepherders, Harry Bitsouie and his uncle, Fred Tsinniginie. These men told the researchers that they regularly used the old trail to go down to Lake Powell for water.

After a hike of 12 miles, Rusho and Cecala found what they were sure was the expedition's camp of November 8. It stood at the base of a dramatic 1,000-foot tower called Tse Tonto. "The only wonder," wrote Rusho, "is that the padres failed to mention the spectacular setting of [the camp]." Pushing on the next day, like the Spaniards before them, Rusho and Cecala lost the trail where it petered out in sand dunes and rock ledges. Striking out where they guessed the Spaniards must have wandered, they ran out of time and water. At the end of the day, the researchers had to confess, "Their campsite that night [November 9] cannot be pinpointed." The weary pair were picked up late in the afternoon by the Bureau of Reclamation boat traveling along a narrow arm of Lake Powell that reaches many miles up Navajo Canyon. Two days later Rusho flew over the country to try to clarify the itinerary by air, but he concluded that the precise route had to remain conjectural.

Starting in the early 1990s, I made many trips into the Navajo Reservation in search of Anasazi ruins and rock art. Each journey required me to get an official permit from the Navajo Nation headquarters in Window Rock, Arizona, which in those days could involve a certain amount of red tape and bureaucratic inertia. But the rewards easily made up for such minor hardships. Most Anglo hikers, I had come to see, were leery of the rez, as if it had the vague feel of a Third World country. But because Navajo taboos about places of the dead had left the ruins relatively unvandalized, with potsherds and lithic tools lying everywhere in place, the payoffs of such outings were often sublime. Whole areas on the reservation were off-limits even with a permit, usually because of the sensitivity of local residents to trespass, but although five or six times I was asked by a Navajo ranger or hogan-dweller to show my permit, I never had a hostile encounter with any of the Diné I met in the backcountry.

For more than two decades I pursued such outings, sometimes on day hikes but often on solo backpacks lasting as long as four days or with companions stretching across as many as twelve. Some of the most enchanted hours I was granted in the Southwest came on such ventures. But in 2017, there was no possibility that Sharon and I might poke into the canyons or traverse the mesas where the Spaniards traveled after November 8. I would have been happy to apply for a permit but, post-cancer, I could not have met the physical challenge of getting to Tse Tonto or Weed Bench or Face Canyon.

On a single day in 2012, however, Sharon and I had set out on a marathon hike from State Highway 98, across a bewildering complex of ridges, cliffs, and sand dunes, and at last entered the green corridor of Chaol Canyon, a tributary of Navajo Canyon. We could spend only an hour and a half hiking up and back down a short stretch of Chaol, but there we found masterly petroglyphs and small waterfalls and cottonwoods with leaves turning gold. Domínguez and Escalante were far from my thoughts back then, but now, as Sharon and I drove out of Page on September 28, I reminded her that on that memorable day five years before we had come very close to—and perhaps walked directly on—the path the starving Spaniards had imprinted as they struggled south from the Crossing of the Fathers.

Having found the old trail again, thanks to the advice of the Paiutes, the expedition followed it for two more days. In places the route had been cunningly improved by the natives with "loose stones and sticks" here, a manufactured "stairway" there. On November 11 the men passed just west of Tsai Skizzi Rock, a 400-foot monolith with a window arch in it that Sharon and I could see just beyond Chaol Canyon as we scrambled down into that sanctum in 2012. The team accepted a waterless camp on the plateau that night because there was an abundance of firewood "to ward off the severe cold we were experiencing." Early the next morning the men found a spring-fed pool covered with a sheet of ice they broke to get drinking water for both humans and horses.

Somehow the padres, or one of their cannier teammates (Miera? Cisneros? Andrés Muñiz?) could deduce from the "vestiges" of Indian activity around the spring that "it is a stopping place for the Cosninas [Havasupai] when they travel to the Payuchis [Paiutes]." So confident were they of this reading of the runes that after a further ride southward of 10 miles, they chose to leave the direct route toward Moqui and veer westward on the trail that led toward the Cosninas. Sure enough, less than three miles onward they discovered "small dwellings or deserted camps and indications that many herds of cattle and horses had been pastured hereabouts for some time."

Some thorny ethnographic puzzles spring from Escalante's account of these days in early November. Since the creation of the Navajo Reservation in 1868, all the country between the Colorado River and the Hopi pueblos has belonged to the Diné. Nor was the government allocation of that massive tract of land an artifical fiat: tree-ring cuttings from old hogans still standing all over this country give dates stretching back into the eighteenth century. For that matter, Miera's map of the expedition unambiguously enfolds this landscape in the "Provincia de Nabajoo." The Payuchis, or Southern Paiutes, generally confined their hunting and gathering to the barren lands north of the Colorado and east of the Grand Canyon. For months, Escalante (as well, probably, as Domínguez) had had a bee in his bonnet about the Cosninas, but then as now the Havasupai homeland lay on the southern slope of the Grand Canyon a full 90 miles southwest of such landmarks as Tsai Skizzi Rock. Why Escalante was so keen to meet the Cosninas he never adequately explains.

Between November 8 and 16, when at last the team reached Hopi, the only natives they met on the trail were Paiutes—the tribal band that had straightened out the Spaniards' confusion and given them directions to the trails leading to Moqui and the Cosninas. Where, indeed, were the Navajos? Even in 1776, it would seem to defy logic to cross the Navajo heartland both coming and going and not meet with a single Diné man, woman, or child. But that is what Escalante reports the team did. It's not possible that the timid trail advisors that Andrés Muñiz and Joaquín conferred with on November 10 were Navajos whom the men mistook for Paiutes, for both interpreters seemed to be able to communicate in a Numic tongue shared by Utes and Paiutes, to which the Navajo language is utterly unrelated. Furthermore, Juan Pedro Cisneros seems to have been able to speak some Navajo. That up to this point he had never interpreted with natives reinforces the strange conclusion that the team managed to avoid all encounters with the Diné.

What *is* possible is that on November 14, somewhere close to present-day Tuba City, Arizona, in a fertile vale the retracers identify as Pasture Canyon, the Spaniards came upon a substantial campsite whose denizens had recently left, and that the padres were absolutely certain they had found a small Cosnina village that was actually a Navajo settlement. Escalante's description of it is vivid and bucolic:

> We . . . arrived at a small farm and camp of the Cosninas, all of it pretty and well arranged . . . ; here this year the Cosninas planted maize, squash, watermelon, and muskmelon. By the time we arrived they had gathered their harvest and, judging from the refuse or scraps of everything we found, it had been an abundant one, and especially that of beans. For if we had made camp here, we could have gleaned half a bushel of it. The farmland is surrounded by peach trees.
>
> Besides the several huts made of boughs, there was a very well constructed little house of stone and mud. In it were the baskets, jars, and other utensils of these Indians. These, judging from the tracks, had gone away some days before, perhaps to look for piñon nuts in the adjacent high sierra toward the south-southwest.

A virtual village with wickiup-style shelters as well as a single mortared building does not sound at all Navajo, but neither does it fit the Havasupai pattern. One wonders why Escalante unquestioningly assigns it to the Cosninas, only one member of whose tribe he had ever met, the year before on his visit to Hopi. After all, none of the Spaniards had ever seen a Havasupai village, so how could Escalante have known what one looked like? It is even barely possible that the recently abandoned encampment might have been a semi-permanent Hopi outlier. The planted peach trees (an import from the Spanish after Oñate's 1598 expedition), the stone-and-mud building, and the baskets and jars stored therein fit a Hopi paradigm better than either a Navajo or a Havasupai one. But as so often on the Domínguez–Escalante trail, the truth of the matter remains unknowable.

Escalante's obsession with finding the Cosninas seems to have been planted on that 1775 visit to Hopi. In the midst of his demoralizing failure to make the smallest inroads into Moqui paganism, he learned that two Cojninas (as he spelled the term in his 1775 diary) were in the vicinity. At last he wangled a two-hour meeting with one of those men. Through an interpreter, he heard the Havasupai say that "all my people . . . are very fond of [the Spaniards], and that you are to say so to all of them." Overjoyed, Escalante replied that he "already loved [the Cojninas] as my sons." He would gladly have traveled with the man westward to the tribe's home village "if he had not found me so ill and without an animal to ride," since his only horse was "completely incapacitated for so long a journey."

This interlude in Escalante's dismal several days at Hopi in 1775 explains the friar's passionate desire to visit the Cosninas the next year, on the homeward leg of his expedition through the Southwest. But "so long a journey" also implies that Escalante knew well how far off the Havasupai homeland lay. The illusion he nursed in November 1776 that the team was virtually next door to that homeland, that they had come upon a Cosnina village whose inhabitants had left only a few days before, was pure wishful thinking.

Be that as it may, on November 14, from the purported Havasupai village, the padres decided to give up their quest for the Cosninas and head south to Moqui. Escalante blames "the lack of supplies" and "the extreme severity with which winter was plaguing us." In hindsight, we can say that it was unquestionably the right decision.

Near today's Navajo settlement of Kaibito, the route of the Spaniards emerges from the deep outback to follow, approximately, routes 20, 89, and 264 toward the Hopi mesas. Across this open plain, dissected by shallow canyons, Sharon and I made no effort to adhere to the path the team took in 1776. Instead we followed the highways past the towns of Tuba City (founded in 1887 by the Mormon missionary Jacob Hamblin) and Moenkopi (founded seven years earlier by Hopi refugees from Oraibi who were seeking better farmland). As the Bicentennial researchers (Rusho, Cecala, and Crampton) admit, the Spaniards' route, so far as it can be excavated, roughly parallels today's highways.

Over the years I'd driven through Kaibito a number of times. No Navajo settlement I'd ever visited seemed more hostile to Anglos. Once, when I asked about road conditions on the dirt County Highway 21 toward Tonalea, I received an answer so vague and yet discouraging that I backtracked on paved State Highway 98 instead. On those drives to Kaibito, I'd salivated as I stared at White Mesa, a massive sandstone dome full of fins and alcoves that I was sure must have once sheltered the Anasazi. Short feeder tracks headed off from Route 98 toward the nearest cliffs, but every one was guarded with "no trespassing" signs. In Crampton's splendid picture book *Standing Up Country* (1964), there are many close-up photos of White Mesa, which I was sure the author had explored to his heart's content. But the regulations for backcountry hiking permits near Kaibito were draconian. In its latest iteration, the language under "Areas Closed to Hiking" states, "Recently, the Kaibeto [sic] Chapter community has prohibited hiking and camping in the entire area of Upper Kaibeto, Navajo Canyon, Choal [sic] Canyon, Kaibeto Creek, Peach Wash, and Butterfly Canyon. . . . These closures are due to trespassing across residential areas." I wish I knew what egregious acts by pushy Anglo hikers had inspired this blanket prohibition, but for all I knew the bad vibes I felt around the town of Kaibito were simply the legacy of the brutal roundup of all the Navajo people and deportation to a concentration camp in eastern New Mexico in the 1860s. I was glad that Sharon and I had caught our tantalizing glimpse of Chaol Canyon before it fell under the stern injunction against visitation on foot.

Between November 12 and 16 the Spaniards suffered grievously from the cold. On the 12th, several "companions" went ahead to build a fire "to warm up Don Bernardo Miera," who, in Escalante's quaint phrase, "was ready to freeze on us and who we feared could not survive so much cold." His new affliction was apparently unrelated to the terrible stomach pains for which Miera had sought the cure of the Paiute shaman on October 22. The next day the team made camp on a nondescript sandstone shelf not far from present-day Tuba City, which the padres named not after a saint but rather El Espino, "because we caught a porcupine today, and here we tasted flesh of the richest flavor."

One dequilled porcupine divided among thirteen men? But the day before, the Spaniards had had no food except for "a piece of toasted hide" from the last slaughtered horse, and Escalante admits that "the porcupine shared among so many only served to whet the appetite." So the men killed and butchered yet another horse, the fifth sacrificed to their ravenous hunger. It took less than two days to devour the no doubt stringy beast. On November 15, the team discovered whole herds of Hopi cattle ranging loose. "All of the companions wanted to kill a cow or a heifer," wrote Escalante. "They kept impatiently insisting that we should let them relieve the need from which we all were suffering by this means." In their desperation, the men argued that the cattle were either "runaways" or "public property," whatever that phrase might mean.

But now the padres insisted on an act of heroic forbearance, as they refused their comrades' demand to kill one of the cattle and feast on juicy beef. A certain respect for the Hopi themselves may have motivated D & E's restraint, along with the discipline the padres had tried to instill in the men by forbidding them to trade with the Indians. But the friars were also afraid that a rustled cow might "cause some trouble between us and the Moqui people and defeat our purpose." That purpose, forged in the crucible of Escalante's unhappy visit to the Hopi the year before, was "to exert anew our efforts in behalf of the Light, and meekness of the Gospel, as against their willful blindness and inveterate obstinacy." Instead, the padres ordered a sixth horse killed.

The next day, November 16, after riding southwest for eight miles, the Spaniards came upon "a well-beaten trail and concluded that it went to one of the Moqui pueblos." Curving back toward the northeast, the men followed this thoroughfare for another 13 miles, until they paused beneath a mesa that Escalante recognized as the site of the ancient Hopi village of Oraibi. As far as we know, only Escalante and Juan Pedro Cisneros among the thirteen explorers had ever been to Hopi before. For the padre, though, the prospect of another visit had to be fraught with both hope and anxiety—most likely more of the latter than of the former. "We ordered the companions to halt at the mesa's foot," he would note in his journal, "that none except those going up with us should approach the pueblo until we gave the word."

Escalante's first encounter with the Hopi had come twenty months before, when several Hopi men had arrived at Zuni, where the padre was stationed, to trade. They invited him to come to their home village some 130 miles to the northwest. In June 1775, eager to missionize among a Puebloan people famed for their resistance to Spanish rule and Christian ideas, Escalante started along the trail. The twenty-six-year-old friar had been assigned to Zuni only five months earlier, and his eagerness was born in some part out of naive idealism. Before he could set out, Cisneros, then the *alcalde*, or mayor, of Zuni, warned him that the Hopi were not to be trusted and that the trail between the pueblos was exposed to the depredations of Navajo raiders. Escalante was authorized by his Franciscan superior to make the journey only after he agreed to a retinue composed of Cisneros, seventeen Zuni men, and a Puebloan from Sandia who spoke Hopi to act as interpreter.

The uneventful journey took only four days. At Walpi, the Hopi village on First Mesa that crowds the western end of a finger of bedrock overlooking precipices of several hundred feet on each side, Escalante was cordially received. It was there that a Hopi man warned him of the Navajo plot to ambush and massacre his team on the way back to Zuni, to which the padre replied (as related in chapter 1) that he had nothing to fear because he "trusted in God Who is infinitely more powerful than all the men there ever were, are, or will be."

Even before arriving at Hopi, Escalante had heard lurid accounts of the "idolatrous abominations" the Hopi were in the habit of performing in their ceremonies. So intense was the friar's commitment to the purity of his own spirit—or, to put it in modern terms, so squeamish was he about native customs—that the first thing he did on arriving at Walpi was to urge its inhabitants "not to neglect their sowings" in the corn fields below the mesa. Escalante's journal from the 1775 trip makes it clear that this goodwill gesture was a dodge to avoid having to watch the dances he was afraid the locals would put on to greet him. He also begged off by citing the persistent "urinary ailment" that so debilitated him. It's striking that in his 1775 diary Escalante refers to that affliction, which almost certainly would cause his premature death, while the 1776 journal never breathes a word about it. When the Walpi folks, no doubt perplexed, agreed not to dance for their visitors, Escalante privately vented his relief: "I was freed from countenancing by my presence (for never with God's grace would I do such a thing) the very thing that deserves to be and I wish to see scorned by those who esteem it."

In the Yuta villages in 1776, Escalante and Domínguez were so eager to spread the Gospel that they had hardly tethered their horses before they started preaching. But in Walpi in 1775, Escalante held off. He had decided that Oraibi on Third Mesa, "which is like a provincial capital," was the focal point of Hopi idolatry. Full of optimism from his friendly reception at Walpi, he set off for Oraibi on June 27, accompanied by Cisneros and the Sandia interpreter but only three Zuni men. He arrived at 11 in the morning.

A young Hopi met the party and escorted them to the "little house they had cleared out for us to spend the night in." There the men waited. "I was surprised," wrote Escalante, "that no one came to see me during the whole afternoon, not even for the sake of novelty." With Cisneros, the padre ventured out "to take a look at the pueblo," then returned to the team's humble guest room. At last, tired of waiting, Escalante sent word to Oraibi's *cacique*, or head man, and his lieutenants "to prepare them for the sermon I wanted to preach to them the next day." He was further disappointed when only a pair of what he perceived as second-rank Hopi officials arrived, accompanied by several old men. Someone made a token apology for the absence of the *cacique*, saying the man was off on a hunt, "which I later learned was untrue." Escalante forged on, speaking through the Sandia interpreter to express his goodwill, "to which they did not correspond as they should have."

Instead, the delegates demanded that "I should tell them once and for all what I wanted to discuss with them." Escalante said he was in no hurry, and would wait for the arrival of the *cacique* to declare his purpose in coming. His auditors doubled down, demanding that the friar immediately declare his purpose, or "they would not come to meet again." Backed into a corner, Escalante stood up, made "the preliminary remarks that I considered appropriate," then haughtily told his hosts "to listen to me with the attention required by a matter so weighty as their eternal well-being or perdition." At this prickly juncture, Escalante turned his anxiety on the interpreter, whom he suspected of soft-pedaling his message for fear of retribution. Only when the Sandia man swore to translate faithfully "even if . . . it was going to cost him his life" did Escalante plunge into his sermon.

The scene that ensued reads in the padre's diary like a nightmare of cultures in collision. The arrogance of the young priest as

he dictated the terms of spiritual survivial to his hostile hosts can be
excused only in the context of the black-and-white absolutism of his
Franciscan faith.

> I began to explain to them the most essential points of our reli-
> gion and those most conducive to my purpose. . . . When I had
> finished, I gave them to understand that I had been sent by
> God to proclaim for Him the eternal glory to which He was
> inviting them even though they had offended Him for so long,
> and the torments with which He would punish them if they
> did not abandon their abominations and, becoming Christians,
> keep His Holy Commandments. I exhorted them with all the
> force and clarity I could, and they replied briefly that even if
> what they had heard from me was true they had no desire to
> be Christians.

In the blindness of his faith, Escalante barely heard what the Hopi
"captain" was trying to say. Refusing to give up, he harangued his
auditors even more forcefully. Their torments in hell, he insisted,
would be all the worse because in their obstinacy they were prevent-
ing all the other men and women in the pueblo from receiving the
light of salvation. The "said captain" fired back with both barrels,
bluntly telling Escalante "that he did not want the Spaniards ever to
live in his land; and for me not to worry myself in going about giving
advice to his people, for none would give ear to me."

Reading Escalante's own diary account of this catastrophic spiritual clash, one cannot help wondering if the padre was ignorant of
the eighteen decades of hostility and violence between the Spaniards
in New Mexico and the Hopi people that preceded his futile visit. Yet
surely, like all Franciscans, he marked history from the terrible *año
ochenta*—the Pueblo Revolt of 1680, when the Hopi had killed their
priest and burned their church to the ground. Surely he knew about
Awatowi, the Hopi village east of First Mesa massacred by other Hopi

in 1700 in large part because that pueblo had allowed the Church to creep back in between its kivas.

Instead, Escalante, who prided himself on his iron control of his temper, railed on against the captain with "bitterness and anger" at his own "sorrow of seeing so great a multitude of souls lost by the ambitious malice of a few." The Hopi were so surprised by Escalante's wrath that they "begged the interpreter to calm me down." Instead, "I left the meeting without taking leave and even without finishing the last word on my lips." Escalante returned to the "little house" the Hopi had assigned his team "feeling very sad." During the next few hours, he learned that the delegation he had met with was spreading the word throughout Oraibi and on to the other Hopi villages that "no one was to listen to my counsels because my aim was to subject them to the Spaniards."

In the depths of discouragement, Escalante was ready to call it quits and head back to Zuni. But instead he lingered for five more days, hoping to find solitary Hopi who might go against the tribal prohibition and at least consider conversion to the True Church. He left Oraibi and stopped briefly at three other pueblo villages on Second and First mesas, where he tried again to gather listeners to hear his sermon. But it seemed his heart was no longer in the effort; in each case "it was no use, for they replied, perhaps to excuse their own malice, that they could not go against the decisions of Oraybi."

During these days, in the diary it is as if Cisneros and the three Zuni men had disappeared. Only the interpreter merits mention, as Escalante recruits him again and again to convey his earnest message. Within this gloom, two rays of hope pierce the padre's hopelessness. One is the two-hour parley with the Cosnina man related above, which would crystallize the determination Escalante nursed through the first four months of the 1776 expedition to make his way to that distant homeland and preach to Indians who might well heed his glad tidings. The other, still in Oraibi, is a strange, furtive encounter with a Hopi man who slipped into the "little house" at daybreak and managed to inquire via sign language whether the friar had any goods to trade. Heartened but confused, Escalante summoned the interpreter, and in the meantime, "to entertain and gratify" his visitor, he mixed up a chocolate drink and offered the man half a cup. After heading off to search for the interpreter, Escalante returned to find the poor Hopi man vomiting the unfamiliar drink. Other Hopis spoke to him, whereupon "he then went away without my being able to discover the purpose of his mysterious arrival, and I did not see him again."

On his final afternoon at Hopi, ensconced again in a small room at Walpi, the village that had given him his auspicious first reception, Escalante observed an event that was for him the last straw. His account of it conveys his shock and disgust at the pagan ritual he was forced to witness:

> I heard . . . a great noise and disturbance in the street. I hastened out to learn the cause and saw some of the masked men they call *entremeseros*, and they are equivalent to the ancient Mexican *huehuenches*. The frightful and gloomy painting of their masks and the height of indecency in which they ran in view of many people of both sexes were very clear signs of the foul spirit who has their hearts in his power. The only part of their bodies that was covered was the face, and at the end of the member it is not modest to name they wore a small and delicate feather subtly attached.

What Escalante saw may have been a Hopi *koshare* dance. The *koshare* are sacred clowns based on the kachinas, supernatural intercessors between men and gods. In the dances, men wear masks and go virtually naked, and much of the humor derives from the parodic reenactment of what Europeans considered "obscene" behavior. "This horrifying spectacle," Escalante ends his account, "saddened me so that I arranged my departure for the following day."

* * *

O<small>N THE AFTERNOON</small> of September 28, Sharon and I drove up the long incline on State Highway 264 that climbs Third Mesa from the west. We stopped briefly at the entrance to Oraibi, which is often touted as the oldest continuously occupied village in the United States. (Walpi on First Mesa and Sky City on the mesa at Acoma pueblo in New Mexico are other contenders for that distinction.) The signs proscribing everything from photography to entering kivas to painting or sketching the village still hint at the xenophobia that unsettled Escalante, though it could equally be called the legacy of pride in Hopi autonomy. As recently as 1975, when Rusho, Cecala, and Crampton visited as part of the Bicentennial survey, a sign at the entrance to Oraibi declared, "WARNING: No outside white visitors allowed. Because of your failure to obey the laws of our tribe as well as the laws of your own, this village is hereby closed."

By 2017, Oraibi had somewhat loosened its antagonism to tourists, though I later discerned the discomfort of certain Anglo passersby in their comments on TripAdvisor. One wrote, "As part of a tour we visited this village and found it to be quite unpleasant. Living on a high mesa does not equate to dumping trash outside one's doorstep, urinating in the street or leaving a dead animal for visitors to smell!" Another, more gently: "I was surprised that a number of people appear to still live there. I saw no one, but at one point was greeted by several dogs."

We checked in at the motel in the Hopi Cultural Center on Second Mesa, planning to spend parts of three days. I'd been to Hopi many times before, but this was Sharon's first visit. The handsome adobe rectangle of guest rooms encloses a plaza in which a small corn field has been planted that conjures up the maize the Hopi grew before the Spaniards came. That evening, in the dining room adjoining the motel, I was arrested by a detailed timeline of Hopi history mounted in the lobby—a display that hadn't been there on my last previous visit.

Peering close, I read a notation that seemed to add a whole dimension to Escalante's experience at Hopi. It read, "1775–1780. Three-year drought; famine and disease widespread. Hopi population drops from 7,500 to 800. Many Hopis scatter to live with other tribes."

The next day we drove to Kykotsmovi to meet with Leigh Kuwan-wisiwma, the longtime chief cultural preservation officer for Hopi. I'd known Leigh for a quarter century, since I'd first interviewed him for my book about the Anasazi and the Southwest, *In Search of the Old Ones*. In 1991 he was still calling himself Leigh Jenkins, before he discarded the Anglo name somebody had inflicted on his family decades before, but his articulate edginess in defense of his people was on full display.

No one doubts that the Hopi are in some part descended from the Anasazi who abandoned the whole of the Colorado Plateau just before 1300 AD. Leigh had been irked by a recent scholarly conference devoted to the abandonment. "They invited me at the last minute," he told me on my first visit. "All these professional archaeologists were debating the question 'What happened to the Anasazi? Where did they go?' I said, 'They didn't go anywhere. They're still around. I can tell you exactly where.'" Now I showed Leigh my Xerox copy of a 1963 article from the *New Mexico Historical Review* by the shrewd historian Eleanor B. Adams, in which I'd found the English transcript of Escalante's 1775 diary of his trip to Hopi. It was titled "Fray Sylvestre and the Obstinate Hopi." (The epithet is ironic. Throughout the seventeenth and eighteenth centuries, the adjective "obstinate" was unfailingly applied to the Hopi—including by Escalante himself.) Leigh glanced at the article and chuckled. "We're still obstinate," he said.

I showed him the passage in which Escalante recoils from the ceremony featuring the nearly naked masked dancers. "It sounds like the Wuwuchim ceremony," he offered. "Anglos often called that a 'horrifying spectacle.' What month was Escalante here?"

"Late June, early July," I answered.

He frowned. "The Wuwuchim is usually danced in November. Maybe it was the Snake Dance. The masked dancers would have been the kachinas. And they're often part of a clowning ceremony, making fun of the people for all kinds of things."

I mentioned the timeline of Hopi history I'd seen in the Cultural Center lobby. Leigh had collaborated with a historian to write all the captions. Now he elaborated on the grim five-year period from 1775 to 1780. "My grandfather's grandfather moved away then," he said. "Went up to Acoma, then to Canyon de Chelly. Eventually he ended up at Isleta. There's a small part of Isleta pueblo that's still called Oraibi." He paused to reflect. "My uncles and my mom passed on those stories."

There was one passage in Escalante's 1775 diary that I had been very skeptical of. In secret, at night, the padre and his Sandia interpreter enter the dwelling of the interpreter's uncle, who confesses that he truly wishes to be baptized and become a Christian. "But if I declare myself now," he says, ". . . I cannot remain here except in great danger of losing everything I have. Neither can I leave, because the father brings no arms to defend me." Despairing of making even a single conversion, Escalante starts to leave, whereupon the unhappy uncle pleads, "If the father could bring Spanish people, build a church, and remain here, I and most of the pueblo would become Christians because many of us wish it. Perhaps it will be God's will that fathers come."

Leigh sucked in his breath. "It was a bad time. The Navajos were attacking all the time, because the Hopi were so weak."

"So perhaps the only reason a Hopi might have welcomed the Spaniards in 1775 was in hopes of defense against the Navajo?" I ventured. Leigh nodded.

I had been dumbstruck to read in the Bicentennial Commission's *Interpretive Master Plan* a recommendation to erect a trail marker tribute to Domínguez and Escalante right on the grounds of the Cultural Center, which in 1975 had recently been built. If ever there was a place on the long circuit of their voyage where the padres were *not* welcome, it was at Hopi. I assumed that this ill-conceived recommendation was only an empty Commission pipe dream.

But Leigh filled in the story. "They actually did build a monument at the Cultural Center, around 1980. It was a big deal. But the monument got pushed over by Hopis. Then it was sledgehammered to pieces." A wry grin tightened the man's lips.

We talked a bit about the several times over the decades when I had interviewed Leigh for books and articles. I'd always found his insights a welcome tonic to the honeyed prose of politicians and developers, and even to the pronouncements of archaeologists who had their own plans for land the Hopi considered ancestral and sacred. We compared our ages. Leigh admitted to being sixty-seven. After thirty years as Hopi's chief cultural preservation officer, he was retiring within the coming months. A recently published anthology of scholarly articles by both Hopi speakers and Anglo ethnographers, titled *Moquis and Kastiilam*, had been compiled as a kind of festschrift to honor Leigh Kuwanwisiwma's lifelong achievement.

I mentioned my cancer, and to my surprise Leigh responded with his own brief account of a new and fairly dire cancer diagnosis of his own. I had noticed that the once-spry man seemed to move about with a hesitant, wincing limp. "Are you in pain?" I asked.

"All the time."

At the end of our long visit, Leigh invited Sharon and me to the Home Dance of his village of Bacavi the following summer. We were both moved. I knew that such invitations were not readily proffered to Anglos. We shook hands. The parting seemed full of an unspoken sorrow.

Back at the motel, Sharon said, "I had no idea how vivid it would be to come here. To think that these were the same towns—even the same houses—that Domínguez and Escalante visited in 1776. In Provo, you just couldn't get any feel for the valley that was the Ute homeland way back then. But here the connection with the natives is still alive."

I was gratified by Sharon's response. "You don't mind that there's no gift shops or McDonald's?" I teased.

Her sidelong look of scorn sufficed for an answer. Sharon went on, "What made Hopi really come alive for me was talking with Leigh."

"Yeah," I said. "You just can't get the same thing from books."

"Exactly. It was like the past was speaking in his bones. The business about his grandfather's grandfather leaving during that bad time, right when the Spaniards came through. Escalante seemed like a real person to him."

"Not unlike the politicians and Anglo entrepreneurs he's fought for the last thirty years," I added. "He's a big reason Hopi has kept its identity intact." I wondered briefly if I was overthinking our meeting with my old friend.

"And it seemed like an amazing honor to be invited to his Home Dance at Bacavi next year," Sharon said. "We should really try to go."

*   *   *

AT MIDDAY ON November 16, 1776, Domínguez and Escalante told the team to wait at the base of the mesa crowned by the village of Oraibi, while they ascended with Juan Pedro Cisneros and most likely Andrés Muñiz. "As we started to enter the pueblo," Escalante recorded, "a large number of Indians, big and small, surrounded us. We kept asking for the ritual headman and war captain in a language they did not know"—presumably Muñiz's Ute. At last Cisneros, switching into his rudimentary Navajo, sorted out the impasse. To a Hopi man who had ordered the Spaniards not to enter Oraibi, Cisneros "spiritedly" responded by asking the man "whether or not they were friends of ours." Somehow that did the trick.

By evening the team had been installed in a domicile in Oraibi, and offered "their customary victuals." Escalante registers no surprise at this turnabout in Hopi hospitality. "Tonight the ritual headman with two very old men came to visit us," he closes his November 16 journal entry, "and having let us know that they were our friends, offered to sell us the provisions we might need. We let them know that we much appreciated it."

The modern-day legacy of the Domínguez–Escalante expedition tends to minimize the dogmatic aggressiveness of the padres' determination to convert every group of natives they met to the Gospel of Jesus and the one true God, while emphasizing the peacefulness and respect the team exhibited in all their dealings with Indians. In the formula of several of the trail-marking monuments we came across in our own retracing jaunt, "Throughout their journey they encountered a dozen native tribes, yet they never resorted to violence against their fellow men."

Thus it comes as a shock—I myself was shocked when I first read the text—to learn that in October 1775, only two and a half months after returning from his discouraging first trip to Hopi, Escalante wrote not to his Franciscan superior, Fray Isidro Murillo, but to Governor Mendinueta himself, recommending a radical solution to the "Moqui problem."

The challenge for all Franciscans in New Mexico, Escalante wrote, was "the redemption of souls which lie in the tyrannical shades of heathenism of the common enemy because of the miserable slavery of sin." What he had learned from his eight-day visit in June–July was that the Hopi "are without hope of giving up their ignorant licentiousness," because they refused to bow "their arrogant heads beneath the gentle yoke of our Lord, Jesus Christ." Those months of reflection, however, had produced a new explanation for this grim state of affairs at Moqui. It was the power-crazy *caciques* and "chiefs" who enforced the anti-Christian stance of the pueblo, as they threatened and suppressed the "many who desire holy Baptism." Those weeks of stewing on his failure must have germinated this delusion.

The solution, as Escalante urged it on the governor, was relatively simple. "The proper means that can and ought to be taken is as follows: with forces of the projected expedition [a military assault on the Gila Apaches far to the southwest of Hopi] they be subdued by arms to the dominion of their legitimate sovereign; that they be brought down from the pueblos to a plain and proper site, and whatever measures considered imperative be taken to require of them the necessary compliance" (torture? execution?). The tactics for such a conquest? "By our seizing and defending the water holes of which they daily avail themselves, because of thirst and need of their flocks, they will be forced to surrender without great fatigue to ourselves."

Seven months later, Escalante had not changed his mind. In May 1776, on the eve of his departure on the expedition in search of a route to Monterey, he wrote a long letter to Fray Murillo, urging the same plan for the total "reduction" of Moqui. And once the "obstinate" Puebloans were "brought down from their peñoles [mesas] to a plain and fit site," they would soon be "without hope of returning to their hateful licentiousness," and ought to be easy targets for "quick and complete conversion by the preaching of the religious [priests] who may be destined for this end."

As the team entered Oraibi on November 16, however, the thirteen men were in a worn-out state verging on desperation. The freezing nights had turned their journey into an ordeal and hunger assailed them hourly, as they had had little more than chunks of horse meat and a few bites of porcupine in their bellies during the previous week. Could the conquest of eternally rebellious Hopi by force of arms still have been part of the Spaniards' agenda, even though they had crawled up to Oraibi as little better than beggars?

Early on November 17, the Hopi who had given the refugees shelter brought them nourishment—"some baskets or trays of flour, beef tallow, maize paperbread [piki bread, a Hopi specialty], and other kinds of food supplies." Escalante insists that the team paid for the food, though by now it's hard to imagine what the Spaniards might have offered that the Hopi would have valued as currency. The men spent only half a day in Oraibi before moving on to Second Mesa. Escalante's succinct journal entry maintains the illusion that the authorities in Santa Fe are still in charge of the exchange. "For lack of an interpreter," he writes, "we were unable to discuss their civil submission as it was opportune and we desired it." (Talk about a toothless chomp, I thought, on the hands that were feeding them!) Somehow, despite the language barrier, the padres got the Hopi's message, which was to "let us know little else than that they wanted to preserve their friendship with the Spaniards."

The next day, in the Second Mesa village of Shongopavi, the padres doggedly resumed their sermonizing. The lecture was interrupted by locals who managed to convey that they understood nothing of what their visitors were preaching, because they themselves spoke no Castilian and the padres no Moqui. Through all the confusion, Escalante once more divined "that they wanted to be our friends but not Christians." At a loss for ways further to enlighten the pagans, D & E tried to give the old man in Shongopavi who had offered them lodging a blanket for his wife, "figuring that in this way they would better appreciate our gratitude and would become more fond of us." The gesture backfired when the brother of the woman for whom the blanket was intended "snatched it away from her and threw it at us with a mean look on his face."

It's hard not to see the meeting at Shongopavi as farce, with the men in tattered blue robes solemnly holding forth in a language unintelligible to their bemused hosts. At least among the Utes, D & E could cherish the conviction that through Andrés Muñiz the Indians comprehended the gist of the message that could save their souls. In a kind of mute acknowledgment of the futility of their preaching, the padres decided to proceed the same afternoon toward First Mesa. There, at Walpi the year before, Escalante had received the only encouragement he could wring from any of the stubborn infidels among the several Hopi villages.

The team reached the foot of First Mesa after dark on November 18. Again Domínguez and Escalante and a few unspecified companions (probably Cisneros and Muñiz) climbed up to Walpi, escorted by some local men, while the rest of the team bided its time below.

Escalante reports that in the ancient First Mesa village the padres' advance guard was "joyfully received." Again the whole team was provided lodging in the house of the "ritual headman."

Later that night, through the counsel of a "backslider Indian" originally from Galisteo pueblo south of Santa Fe, the padres got their first real inkling of what was going on at Hopi to explain the curiously mixed reception the Spaniards had received. The "very old" Galisteo man told the friars that Hopi was "currently engaged in a cruel war with the Navajo Apaches, and that these had killed and captured many of their people." Thus whatever warmth the team felt at Walpi sprang from a beleaguered nation that saw in the ragtag band of Spaniards a party "through whom they might beg the lord governor for some aid or defense against their foes." The Galisteo elder, who evidently spoke Spanish, even volunteered to travel with the team to Santa Fe to plead for a Spanish alliance against the Navajos.

Reading this passage in Escalante's journal, I saw vividly mirrored the onset of the five years of famine and warfare documented in Leigh Kuwanwisiwma's timeline in the Cultural Center lobby. Without being able to grasp the full horror of the Hopi's plight, Domínguez and Escalante pounced on the opportunity. Back in their peremptory mode, they ordered the Galisteo go-between and his Walpi friends to summon "someone in authority" from "each of the six [Hopi] pueblos" to meet the next morning "to talk over and to discuss it all, and to decide on what was best."

On November 19 the conclave opened in one of the kivas in Tano, the gateway village to Walpi. According to Escalante, the representatives from all six of the proud Hopi villages "begged us to do everything possible in their behalf."

This was the chance for which all true Franciscans lived—to bring the Word to the benighted heathen and save their souls while ensuring complete submission to Spanish rule. Domínguez and Escalante confidently laid out the terms of their agreement to intercede with Goveror Mendinueta on behalf of the Hopi. Sensing that despite their bedraggled condition, the team had gained the upper hand, the padres harangued the six pueblo spokesmen with the full righteous sanctimony of their faith. In Escalante's unflinching record of that assault, there is a hint of the Machiavellian—a nasty side of the bargain which until now had been entirely absent from the over-earnest twenty-seven-year-old's dealings with natives:

> We answered them by saying that we would be by their side
> in everything, because we loved them as one does his children,
> and that we very much sympathized with their troubles, but,
> since God alone is the one who can do everything and governs
> all, that they could not rid themselves of their sufferings so long
> as they persisted in their infidelity and did not cease offending
> Him. We went on expounding to them the gravity of eternal
> punishments, that if they failed to submit to the Christian reli-
> gion, they would have to suffer without letup in hell—we tak-
> ing advantage of the afflictions which they had just brought up
> for greater clarity and force.

The padres were utterly unprepared for the Hopi response. Between the lines in this November 19 entry in Escalante's journal— the last substantive passage in the five-month record of the great journey—the courage of the Hopi pueblos even at their lowest ebb shines through. Submit to the true religion, D & E promised, and the Hopi would "enjoy continual and sure recourse to Spanish arms against all infidels who should war against them." From the padres' point of view, the bargain was win-win. In one stroke the Hopi could ensure their eternal salvation and gain an ally equipped with swords and firearms to crush the savage Navajos. "Three times we made our plea," wrote Escalante, choking on his incredulity, "exhorting them to submit themselves to the church's bosom by impugning and demon- strating as vain and false the reasons they gave for their not convert- ing to the faith."

The Hopi parried every argument the friars brought forth. They had seen padres before who tried to manipulate them into bending to Spanish rule, and "they never had wanted it then or now." (No doubt the glorious memory of the Pueblo Revolt, only ninety-six years in the past, gave the pueblo spokesmen backbone to resist.) Besides, in the world of the greater Southwest, "there were many more gentile nations than there were Christian folk," so the Hopi "wanted to be on the more numerous side." And the three mesas lay at too great a distance from Santa Fe for the Hopi to harbor any confidence in Spanish arms. The six spokesmen queried one another. The conclusion was uniform: "They recalled the traditions of their forebears . . . concluding that it was better for them to undergo their present calamities and hardships" than to sell their souls to the oppressor. "They solely desired our friendship but by no means to become Christians, because the ancient ones had told them and counseled them never to subject themselves to the Spaniards."

At last the padres recognized total failure. "We withdrew quite crestfallen back to our lodgings," wrote Escalante, "after seeing how invincible was the obstinancy of these unfortunate Indians." I heard Leigh Kuwanwisiwma's gently mocking riposte: "We're still obstinate."

All the life goes out of Escalante's journal after this setback. The next day the thirteen men headed off for Zuni. It took them five days to ride the 130 miles that stretched between the two farthest western pueblos, along a track that Escalante and Cisneros had ridden both ways seventeen months before. The journal entries for these five days are curt and spiritless. Winter seemed to have arrived, with snowstorms and plunging temperatures. On November 24 "it was so cold that we feared we could end up frozen in the narrow valley" of the dried-up Rio Puerco. Later than day, the team arrived at Zuni "extremely exhausted when it was already dark."

In a real sense, the expedition ended here.

THE LEGACY

In the long view of history, what did the Domínguez–Escalante expedition accomplish? What, indeed, was its legacy? How would the discovery of the American Southwest have been different had the padres and their ten companions never set out from Santa Fe in 1776, determined to find a route to Monterey?

In 2017 and 2018, when friends asked me what the book I was working on was about, I often resorted to a shorthand résumé: "It's the Spanish Lewis and Clark," I would suggest, "a quarter century *before* Lewis and Clark."

No American saga has been wreathed in richer glory than the Corps of Discovery expedition President Thomas Jefferson sent westward in 1804. Even as Lewis and Clark were on their way homeward from their great voyage of exploration, Zebulon Pike set out at the head of his own government-sponsored enterprise, aimed at reconnoitering the vast territory beyond the Mississippi River and well to the south of the route Lewis and Clark had chosen. Despite the many peaks, creeks, and counties named after Pike today, his journey has never basked in the glow of historical adulation that shines eternally on Lewis and Clark. In part this neglect can be blamed on the crowning ignominy of Pike's venture, as he was captured by Spanish authorities in Santa Fe and shipped to Chihuahua for interrogation before being verbally spanked and sent back to his own people.

Thirteen years passed after Pike's journey before Stephen G. Long was launched on the next official American jaunt into the limitless West, in 1820. His charge was to discover the sources of the Platte, the Arkansas, and the Red rivers, none of which he accomplished. One of his actual achievements was the first ascent of Pikes Peak, which Pike himself had declared unclimbable. Long's published report of his voyage is a testament to discouragement and pessimism. Memorably, he wrote that the Great Plains all the way from Nebraska to Oklahoma were "unfit for cultivation and of course uninhabitable by a people depending upon agriculture."

Despite the encomiums of Willa Cather, Laura Ingalls Wilder, and Ian Frazier, I've always found the Great Plains, which I crossed as fast as I could drive by auto a couple of dozen times in the 1960s and '70s, bleak and depressing and monstrously unrelieved. Sir Richard Burton, on his journey to check out the Mormons in Salt Lake City in 1860, was of like mind, declaring that to survive crossing the Plains by mail wagon one must resort to opium.

In short, the notion that Lewis and Clark laid the groundwork for the inevitable expansion of the United States "from sea to shining sea" rests on a shaky foundation. John Colter was a member of the Corps of Discovery who, on the way back east, quit the company to head back into the wilderness the team had only begun to discover. His desertion triggered a thirty-two-year cavalcade of exploration of the West in the form of freelance entrepreneurs bent on getting rich by trapping beavers to be sold to the markets back east. The Anglo discovery of Yellowstone was made by Colter, whose outlandish tales of exploding geysers and boiling mud pools earned his fantasy landscape the nickname Colter's Hell. As a brotherhood, the mountain men were mostly illiterate, unconcerned with history, and not particularly patriotic. Many of them were French or Spanish. Only in the 1840s, with the expeditions of John C. Frémont, a new fascination with Oregon and California as dreamlands in which to start a new life, and above all the discovery of gold, did westward expansion turn into America's manifest destiny.

The ambition behind the Spanish quest to link Santa Fe with Monterey was every bit as imperialistic as Jefferson's designs on the American West. Yet, for many reasons, after 1776 the course of history in New Spain took a diametrically different path.

When the Domínguez–Escalante expedition reached Zuni on November 24, the junior friar was at last back on home ground, having been assigned to the mission there a year and a half earlier. He and Domínguez lingered at Zuni for another nineteen days before setting out for Santa Fe—exactly why, the journal does not make clear. Nor does Escalante account for what happened to the padres' eleven companions after they got to Zuni. Scholars have assumed that the other men made their own way back to Santa Fe, probably long before the padres returned. By 1776 the trail, after all, was well-known and often traveled.

From Zuni Domínguez wrote a letter to Fray Isidro Murillo, briefly summarizing the team's adventure and promising a fuller narrative in the journal the padres would bring back to Santa Fe. In the letter he lays out the obvious reasons for giving up the quest for Monterey— lack of provisions, cold, and the discouraging fact that not even at the point of their farthest westward push "did we find any information whatsoever about the Spaniards of Monterey." Domínguez confesses the failure to dent the Hopi obstinacy about not becoming Christians, but near the end of the letter he makes a case for both settlement among and conversion of the Utes and for trying again to establish a trade route to California. "From the lake [Utah Lake] to near the Río Colorado," he writes, "there is an extremely beautiful road, and entirely free from enemies. With regard to Monterey, according to what we observed and through all the land we traveled from the lake, it is possible to travel safely with a very small force." This letter to Murillo is the only surviving commentary in Domínguez's hand on the journey he had co-led, though scholars argue about how big a contribution he made to Escalante's writing of the official journal.

It was not until January 2, 1777, that Domínguez and Escalante finally reached Santa Fe. The next day they presented the journal to their Franciscan boss, Fray Murillo, and to Governor Mendinueta. In front of these worthies they formally signed the manuscript, declaring in its last line that "everything contained in this diary is true and faithful to what occurred and was observed during our journey." They also presented the deerskin painting on which the Timpanogotzis had illustrated their best warriors in battle with the Comanches, which the team had carefully carried through all their trials from Utah Lake back to Santa Fe. (Where is that relic today? Gathering dust in some drawer of a neglected archive in Mexico City? Or long since thrown out as trash?) That diorama on deerskin had been given to the padres as a token of the Timpanogotzis's sincerity in wishing to become Christians, and as such D & E handed it over to the Franciscan Custodian and the Governor as proof that the Yutas were hungry for conversion.

For D & E, blazing the trade route to Monterey was ultimately of secondary significance. What they clung to was the hope that their superiors would see the value of returning to that newly discovered land, where the padres and other Spaniards could build towns and establish missions and fulfill their promises to return and bring eternal salvation to the infidels. Whatever Murillo thought about this proposal, Governor Mendinueta promptly squelched it. Even before the expedition, he had cast a jaundiced eye on the padres' ambitions to found new missions in the wilderness. "If there are not enough fathers for those already conquered," he had said then, "how can there be any for those that may be newly conquered?" By January 1777, he had not changed his mind.

The record does not show whether Domínguez and Escalante gave up their missionizing dream after that meeting. But Miera y Pacheco had not abandoned his own rather grandiose plans for how

New Mexico might take advantage of the newly discovered lands. On October 26, 1777, he addressed a lengthy proposal not to Mendinueta or Murillo but to the King of Spain himself. He paid lip service to the importance of religious conversion: "It is certain, My Lord, that many tribes desire the water of baptism . . . for these people, with tears in their eyes, manifested their ardent desire to become Christians." But ultimately, the key to expanding the empire of New Spain into the great Southwest was military. Miera built his vision on the vital need to establish three presidios—massive forts that would take the shape of walled cities. With those three, Miera would guarantee Spanish control of the vast domain stretching between Santa Fe and Monterey.

One presidio should be built at the mouth of the Gila River, where it flows into the Colorado. This locale, far to the southwest of any stage of the D & E circuit, had been the arena of a previous military campaign in which Miera had played a key role. From that fortress, the Spaniards could subdue the Gila Apaches, who had already caused so much trouble in the no-man's-land between Sonora and New Mexico. A second presidio would be plunked down right on Utah Lake, in the heartland of the Timpanogotzis Utes. As Escalante had in his "Description of the Valley," Miera rhapsodized about the region as "the most pleasing, beautiful, and fertile site in all New Spain." The great lake on the edge of that homeland abounded in "many varieties of savory fish, very large white geese, many kinds of ducks, and other exquisite birds never seen elsewhere, besides beaver, otters, seals, and some strange animals which are or appear to be ermines, judging by the softness and whiteness of their furs." The old soldier went on to extol the river that he had drawn flowing westward out of the even larger lake to the north (today's Great Salt Lake), even though none of the team had seen it, but which he assured the king was "very large and navigable," and which led to some "very large settlements in which lived civilized Indians." Such a river, of course, does not exist.

The third presidio, curiously, should be built at the junction of the Navajo and Las Animas rivers, "along the beautiful and extensive meadows which its margins provide for raising crops, together with the convenience of the timber, firewood, and pastures which they offer." Curious, because despite the cartographer's acumen, the Navajo and Las Animas rivers never meet. Perhaps Miera meant the junction of the Navajo with the San Juan, near which the team had established its Nuestra Señora de las Nieves camp on August 5, where Escalante saw only "good prospects for a moderate settlement."

No matter. The ultimate purpose of this third presidio, in Miera's starry-eyed plan, was to be a concentration camp for all the Hopi people, after they had been "brought down by force from their cliffs" on the three mesas in faraway Arizona. Miera thought a bloodless siege of Moqui by soldiers guarding the water holes on the plains below Walpi and Oraibi would convince the obstinate Hopi to "surrender and do whatever might be required of them." As industrious Indian slaves in the presidio on the Navajo River, the Moqui would buttress "a rich and strong province, adjoining New Mexico and expanding toward these new establishments [on Utah Lake]." Miera's plan was Escalante's scheme of conquest by siege added to forced removal to an alien land. In its ruthless totalitarianism, it anticipates the Long Walk of the Navajos beginning in 1863 and their five-year incarceration at Bosque Redondo.

Needless to say, nothing came of Miera's cockamamie proposal. It's doubtful whether the King of Spain ever responded to the letter advancing it.

After 1777, Miera, Domínguez, and Escalante never again went on record urging a second try at establishing a route from Santa Fe to Monterey, let alone the building of presidios and towns and missions along the way. Domínguez went back to work on his comprehensive survey of the existing missions of New Mexico, compiling that massive document by August 1777. In the words of his modern editor, Domínguez's "lengthy report was filed away with a sarcastic notation and forgotten." It was rediscovered only in 1928 in a dusty archive in the Biblioteca Nacional in Mexico City. It survives today as one of the two or three most valuable accounts of life in eighteenth-century New Mexico. Domínguez himself pops up in El Paso in 1778, then disappears from the record for seventeen years. His last written utterance emerges in 1795 in the form of a short, obsequious plea for a sinecure as "definitor" (a sidekick or yes-man to the head priest) in the benighted outpost of Janos on the northern frontier of the state of Chihuahua. He died at Janos sometime before 1805.

Bernardo Miera y Pacheco compiled his extraordinary map covering the route and discoveries of the 1776 expedition. It was recopied by himself and others, with some additions. As well as a priceless record of the five-month journey into the unknown Southwest that the motley team performed, it survives as a cartographic work of art in its own right.

In 1778 Juan Bautista de Anza became governor of New Mexico. His predecessor, Mendinueta, was wildly unpopular in Santa Fe. During his reign he had cut off trade with the dangerous Comanches, but as their antagonist he proved a feckless warrior. In 1779 Anza amassed an army of 600 soldiers, later reinforced with 200 Utes and Jicarilla Apaches, to ride out onto the plains in pursuit of the main Comanche band, under the leadership of their legendary chief, Cuerno Verde. Miera was almost certainly a member of that expedition, but since Anza never bothered to name even his principal lieutenants in his reports, we cannot be absolutely sure that Miera was on board. Still, the anonymous map produced to accompany the report bears Miera's unmistakable stamp.

The two men were not only close friends, they were distant cousins. Anza gave Miera the official epithet *distinguido* to add to his title, and he left the best description we have of the mapmaker. In 1779, wrote Anza, Miera was "five feet tall, sixty-five years old, his faith Apostolic Roman Catholic, and his features as follows: gray hair and eyebrows, blue eyes, rosy fair complexion, straight nose, with full gray beard." (Would that we had a description of either Domínguez or Escalante half so detailed!)

The war against the Comanches was a great success. Anza rode back into Santa Fe carrying aloft Cuerno Verde's headdress ("a green horn in his forehead, fixed in a . . . tanned leather headpiece") like a trophy scalp, as a "delirious" crowd in the plaza cheered the soldiers. According to historian Pekka Hämäläinen, the defeat of Cuerno Verde marked the beginning of the end of the century-long Empire of the Plains during which the Comanches terrorized all enemies, including the Spaniards.

Miera was almost certainly a soldier in that victorious army. He had, alas, only six more years to live, succumbing at the age of seventy-one in Santa Fe in 1785. His incomparable maps and the altar screens and statues for churches that survive furnish the legacy of the man biographer John Kessell calls "one of the most versatile and fascinating figures" of eighteenth-century New Mexico.

The excruciating "urinary ailment" of which Escalante complained in his 1775 diary, but all hints of which he stoically expunged from the much longer journal of the 1776 expedition, almost certainly caused his premature death. Whether, as Kessell believes, Escalante was stricken with pancreatic or bladder cancer or some other incurable disease, we will never know. After the great expedition, he stayed in New Mexico for three more years, serving as missionary to various pueblos. In 1780, he requested permission to make the long ride to Mexico City for treatment for his recurring malady. He never got there, dying in April in the ex-mining town of Parral in southern Chihuahua. He was only thirty years old.

*   *   *

AS RECOUNTED IN chapter 8, the Domínguez–Escalante expedition should be seen as a courageous campaign by two idealistic priests to save Franciscan honor in a colony rife with the corruption and incompetence of their missionary brethren. That the team failed to reach Monterey can hardly be held against them. Not even the Timpanogotzis living in what Marshall Sahlins has called "aboriginal affluence" on Utah Lake really comprehended the topographic obstacles that lay between the farthest western stab the team made in October 1776 and the Pacific Ocean—not the least of which was the lordly chain of the Sierra Nevada, which stretches from north to south a full 350 miles beyond the dreary sagebrush plain where the casting of lots dictated the retreat to Santa Fe.

It was not only the church in New Mexico that had fallen into torpor by 1776. Spain itself, the most powerful nation in Europe in the era of Cortés and Coronado, had slid into second-rate status compared to France or Great Britain by the end of the eighteenth century. It was not merely Mendinueta's timidity that ruled out a further expedition in quest of a route to Monterey, much less the building of towns and missions along the trail pioneered by D & E. The monarchy in Spain was losing its grip on the New World, or at least on the northern frontier where it had once dreamed of consolidating its empire. Only forty-four years after the padres handed over the deerskin pledge of Ute allegiance to the authorities in Santa Fe, Spain altogether gave up its hold on that northern frontier, as Mexico gained its sovereignty in its war of independence in 1821. Within a decade, thanks largely to the exploits of Antonio Armijo, the Spanish Trail (which should really be called the Mexican Trail) solidified a trading route to California far more practical than the wandering path the padres had forged in 1776.

Yet even the Spanish Trail was soon to become an American trail. There was no quenching the relentless tide of trappers and miners and settlers a country bursting with ambition sent westward from St. Louis through the first decades of the nineteenth century. It's worth remembering that when Brigham Young led his persecuted Saints into the valley of the Great Salt Lake in 1847, he was invading a foreign country. But only a year later, Mexico ceded its last-gasp hold on what would become the American Southwest to a nation enthralled by its God-given charter of manifest destiny. That surrender would be completed with the Gadsden Purchase in 1853.

Historians love to play the game of what-if. If the United States had failed to spread its dominion all the way to the shores of the Pacific, would Lewis and Clark be as forgotten today as Domínguez and Escalante are? If in 2018 Oregon belonged to Great Britain, Alaska to Russia, and California to Mexico, would the daring pioneers of the Corps of Discovery be relegated to the footnotes of North American exploration?

Yet the lasting value of a voyage like that of Domínguez and Escalante does not hinge on whether or not it paved the way for conquest and empire. Even history books for kids no longer tout Columbus as having "discovered" America. Leif Erikson's inspired determination around 1000 AD "to sail beyond the sunset, and the baths of all the western stars" led to no enduring Viking settlement in North America. By the fifteenth century even the Danish colony in Greenland had gone extinct. Domínguez and Escalante, of course, did not "discover" the Southwest. Native Americans had thrived there for more than ten millennia before 1776. But they were the first Europeans to explore that majestic and difficult region of canyons and rivers and stark plateaus, and that is a distinction that the feckless decades of Spanish misrule that followed their unrepeated *entrada* cannot dim.

As Sharon and I drove out of Hopi on the road toward Zuni on September 29, I mused about how to sum up the padres' achievement. For two unlikely feats they have been justly commended by later writers and travelers. The first is that, for all the desperate vicissitudes to which they were reduced by the pitiless country they explored, they lost not a single man. In fact, they brought back an extra "companion," in the person of Joaquín the Laguna, who for reasons only he knew stayed with the team all the way, and seemed unfazed as he entered an unimaginable new life in Santa Fe. (Domínguez was quick to boast of this addition in his letter to Murillo from Zuni, writing that "this has sweetened the inevitable bitter things that so long a journey offers, because we have now assured the safety of his soul.") Despite all the complaining Escalante indulged in as the "experts" led the padres astray time and again, or got lost overnight, there's no avoiding the conclusion that this small and ill-equipped party of Spaniards looked after one another. You cannot say the same of the armies led by Coronado, Oñate, or Vargas.

The other achievement is that indeed they "never resorted to violence against their fellow men." Even the equally peaceable Lewis and Clark team ended up killing two Indians when, on the Marias River in present-day Montana, the men chased a group of Blackfeet they suspected of trying to steal their horses. Meriwether Lewis shot one man, and a soldier stabbed another to death. For almost a century thereafter, the Blackfoot nation harbored a seething hatred of Americans, even while they traded on friendly terms with Canadians.

Escalante's recommendation that obstinate Moqui ought to be brought to heel by force of arms seems in the end to have been an empty threat. No matter how "crestfallen" the padres were after the implosion of the oratory by which they sought to convert the Hopi through the sheer power of what they thought was reason, Escalante's journal in November never hints at a final solution by force to be meted out by Governor Mendinueta's soldiers. The padres gave up instead—and in their ignominious retreat, Escalante had the honesty to present the Hopi point of view so clearly that we can cheer from the sidelines 241 years later.

To be sure, twelve men with a few muskets, no armor, and only Miera's experience in a real military campaign presented no threat to Utes, Hopi, or even "cowardly" Paiutes. The wonder is that somewhere along the trail the party was not wiped out by Indians who might have coveted the expedition's meager belongings or simply resented white men trespassing on their homeland. The team seems to have glided along under the spell of a magic charm against harm, whether or not a Franciscan God was in charge of looking out for them.

For the modern observer, as for the reader of Escalante's journal, the hardest thing to swallow is the padres' self-righteous condescension toward the natives, linked as it is to their adamantine determination to turn every Yuta or Moqui they met into a dyed-in-the-soul Christian. Many times as I read out loud to Sharon a passage in which Escalante reports that he and his fellow friar told some band of Indians that "we loved them as our children," or waxes outraged that the natives danced almost naked or used a shaman's mumbo-jumbo to cure a sick man, I couldn't resist sighing or snickering or editorializing, "Can you believe their arrogance?" But just as often, I caught myself on the brink of my own condescension, as I reminded myself that I needed to see these encounters through the lens of historical perspective.

In 2018, despite the dogged persistence of racism and xenophobia in America, we tend to take as a self-evident truth the idea that a culture or a people can only be judged in terms of its own mores and beliefs. Yet cultural relativism was an invention of the late nineteenth century. Yes, Jean-Jacques Rousseau published his *Discourse on the Origins of Inequality among Men* twenty-two years before D & E took off from Santa Fe, and Europe during the Enlightenment of the last half of the eighteenth century took seriously the notion of the noble savage (a term Rousseau never used, though he championed the idea). But the lofty theorizing of French *philosophes* and the poetry of the English Romantics hardly trickled down to the remote northern frontier of New Spain. Even among Spaniards in New Mexico, no one was less inclined than its Franciscan priests to view Indian dances and idol worship as a viable alternative religion. For D & E, as passionate and dogmatic as any Franciscans, the devil was literally present in the kiva and the wickiup.

The generally received notion of today that a culture can only be judged in terms of its own internal logic was a radical idea in 1899, when Franz Boas began teaching anthropology at Columbia University. Such protégés as Margaret Mead, Ruth Benedict, A. L. Kroeber, Edward Sapir, and Zora Neale Hurston carried his teachings into the real world from Samoa to the Yahi-Yana hideout of Ishi, "the last wild Indian in North America." As Matt Liebmann explained to me, Boas drove home in vivid fashion his doctine of cultural autonomy by reorganizing the exhibits at the American Museum of Natural History. Before Boas, the glass cases taught the steady and inexorable progress of humankind from Stone Age to Gunpowder, from Savagery through Barbarism to Civilization. Boas dismantled this tendentious apparatus and reorganized the exhibits to treat each region of the world separately, in terms of its own development of everything from tools to customs to cosmogony.

Domínguez and Escalante may have been rigidly doctrinaire about the unbridgeable gulf between heaven and hell and about the absolute truth of the Bible as further explicated by Saint Francis. But they were almost entirely without guile, and they were full of humility about their own failings as men and priests. Escalante closes a typical letter to Fray Murillo thus: "Your most affectionate and useless subject kisses your Reverend Paternity's hands." He opens his letter to Murillo reporting the 1775 visit to Hopi by claiming that "the knowledge that my sins were responsible for its failure causes me great chagrin and mortification."

An ancillary virtue of the black-and-white morality the padres brought to their Indian encounters is that the journal nowhere veers near the modern-day caricature of Native Americans living in wise and stoic harmony with the earth and with their fellow man. In Escalante's account, the Hopi are in all-out war with the Navajos, the Sabuagana and Laguna Utes constantly raid against and battle with the Comanches (whoever that enemy was), and the Paiutes seem to lurk in fear of all strangers.

In almost six weeks of riding along with Escalante, I'd gotten used to his foibles: his incredulity that infidels didn't at once see the transparent truth of the Gospel and its promise of eternal life, his I-told-you-so disgust when the "experts" led the team astray, his dogged humorlessness. I had come to find his quaint locutions charming: how Miera "was ready to freeze on us," or how after cutting their porcupine into thirteen pieces "we tasted flesh of the richest flavor," or how the Hopi man flung the blanket back at the Spaniards "with a mean look on his face." Escalante's squeamishness about the human body was like that of a Victorian maiden aunt, as he averted his eyes from the G-strings of the Paiute women "barely covering what one cannot gaze upon without peril" or as he managed to notice the "small and delicate feather subtly attached" to "the end of the member it is not modest to name" of the Hopi dancers.

Escalante was a chronicler without pretense or affectation. He never tried to put a spin on a failure in order to transform it into a partial success. Though he could tell Indians he'd just met that he loved them as his children, he tasted real grief when the teaching of the padres failed to win any converts. The dawning realization that he would almost certainly have to break his promise to the Timpanogotzis to come back and live with them and build them a church hums like a pulse of sorrow throughout the last two months of the journey. By the end of our long drive, Escalante almost seemed like a third passenger in our SUV. Though he wouldn't have been my first choice as a companion on our road trip, by the time we reached Zuni he felt almost like a friend.

The journey of Escalante and Domínguez and their tenacious teammates is not unique in North American history, but the combination of the voyage and Escalante's diary is. Lewis and Clark's journals are packed with detail, so much so that the shape of the exploit often gets lost. Oddly, Clark's semiliterate, unpunctuated jottings are often blunter and truer than Lewis's more learned entries, and Clark sometimes fills in incidents that Lewis smooths over or omits altogether. It takes a historian such as Stephen Ambrose to tell the story whole.

The amazing eight-year traverse of the continent from Florida to Sinaloa from 1528 to 1536 by Cabeza de Vaca and his three tough comrades is arguably the most extraordinary voyage of discovery ever undertaken in North America. But Cabeza de Vaca's diary is so sketchy, so vague, and ultimately so unreliable that scholars ever since have wrangled not only over where the four refugees went but over what they did during those eight years of survival.

John Wesley Powell's classic *The Exploration of the Colorado River and Its Canyons* may be the liveliest and best-written narrative of an epic North American voyage of discovery ever penned. But the skill of the telling derives in large part from the ways that Powell turned his "journal" into a semifictional account, as he interweaves incidents from both his 1869 and 1871–72 trips, overdramatizes some hair's-breadth escapes and neglects to mention others, and in painting the team as a platoon of loyal comrades streamlined to the will of their captain glides over the constant antagonisms and near mutinies that would have made the true story even more fascinating. (There is one other narrative of discovery in North America that I would put alongside Powell's in the ranks of the greatest expedition books. That is Samuel Hearne's *Journey to the Northern Ocean*, published in 1795—his account of the first European descent of the Coppermine River in arctic Canada. But that book is virtually unread today. I urge the curious aficionado to seek out a copy.)

All in all, I know of no combination of pathbreaking journey and first-person narrative in the short history of European and American exploration of our continent quite in Escalante's league. At the finish line of our own journey, our odometer read 3434, almost exactly double the mileage the Spaniards racked up. If we were left puzzled by all kinds of fundamental questions the padres' strange *entrada* raises, still, that uncertainty was suffused with admiration. And in memory, our own journey in homage to the padres fades only very slowly—maybe not at all.

*　*　*

SHARON AND I spent September 30 at Zuni, but nothing we did there evoked the spirit of the 1776 adventure the way even ten minutes of chatting with Leigh Kuwanwisiwma at Hopi had. On a late

Saturday morning the visitor center was closed, as was the A:shiwi A:wan Museum and Heritage Center. The whole town, in fact, felt closed, except for the Giant gas station–cum–Subway, a few jewelry shops, and the yard sale on the porch of the modern church where we could have bought used T-shirts for 25 cents each. Instead of the stern "no photography" sign at the entrance to Oraibi, we read the gentle suggestion on the window of the visitor center, "Consider capturing visual memories instead of photographs!"

Only the old mission church seemed to reverberate with echoes of the Domínguez–Escalante expedition. Originally built in 1629, it had fallen into decrepitude by 1821, when Spain ceded its colony to Mexico. The National Park Service restored the buiding in the late 1960s and early 1970s, but on this genial morning in 2017 it was locked up tight and looked as though it had been for months. Sharon and I stood just outside the gates, gazing across the weed-strewn cemetery as we took in the lopsided grace of the adobe building. It was not hard to imagine Escalante giving sermons and hearing confessions here in the spring of 1775, before he set out on his first trip to Hopi. But it *was* hard to see Zuni as it must have felt to Spaniards back then, exiled to the far western outpost of what John Kessell called "the Siberia of New Mexico." During our several hours at Zuni, four locals came up to our vehicle to beg for money. One leather-skinned oldster asked for "a dollar so I can get a drink."

We drove on. No longer was there any incentive to match our journey to Escalante's diary, for he barely recorded his eventual trek with Domínguez back to Santa Fe. The two-sentence entry for December 13 actually covers four days' travel across 79 miles from Zuni to Acoma. We stopped at El Morro, or Inscription Rock, the astonishing 200-foot-high sandstone buttress on which hundreds of passersby have carved their names and messages, from the beginning of the seventeenth century through the beginning of the twenty-first. I'd stopped there several times before, but for Sharon this bulletin board of history, unique in the United States, was a revelation. About fifteen years before, as I researched a book about the Pueblo Revolt, I'd dutifully transcribed the vaunts of Oñate and Vargas at El Morro. In 1605, seven years after Oñate took possession of the fledgling colony of New Mexico, calling himself *el adelantado* (a title bestowed on someone who had "conquered" a new land), he had recorded his passage on the way back from "the discovery of the South Sea," since he'd completed a voyage from Santa Fe to the Gulf of California. Vargas, the architect of the Bloodless Reconquest from 1692 to 1696, had deemed it fitting to carve into the stone his claim that he had retaken "all of New Mexico" from the treacherous Puebloan rebels not only for the Holy Faith and the Royal Crown, but "at his [own] expense."

As we slowly walked the Park Service path along the base of the monument on a windy day with the tang of autumn in it, I noticed an inscription I'd previously overlooked, one that ironically anticipated D & E's mission. In August 1716, the then governor of New Mexico, Féliz Martínez, had bragged that he was en route with the Franciscan Custodian of the colony (Murillo's predecessor) to carry out "the reduction and conquest of Moqui." Martínez, as it turned out, had no more luck with the obstinate Hopi than D & E would have six decades later.

In all likelihood, the padres passed by El Morro on December 13, 1776. They may have camped there, for the deep tank or pool filled by a waterfall spilling off the summit of the buttress made for one of the most reliable waypoints on the road between Zuni and Santa Fe. But if they stopped at El Morro, they didn't bother to record the event in stone. Inscriptions, much less boastful ones, weren't the padres' style, they who had carved only *"paso por aqui"* and the year as they stumbled down the slickrock ramps toward the Crossing of the Fathers a month before. On the banks of the Green River, Joaquín Lain had used his adze to chisel out his name, the date, and a pair of crosses in a sturdy cottonwood tree in September, but despite Herbert E. Bolton's wishful thinking in 1950, that piece of sylvan annotation had long since crumbled into the soil.

On the homeward stretch from Zuni at the end of September, I did a lot of thinking about the journey Sharon and I were about to complete. There's no getting around the fact that the Domínguez–Escalante expedition ended not with a bang but a whimper. Our own forty-day pilgrimage (actually thirty-nine) was also heading toward a whimpering finish line. We did not even plan to return to Santa Fe, since we had rented our RAV4 at the Albuquerque airport, from which we would fly home on October 4. We wanted to camp out one more night on the trail, whether or not our bivouac corresponded in any way with the padres' December dash back to Santa Fe.

I realized that our own "expedition" was the longest continuous journey in quest of any kind of goal that the two of us had ever taken together. When we were still in our twenties, between 1968 and 1971, Sharon had been my partner on four Alaskan expeditions—one a kayaking trip on the Tikchik Lakes in the southwestern corner of the state, the other three climbing expeditions with other men who would team up with me to attempt unclimbed peaks in the magnificent Brooks Range north of the Arctic Circle. Those trips had lasted between eighteen and thirty-three days, so our Domínguez–Escalante jaunt was actually the longest single-purpose journey we had ever shared. It seemed fudging a bit to call it an expedition, especially since we were never that far from the next motel or McDonald's. But it had the true intensity of a search. Every day—every hour on the road—we were trying to solve a puzzle that required mapping a 241-year-old diary onto a landscape that had been radically transformed since 1776 in some ways, in others hardly at all.

As we drove slowly toward Albuquerque, I realized that our trip also fit my paradigm for the kind of quest that I had discovered in the Southwest as I sought out prehistoric ruins and rock art panels. Unlike a climbing expedition, our retracing of D & E was in pursuit of an Other—in this case, not the Anasazi cosmos but a wilderness full of unredeemed strangers to which a pair of

Franciscan priests brought a vision almost as alien to Sharon's and my thinking as the one blazoned forth in kachina masks etched on sandstone walls. Escalante's journal was our Rosetta Stone, but even through its kaleidoscopic lens it was hard to see the Satan lurking just beyond the drumbeat of an Indian dance that the padres were sure was there.

On our Alaska trips, I had always been the partner in charge. When my cronies and I went off to climb Igikpak or Shot Tower, Sharon waited at base camp, her ear cocked for the snuffling grunt of a grizzly bear wandering near or the joyful banter of climbers coming back exhausted from a first ascent. On the D & E trail, thanks to the ravages of my cancer, Sharon and I were truly equal partners. If anything, she was in charge, trying to figure out what to do when my nausea or fatigue threatened the day's program, arranging blood draws in Durango and Provo, fixing meals I could eat with my saliva-less mouth and throat, sorting out my dozens of pills and reminding me to take them, and hugging me back to sleep when a nightmare woke me drenched in sweat. And, yes, driving our SUV at least two-thirds of the time.

Ten months after our trip, in July 2018, as I was writing the last pages of this book, I got bad news. The Pembrolizumab that had held the metastasized cancer in my chest nodules in check for two years seemed not to have stopped a new growth in nodules on my adrenal glands. It was the second metastasis of throat cancer, and its appearance in a different part of my body boded ill. My oncologist opted to start infusions of Pembro again, but I could see that she wasn't optimistic.

Yet even the previous fall, by the end of our D & E circuit, I had felt the weight of mortality hanging over me. The bad days when it was hard to get back in the SUV and keep going portended the decline into helplessness, hospitalization, and death that was never far from my thoughts. Often I wondered if Escalante, who must have suffered every day from the "urinary ailment" that probably prefigured his death, rode onward with a kindred sense of doom. But he had one advantage over me: he was certain of the far better world that lay on the other side.

*   *   *

AT THE END of our journey in early October 2017, Sharon and I were three and a half weeks shy of our fiftieth wedding anniversary. Like any long-married couple, we had traversed alpine ridges of transporting joy during those years, and slogged through swamps of anger and estrangement. By staying together, we had of course locked doors to alternate lives we might have explored had the option of chucking it in and starting over seduced us with its illusion of freedom.

All my adult life, I have been tantalized by the vision of intimacy embodied in Robert Browning's poem "Two in the Campagna." It seems to speak directly to the craving for love vexed with doubt and distraction that is like a blueprint for my life with Sharon. The poem begins:

I wonder do you feel today
As I have felt since, hand in hand,
We sat down on the grass, to stray
In spirit better through the land,
This morn of Rome and May?

But "Two in the Campagna" is no simple love poem. "Help me to hold it," the speaker pleads to the woman beside him, as Browning launches on a tour de force of metaphor, the "thought" he tries to hold skimming from fennel to "brickwork's cleft" to five "blind and green" beetles groping for nectar inside a flower, alighting briefly on the "grassy slope" on which the lovers lie. The poem is about the almost-meeting of souls, the desire to merge completely with the other, which the speaker can never quite realize.

No. I yearn upward, touch you close,
Then stand away. I kiss your cheek,
Catch your soul's warmth—I pluck the rose
And love it more than tongue can speak—
Then the good minute goes.

That poem has always seemed to capture the depths of love I felt for Sharon crossed with the futility of love, of the impossibility of finding true contentment with any other person. The poem ends with a characteristic Browning outcry:

Only I discern—
Infinite passion, and the pain
Of finite hearts that yearn.

But during our thirty-nine days on the road from New Mexico to Colorado to Utah to Arizona and back to New Mexico, much of that despairing "almost-perfect" stasis between Sharon and me seemed to transmute into something quieter and less troubled—something not, in Browning's phrase, "to catch at and let go," but rather "to catch at and hold." Yes, we had our little squabbles along the road, our arguments about where to stop for lunch or whether to spend an hour hiking along a creek that D & E might have skirted way back then, even those all-too-normal marital blackouts when one of us got so caught up in our own thoughts that we heard not a word the other was saying for three minutes at a time.

Yet as the end of the journey loomed in the image of the Albuquerque airport, and neither of us wanted the trip to end, I realized that this mini-expedition was the best thing we had ever done together. I didn't need to ask Sharon if she felt the same way.

Late in the afternoon of October 1, we turned off State Highway 53 and drove south on the dirt road that skirts El Malpais

National Monument on the west and the Chain of Craters on the east. Spaniards long before D & E named the black smother of congealed lava covering 462 square miles of what was once ponderosa forest El Malpais, or the Badlands. From such mini-volcanoes as Cerro Lobo and Cerro Chato in the Chain of Craters, wave after wave of eruptions shook the land over the last million years, the last substantial flow spreading the molten magma from the earth's interior only 3,000 years ago. The Spaniards avoided El Malpais, but the Puebloans who lived nearby embraced it long before Coronado. Old secret trails through the lava tubes connected Acoma pueblo to Zuni, and archaeologists are still finding pottery and projectile points in the most arcane bends of the tunnels that reticulate the igneous labyrinth. Here lay one more corner of the Southwest outback I had promised myself I'd explore, and that I now must forgo.

We were not in a national forest but rather in the El Malpais National Conservation Area, set aside only in 1987 by the Bureau of Land Management. We drove back and forth, looking for the most genial site we could find for our last campout on the D & E trail. The usual hodgepodge of private inholdings, replete with barbed wire and "no trespassing" signs, bordered the fenceless pine-needle swards where we guessed no one would object if we pitched our tent. A few cows greeted our SUV with stupefied gazes. The stiff wind that had buffeted us at El Morro was fitfully dwindling, and when the sun left us at 6:30, the air took on a sudden chill.

At last we chose a mediocre campsite with little in the way of a view. In recent years a forest fire had scorched the hillside behind us, and I thought I could still smell a faint char when the breeze swept in the right direction. It was Sunday evening. The only other vehicles on the road were woodcutters with their truck beds loaded with logs and ATVers with their buggies strapped onto trailers, all of them headed home after a weekend tinged with the early threat of winter. "Doesn't anybody camp out any more?" I wondered out loud as Sharon set the plates on our Walmart folding table.

Dinner was hot dogs with yellow mustard and diced onions and baked beans out of a can. It was the same meal we'd had several times before on our trip, but with my choices so limited by the cancer-zapping rays two years earlier, I savored every bite. I drank a bottle of Bohemia beer from Mexico, Sharon a glass of rosé from California, the rosé of Provence that we preferred being hard to come by in the liquor stores of Gallup. After dinner we lit our usual small fire of ponderosa branches.

It had rained hard two days before and the air felt scrubbed clean, its blue the color I remembered from my childhood in Boulder. A three-quarter moon crept up the eastern sky, ducking in and out of the trees. We talked about this and that, and then we just stared into the flames, studying the sparks flung upward and the blue jets of oxidized carbon as if they spoke a language we were just learning to read. We had the whole forest to ourselves.

I got up to pee around 4:30 in the morning. It was cold outside the tent, and I wanted to hurry back to my sleeping bag. But the moon had set, and the stars were sharper than they had been at any time on our whole trip. I lingered, gazing at Orion and Canis Major in the east, wondering if the pinpoint of Sirius had ever looked quite so cold and bright.

As a kid, long before I felt the pull of mountains, the wilderness of the universe had captivated me. That my father was an astronomer had something to do with it, but the constellations seemed to pulse with a demand I could feel in my nerve endings. I needed to get out there, to travel endlessly through space, to reach the stars that hung immobile in the sky each night, to find out what was there. Somewhere among those infinite spaces there was an answer to a question I could not yet formulate.

I turned back to the tent, assailed by a rueful memory of the moment when I first realized—was I seven or eight?—that I would never get to travel into outer space, that Sirius was too far away. That I would be bound by our humdrum earth for the rest of my life.

Inside the tent, I crawled back into my sleeping bag, embracing the tingle of warmth my body had left in its nylon and down. It didn't matter, did it, that the cosmos was beyond our reach. In my seventy-four years, I had gone someplace far and strange and wonderful.

I put my arm around Sharon, and heard her murmur in her sleep. We had gone someplace together. We didn't need a map to tell us where.

Acknowledgments

WHEN I FINISHED WRITING MY LAST BOOK, *LIMITS OF THE Known*, in February 2017, I had my doubts whether I would ever write another one. Seven months earlier, I had learned that my stage 4 throat cancer had metastasized to my lungs. In cases like mine, the immunotherapy drug my oncologist put me on had a success rate of only 15–20 percent.

Yet during the spring of 2017, Sharon and I survived not only "normal" life in Watertown, Massachusetts, but hiking trips to Tucson and Cedar Mesa, then a rock climbing outing with old friends in California. By the beginning of summer, I was thinking about a new book. In August my doctor declared that, against the odds, the immunotherapy had seemed to halt the growth of the cancer cells on my lungs.

I wanted to make a long journey with Sharon, partly because we had grown closer than ever during the past two years, in which she had given up her career as a psychoanalyst to nurse me from one crisis to the next. My first thought was an aimless road trip around the West. For all the journeys and expeditions I had pursued during the previous fifty-plus years, I had never concocted a voyage out of driving from one place to another. The car had always been a means to an end.

But would a lazy ramble from Montana to Arizona make for a readable book? In the midst of my doubts, the old story of Domínguez and Escalante reawoke in my brain. Yes: I would retrace their amazing 1776 journey across the American Southwest, nearly all of which was repeatable by road, and carry on a running dialogue with the Franciscan missionary who kept such a rich and quixotic journal of that ambitious quest.

I tried the idea out on my agent, Stuart Krichevsky. Though we'd become good friends through the course of two decades and fifteen books together, I knew that Stuart was no literary yes-man. I'd also learned to trust his judgment. Whenever he frowned and uttered an unequivocal "no" in response to my latest pipe dream, I would drop it after only the feeblest protestations. (Though I'll always wonder, Stuart, what might have been if you'd let me compose my tributes to Schubert and the 1955 Brooklyn Dodgers.)

To my delight, Stuart was gung-ho about D & E, though he knew only the barest outline of their story. At once I booked our flights to Albuquerque and plotted Sharon's and my itinerary for September 2017. If Stuart was on board, I knew I could also count on his loyal and efficient assistants, Laura Usselman and Aemilia Phillips. A month after Sharon and I finished the D & E journey, we spent one of the happiest evenings of our year with Stuart at the Banff Mountain Film and Book Festival, where he organized a soirée with two of his newer writers whom I'd nudged in his direction, the immensely talented adventurers Roman Dial and Kate Harris.

It takes, of course, not only an agent but a publisher to make a book happen. My friendship with Starling Lawrence at W. W. Norton and Company was only five years and four books old, but when he waved his starter's flag at D & E, I realized that our road trip was ready to launch. Cancer could wait.

I've had several excellent editors during my nearly four decades of writing books for a living, but Star Lawrence is in a category of his own. As an editor, he's a New York legend, and as a novelist himself, he's a provocative (if underappreciated) visionary. His faith in my latest boondoggle thus came with the imprimatur of a man who cared deeply not only about stories but about words, and whose caustic appraisals of bad books were balanced by his quiet enthusiasm for good ones.

At Norton, Emma Hitchcock and Nneoma Amadi-obi admirably performed all the machinations it takes to bring text to print, and Erin Lovett served as a hearty and diligent publicist. I also benefited from Allegra Huston's usual impeccable and insightful work as my copyeditor. It's great to have a reader who catches all my glitches and at the same time responds to the narrative.

While I wrote *Limits of the Known*, I was so weakened and handicapped by cancer that I had to hire an assistant to perform all kinds of research for me. I lucked out big-time in recruiting Madeline Miller, a post-doc in earth and planetary sciences at Harvard who is also a climber, a scuba diver, and a brilliant sleuth. This time around, though I felt stronger and could travel, I knew I needed another assistant to help me dig through the arcana that would deepen my understanding of the 1776 exploit. Again I lucked out big-time, when Adam Stack signed on. A newly minted Harvard PhD in anthropology, Adam too is a climber and outdoorsman, and he saved me many a fruitless hour by untangling such knots as the identities of Ute tribes recorded in Escalante's journal. Adam also drew the excellent map of the expedition on page x.

Both before and after our journey on the D & E trail, I consulted with Stephen Lekson and Matthew Liebmann, two of the smartest and most original archaeologists in North America. Both Steve and Matt have become mentors to my passion for the prehistoric and historic Southwest. I've always felt a sense of awe about such scholars, whose insights about what was going on in Chaco in 1100 AD or Jemez in 1680 are so much deeper than mine. The pros in the field can be dismissive of dabblers like myself, but Matt and Steve have always shared their wisdom with me unstintingly and showed the keenest interest in whatever lark I might be pursuing.

Two first-rate scholars of Southwestern history, Rick Hendricks in Santa Fe and John Kessell in Durango, met with me during our trip and gave me valuable insights. In Bluff, Utah, old friend Jim Hook put me onto a rare and anomalous grove of cottonwoods that may have sprouted about the time the padres were in the field. (Those trees are still going strong at the unthinkable age of 240.)

During a short break in our journey, Sharon and I joined up with Emmett Lyman and Sarah Keyes, two rabid climbers in their late thirties who've become good friends. With them carrying all our gear, we accomplished a three-day backpack to one of the most stunning Anasazi ruins in the Southwest, a journey I thought I would never make again. That idyll deepened my rapport with the wilderness into which D & E had plunged. And on the San Juan River, Emmett gracefully scrambled up a cliff to take the close-up photo of the haunting Navajo petroglyph (see photograph in insert), which may echo the passage of the padres so long ago.

As they have so often before, Matt Hale and Ed Ward read my book in manuscript and gave me "feedback." In Santa Fe, as we prepared for our trip, Sharon and I spent several happy days with Irene Owsley, an ex-student of mine who's become a first-rate photographer. Irene's enthusiasm for Southwest mysteries gave us the kind of boost we needed to set out on the road.

Finally, how can I ever express my debt to Sharon? Every day of our thirty-nine-day journey, she took care of me in one way or another, from cooking hot dogs on our Coleman stove to driving while I pawed through my books to demanding blood draws at hospitals to ensure that my sodium level hadn't dropped to a lethal low, as it had just a year before. But each day on the road was like another class in our endless seminar in all things Domínguez and Escalante.

In July 2018 I learned that my cancer had returned, in the form of a metastasis to my adrenal glands. I went back on the immunotherapy drug that had stopped the growth of the nodules in my lungs, but whether it will work its magic a second time remains uncertain.

This is the first book among the thirty-odd I've written in which Sharon is a central character. I hope it does justice to her intelligence, her insight into motivation, her compassion for the unfortunates of the world. I think she knows how deeply I love her. And she must sense how grateful I am in knowing that whatever the course of my illness, I will have spent the last years of my life at her side.

Bibliography

Adams, Eleanor B. "Fray Silvestre and the Obstinate Hopi." *New Mexico Historical Review* 38, no. 2 (1963).

Bowden, Henry Warner. *American Indians and Christian Missions: Studies in Cultural Conflict*. Chicago: University of Chicago Press, 1981.

Briggs, Walter. *Without Noise of Arms: The 1776 Domínguez–Escalante Search for a Route from Santa Fe to Monterey*. Flagstaff, AZ: Northland Press, 1976.

Cervantes, Fernando. *The Devil in the New World: The Impact of Diabolism in New Spain*. New Haven, CT: Yale University Press, 1994.

Daniel, E. Randolph. *The Franciscan Concept of Mission in the High Middle Ages*. Lexington: University Press of Kentucky, 1975.

DeVoto, Bernard. *The Course of Empire*. Boston: Houghton, Mifflin, 1952.

Domínguez, Francisco Atanasio. *The Missions of New Mexico, 1776*. Translated and annotated by Eleanor B. Adams and Angelico Chavez. Albuquerque: University of New Mexico Press, 1956.

Galgano, Robert C. *Feast of Souls: Indians and Spaniards in the Seventeenth-Century Missions of Florida and New Mexico*. Albuquerque: University of New Mexico Press, 2005.

Gregory, David A., and David R. Wilcox, eds. *Zuni Origins: Toward a New Synthesis of Southwestern Archaeology*. Tucson: University of Arizona Press, 2007.

Guernsey, Samuel James. *Explorations in Northeastern Arizona.* Cambridge, MA: Peabody Museum of Archaeology and Ethnology, 1931.

Hämäläinen, Pekka. *The Comanche Empire.* New Haven, CT: Yale University Press, 2008.

Hill, Jane H. "The Zuni Language in Southwestern Areal Context." In *Zuni Origins: Toward a New Synthesis of Southwestern Archaeology,* edited by David A. Gregory and David R. Wilcox. Tucson: University of Arizona Press, 2007.

Jackson, William Henry. *Time Exposure: The Autobiography of William Henry Jackson.* New York: G. P. Putnam's Sons, 1940.

Kessell, John L. *Miera y Pacheco: A Renaissance Spaniard in Eighteenth-Century New Mexico.* Norman: University of Oklahoma Press, 2013.

———. *Whither the Waters: Mapping the Great Basin from Bernardo de Miera to John C. Frémont.* Albuquerque: University of New Mexico Press, 2017.

Lavender, David. *One Man's West.* Lincoln: University of Nebraska Press, 1977.

MacGregor, Greg, and Siegfried Halus. *In Search of Domínguez & Escalante: Photographing the 1776 Spanish Expedition through the Southwest.* Santa Fe: Museum of New Mexico Press, 2011.

Miller, David E., ed. *The Route of the Domínguez–Escalante Expedition, 1776–77.* Domínguez–Escalante State/Federal Bicentennial Committee, 1976.

Norris, Jim. *After "The Year Eighty": The Demise of Franciscan Power in Spanish New Mexico.* Albuquerque: University of New Mexico Press, 2000.

Ortman, Scott G. *Winds from the North: Tewa Origins and Historical Anthropology.* Salt Lake City: University of Utah Press, 2012.

Posada, Alonso de. *Alonso de Posada Report, 1686.* Translated and edited by Alfred Barnaby Thomas. Pensacola, FL: Perdido Bay Press, 1982.

Rusho, W. L., and C. Gregory Crampton. *Lee's Ferry: Desert River Crossing.* Salt Lake City: Tower Productions, 1998.

Sánchez, Joseph P. *Explorers, Traders, and Slavers: Forging the Old Spanish Trail, 1678–1850.* Salt Lake City: University of Utah Press, 1997.

Saunt, Claudio. *West of the Revolution: An Uncommon History of 1776.* New York: W. W. Norton, 2014.

Sheridan, Thomas E., et al., eds. *Moquis and Kastiilam: Hopis, Spaniards, and the Trauma of History, Volume I: 1540–1679.* Tucson: University of Arizona Press, 2015.

Simmons, Virginia McConnell. *The Ute Indians of Utah, Colorado, and New Mexico.* Niwot: University Press of Colorado, 2000.

Smith, Melvin T. *Dominguez–Escalante Trail Bicentennial Interpretive Master Plan and Final Report.* Salt Lake City: 1976.

Thomas, Alfred Barnaby, ed. and trans. *Forgotten Frontiers: A Study of the Spanish Indian Policy of Don Juan Bautista de Anza, Governor of New Mexico 1777–1787.* Norman: University of Oklahoma Press, 1932.

Tiller, Veronica E. Velarde. *The Jicarilla Apache Tribe: A History.* Albuquerque: BowArrow, 2000.

Utah: A Guide to the State (WPA Guide). New York: Hastings House, 1941.

Vélez de Escalante, Silvestre. *The Domínguez–Escalante Journal: Their Expedition through Colorado, Utah, Arizona, and New Mexico in 1776.* Translated by Fray Angelico Chavez, edited by Ted J. Warner, foreword by Robert Himmerich y Valencia. Salt Lake City: University of Utah Press, 1995.

———. *Pageant in the Wilderness: The Story of the Escalante Expedition to the Interior Basin, 1776.* Translated and edited by Herbert E. Bolton. 2nd ed. Salt Lake City: Utah State Historical Society, 1972.

The WPA Guide to 1930s Arizona. Compiled by the workers of the Writers' Program of the Work Projects Administration in the State of Arizona, foreword by Stewart L. Udall. Tucson: University of Arizona Press, 1989.

The WPA Guide to 1930s Colorado. Compiled by workers of the Writers' Program of the Work Projects Administration in the State of Colorado, with a new introduction by Thomas J. Noel. Lawrence: University Press of Kansas, 1987.

The WPA Guide to 1930s New Mexico. Compiled by the workers of the Writers' Program of the Work Projects Administration in the State of New Mexico, foreword by Marc Simmons. Tucson: University of Arizona Press, 1989.

Index